ON TRIAL

Reagan's War
Against Nicaragua

ON TRIAL

Reagan's War Against Nicaragua

Testimony of the Permanent Peoples' Tribunal

Edited by Marlene Dixon

Foreword by Harvey Cox

Synthesis Publications   *San Francisco*

English translation of poem by Ernesto Cardenal (excerpt from "Canto Nacional," "National Song,") from the book *Nicaragua in Revolution: The Poets Speak,* reprinted courtesy MEP Publications, c/o Anthropology Dept., University of Minnesota, and Marc Zimmerman.

Map of Nicaragua reprinted by permission of Westview Press, from *Nicaragua: The Land of Sandino* by Thomas W. Walker. Copyright © 1981, Westview Press, Boulder, Colo.

Cover photo: San Rafael del Norte, Nicaragua, following an August 1983 contra attack. From the exhibit at the session of the Permanent Peoples' Tribunal on U.S. intervention in Nicaragua, Brussels 1984.

Design: Vanda Sendzimir

Library of Congress Cataloging in Publication Data

International League for the Rights and Liberation of Peoples. Permanent Peoples' Tribunal.
    On Trial.
    Based on the proceedings of the Permanent Peoples' Tribunal session on Nicaragua held in October, 1984 in Brussels, Belgium.
    1. United States — Foreign relations — Nicaragua — Congresses. 2. Nicaragua — Foreign relations — United States — Congresses. 3. Reagan, Ronald — Congresses. 4. United States — Foreign relations — 1981-   — Congresses. 5. Nicaragua — Politics and government — 1979-   — Congresses. I. Dixon, Marlene, 1936-   . II. Title.
E183.8.N5I56   1985   972.85'053   85-7974
ISBN 0-89935-043-7
ISBN 0-89935-042-9 (pbk.)

Published by Synthesis Publications
2703 Folsom Street, San Francisco, CA 94110

Printed in the United States of America
10 9 8 7 6 5 4 3 2 1

ACKNOWLEDGMENTS

The editor wishes to thank the following people for their contribution to this book:

François Houtart, Director of the Centre Tricontinental in Louvain-la-Neuve, Belgium, for invaluable assistance during the Tribunal and in assembling material for this book, as well as clarifying many questions related to it.

Gianni Tognoni, Secretary General of the Permanent Peoples' Tribunal, for facilitating permission to publish this English edition of the proceedings, providing documents of the session, and other very important assistance.

Professor Richard Falk of Princeton University for reviewing, correcting, and clarifying the English version of the Tribunal's lengthy judgment with great care.

Staff members, colleagues, and friends of the Institute for the Study of Militarism and Economic Crisis, in particular:

Elizabeth Sutherland Martínez, for editorial assistance that included reviewing the material available, coordinating translations and transcriptions, and preparation of the final text.

Alicia Aicardi, Armando Aparicio, Matthew Bailey, Laird Boswell, Jeffrey Caden, Suzanne Dod, Carmela Echeveste, Betty Ferrer, Elsa Frausto, Eileen Hoye, Helena Méndez, David Meyers, Maurice Rosen, Rebecca Schwaner, Christina Shellcroft, and Janja Stanich for Spanish and French translation assistance.

Jane Armbruster, Gary Harrison, Yvonne Keller, Isabel Leiva, David Meyers, Don Reneau, Jean Taylor, and Jacqueline Wilson for editorial assistance, including transcription of tapes.

For assistance with specialized terminology in the translations: Daniel Arbus of the Lawyers Committee on Nuclear Policy, Colin Danby and Cecilio J. Morales, Jr., of the Council on Hemispheric Affairs, and Peter Oliver of the McGill Law Journal (Montreal).

Photographers in the exhibit on display during the session of the Permanent Peoples' Tribunal on U.S. intervention in Nicaragua. All photos in this book are by them except those credited to Andrew Ritchie.

CNCD (the National Center for Cooperation and Development), Brussels, for providing prints of the photographs from the Tribunal exhibit.

Paola Gaiotti Oxenius of Cologne, Germany for providing tapes of the session.

The Central American Historical Institute, Washington, D.C., for research assistance.

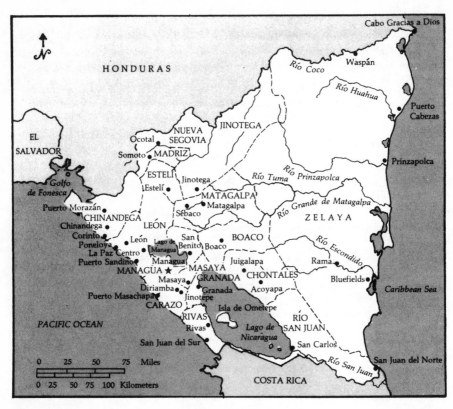

Nicaragua

Contents

Foreword

by Harvey Cox

One of the most ominous developments in recent American history has been the decline in the United States government's respect for the institutions of international law. On the one hand, this development should not have come as a surprise. For the past five years, those forging American policy have done so with the announced intention to pay less attention to world opinion (what the Founding Fathers called "a decent respect for the opinions of mankind"), but rather to shape American policy exclusively in the light of their own views of what is in the best interests of the United States. Obviously, from this perspective established practices and procedures of international law take a decidedly back seat. On the other hand, however, the present administration came into power on a wave of promises to restore respect for law and order and to turn back what its leaders described as a growing contempt for tradition, civility, and the rule of law. The result has been a curious mixture of law-and-order rhetoric and flagrant disregard for the law and legal institutions where they do not seem to serve the purposes of the policymakers.

Nowhere has this ambivalence, or perhaps even duplicity, been better illustrated than in the United States' dealing with its neighboring republics in Central America. The United States is bound to these countries by a web of treaty obligations, both bilateral and multilateral. According to the U.S. Constitution, these treaties have the force of law. Under American legal codes, to violate such treaties is just as much a criminal offense as violating a law which governs the domestic conduct of citizens. Such violations are punishable by established criminal procedures. Yet the United States has openly flaunted these treaties on numerous occasions, while at the same time mounting a fervid global rhetorical campaign against "international terrorists and outlaws." In other words, while acting as prosecutor, judge, jury, and as sometimes executioner of other nations and groups for their alleged violations of international law, the United States has become a kind of international scofflaw (one who contemptuously violates the law).

Harvey Cox is Victor S. Thomas Professor of Divinity at the Harvard Divinity School and author of eight books, most recently Religion in the Secular City *(Simon & Schuster, 1984).*

The apex of this disregard for international law and justice came, of course, with the U.S. government's refusal to accept the jurisdiction of the World Court in the case involving the United States' mining of Nicaraguan coastal waters. Here the pattern of response was typical. At first our government denied such activities had taken place; then it defended them as necessary in view of the security threat posed by Nicaragua; then it announced it would not respect the Court's jurisdiction; then it disclosed that the mining had been terminated anyway. In the course of rejecting the Court's jurisdiction, however, the U.S. government raised the most serious question to date about its commitment to an international community of law. The refusal also appeared bizarre and contradictory to observers who remembered that the United States had severely criticized Iran for rejecting the Court's jurisdiction in the case of the American hostages in 1979. To be a scofflaw is one thing, but when a scofflaw makes himself the chairman of the law-and-order committee and continues to be a scofflaw, then we are faced with a form of hypocrisy bordering on schizophrenia.

This year marks the anniversary of the Nuremberg Tribunal, organized just after the end of World War II. The purpose of that Tribunal was to bring the existing resources of world law to bear on the men who had led Nazi Germany during the years of the Third Reich.

Three major elements of international law, which had been recognized for many years, came forcefully to the forefront as a result of the Nuremberg proceedings. The first was that governments themselves can become criminal governments. To violate international law under the color of law or for reasons of state does not exculpate a government from the guilt of its punishable actions.

The second element that came into prominence at Nuremberg was that when one government becomes an outlaw, it is the duty and obligation of the other nations to protect the citizens of that nation, and of other nations that might be affected, from its criminal activity. This principle of international enforcement suggests that in such cases, intervention is not just allowable; it is obligatory. It is the equivalent of the well-established idea that if one knowingly allows a criminal action to take place when one could have done something to prevent it, one becomes a kind of accessory to the crime.

The third and possibly most important idea that gained focus at Nuremberg was that every individual is responsible for the actions he or she carries out. Appealing to the fact that one acted under superior orders is insufficient grounds for acquittal.

In the present stage of history, in which governments are often still the principal culprits in the violation of domestic and international law, it is especially important to remember that even when there is no available agency to enforce it, the law remains the law. We would find it strange indeed if individuals or corporations could, as the United States did in the coastal waters mining case, simply decline to grant jurisdiction to the court. The victims of official government-sponsored terror in El Salvador and Chile and other places must occasionally long for a court to which they could summon their tormentors. The present structure of international power, however, does not always allow this to happen. Governments can prosecute criminals, but when a government itself engages in criminal acts, who will call it into account? Still, even if the courts are corrupt, the police venial, and the juridical system a shambles, people tend to recognize that there is such a thing as right and wrong and that authentic law should seek to enforce human rights.

There are ancient and venerable philosophical traditions which undergird this conviction. These are sometimes discussed in terms of the *lex naturale* (natural law) or the *lex gentium* (law of the peoples). Natural law in this context means that all rational human beings have an innate capacity to recognize good and evil. In some traditions this capacity is believed to be endowed by God, while in others it is an integral part of human nature. In either case, encoded or positive law must reflect and enforce this more basic law. Even if it does not, the law remains, and its enforcement becomes the obligation of the people.

This book provides the reader with the record of an instance in which the people themselves, exercising this ancient legal and moral obligation, one enshrined more recently in explicit international law, have acted together to bring a government to the bar of justice.

The Permanent Peoples' Tribunal is not a mere political show trial producer. It has organized legal proceedings according to the strictest interpretation of existing international law, but has done so only where governments themselves have failed to protect their citizens (or the citizens of other countries), or where governments themselves are the alleged violators or where governments have colluded to prevent international organs of justice from executing their responsibilities. The Tribunal has heard cases regarding the governments of the Philippines, El Salvador, and Guatemala. It has heard the complaint of representatives of the people of Afghanistan against the U.S.S.R. In the present volume, we have the record of its session in response to the complaints of the people of Nicaragua about the actions of the United States.

I think any fair reader will conclude that the record here presented speaks for itself. But in reading the eloquent, moving, and sometimes infuriating testimony, it might be well to remember that in addition to the case against the conduct of the United States, something else is at issue here. It is the even more basic question of what principles of conduct should govern the relations of nations and peoples with each other.

This book is not just a scathing indictment of U.S. misconduct — which it is — it is also a courageous assertion that in an age of outlaw govern- ments the people themselves are not without a voice. The people them- selves can still fulfill their duty as citizens and as human beings to bring the wrongdoer, even in absentia, to the bar of justice. Even if the present rulers of America can disdain its founding documents, ". . .a decent respect for the opinions of mankind. . ." still obliges the people to speak.

Preface
Marlene Dixon

As I sat down to write a preface for this book I felt at a loss. The legal, ethical, moral and political issues had been presented at the Permanent Peoples' Tribunal in Brussels, by persons more qualified than I by direct experience — the Nicaraguans themselves. What could I possibly add to what they had presented to the peoples of the world at the Tribunal? Yet, if I am a citizen of the United States I bear the responsibility for its policies so long as I fail to oppose them. To speak only of the ethical and humanitarian abstractions by which we explain our behavior would miss the point, for when I speak of obligations, what comes to mind are faces, expressions, joy and grief, and the persistent question I must ask myself: who still lives? who has died?

In January, 1983 I first went to Nicaragua as a guest of the ASTC, the new Sandinista Association of Cultural Workers. I was very fortunate, for the ASTC and their Secretary General, Rosario Murillo, are the best of hosts even in the most difficult of times. Rosario went out of her way to enable me to meet with many of the journalists and scholars who were deeply involved in the new Nicaragua. I was doubly fortunate, for I was also able to meet many people working in the other new institutions of the revolution. Most of the workers and professionals and plain citizens I met at that time were triumphant after the great successes of the literacy campaign and the growing mass health infrastructure. These were the immediate post-revolutionary goals — the development of the quality of life and health of the people at large — and all the people I met, in all walks of life, were buoyant with pride in their accomplishments. Somoza had left the nation in ruins, stolen the state funds, left a crushing debt which had benefited only his family, cronies and the brutal National Guardsmen who were the "Somoza SS" and today's Contras (counterrevolutionary forces), Reagan's "Freedom Fighters." After the earthquake of 1972 (which killed 5,000 people) Somoza had stolen the aid funds and refused to rebuild the city — all that one sees are ruins and brick roads built with Somoza bricks, from Somoza's factory, built to go nowhere, built to fatten Somoza's bank account. The ruins of most of the capital city of Managua speak more eloquently than words of the challenges that faced the young revolution, and the enormous task of economic construction

(with no adequate existing infrastructure — no schools, hospitals, universities, housing). Those ruins always haunt me, not only for the tragedy
of the earthquake itself, but because the ruins stand for the pitiful economic vulnerability of this tiny new nation.

Toward the end of my stay I was given a rare opportunity to observe
first hand the preparations which were being made by the CIA and Somoza
ex-Guardsmen who were to become known as the Contra. I remember
how skeptical I was that the U.S. would attack Nicaragua (with the
memories still fresh in my mind of Vietnam) but I was about to receive
an education in the realities of post-Vietnam warfare, the use of mercenary troops as proxies in the CIA's "secret war" against Nicaragua. After
a long meeting with Captain (now Sub-Comandante) Sánchez concerning the military threat posed by the United States and its proxy armies
of Contra mercenaries concentrating in Honduras, he asked me if I wanted
to observe the Contras first hand. I immediately accepted. The next morning at 5 a.m. our group of four prepared to leave for the front. It was
to be this trip that would teach me, unforgettably, just what ¡No Pasarán!
means to the people of Nicaragua.

It was late afternoon when we reached a rocky hilltop observation post
outside of Jalapa, overlooking the Honduran border. At first the
atmosphere of the post was grim, as heavily armed men moved in and
out from patrol. From this observation post I could clearly see the movement of men and material to a camp in the valley below. I began talking
to a small group of off-duty soldiers, asking them what they thought and
how they felt manning this outpost facing the Contras below. These were
very young men, peasants mostly and veterans of the revolutionary war.
They were so very eloquent, speaking of their homes and families and
the so-recent memories of the Somoza terror. I recall how bitter they were
about a group of French journalists who had been brought up to another
point along the border, and who had baited them about being puppets
of the "communists." Clearly remembering the French journalists, the most
articulate of the soldiers was very eager that we understand what they
as soldiers felt, that they were Sandinistas and they were defending their
country, and their revolution, against that other image of Somoza, the
mercenary ex-Guardsmen with their U.S. military supplies. On this particular day, there were trucks and supplies moving on a mountain road
to the Contras below us — and indeed it would only be a few months before
these men would be engaged in war and the trenches in the provincial
town of Jalapa would be filled with the dead and the dying.

As we talked that afternoon, more and more young men coming off
duty joined us in the rocks, some adding their thoughts and observations
about their lives and the war that was coming, some simply listening or
asking for news from the capital or whether the people of the United States

really wanted to destroy the revolution. So young these men, some only boys, yet they knew what they were defending, they were vibrant with hope and determination and defiance to defend the new Nicaragua, "their" Nicaragua. I shall never forget their quietness, or their eloquence, or that they carried the weapons that protected me from the Contra snipers on neighboring hilltops. I returned from that afternoon determined to tell the people of the United States that Nicaragua was at war, and the United States was the aggressor, and these young men had a right to their lives and to command their own destiny. I wonder now: which of those young men still lives? What has become of those whom I knew such a short time, yet taught me so much.

I visited the outpost near Jalapa in January of 1983. In October of 1983 I attended the XVth Latin American Congress of Sociology in Managua. It was a different Managua than one sees now. The economic terrorism of the United States had not yet bitten into the heart of the country. One cannot imagine the tragedy of a nation of a little over 2,800,000 people (about the same as the population of Los Angeles) with a land area only about the size of the State of Iowa, with an economy based upon coffee and bananas, with only 7% arable land and no economic development beyond the ranchos and plantations of Somocistas. Only six years ago an ugly, neglected land of totalitarian brutality and terror. One has to ask what great power in the world could rationally be threatened by this tiny, impoverished nation? The revolution faced having to build everything a small modern state might need, schools, hospitals, diversified economic development — everything, and pay off Somoza's enormous foreign debt as well. The policy of the United States, to use the Somocista mercenaries to destroy the economic basis of the new Nicaraguan state, is an evil and irrational policy of such brutality and cruelty that it numbs the sensibilities and leaves one outraged that such monsters call themselves the government of the United States and a policy of total destruction against Nicaragua a "freedom struggle."

In October of 1983 it was still possible to be full of boundless hope and enthusiasm for the new society that the young people of Nicaragua were so involved in building. There was time for outdoor dinners to speak of hopes and dreams, of music and the beauty of the rugged landscape. War was on the horizon, a constant threat, but not yet an obsession, not yet the dominant reality of everyday life. The young people who were attending the sociology conference were asking how sociology could serve the needs of revolutionary reconstruction, asking aging radical academics like myself to give lectures on radical sociology. . . it was at this time that I met a young woman, a sociology student, whose job it was to help foreign visitors get around from place to place (when the fuel shortage made it very difficult). Lucia was a lovely girl, who went far beyond the call of duty to assist me and who spoke of her school, and her studies, her hopes and husband, the promise she saw in the new society she hoped to be part of building. I mentioned that I would give much for a bottle of cologne, and she laughed, saying a bottle of cologne would be a miracle to find in the marketplace. Later, I sent her a bottle, for what young woman should go without perfume?

It was during that October sociology conference that the United States engineered the Contra bombing of the port of Corinto. For me, at least, the attack on Corinto was the beginning of the ugly and evil war against the livelihood and economic survival of a whole people. In this attack, CIA-trained terrorists used sophisticated explosives to destroy 3.2 million gallons of gasoline, oil and diesel fuel and hundreds of tons of desperately needed food and medicines. In the aftermath of the attack on Corinto I discovered that Lucia was more than a helpful friend and enthusiastic young student — she was also a soldier, and was called up with her unit of the militia in response to the Corinto attack. It would be units like these that would soon be sent to defend the coffee harvest and the drying plants from terrorist attacks and senseless kidnappings and slaughters. It would be the young people, students and urban workers and small farmers, who would be dying in the defense of the nation against United States aggression. Corinto was the end to the great plans, hopes and dreams for peace and peaceful, constructive national development. Corinto, for me, signaled the inevitable end of the naiveté and idealism of youth and its generosity toward foes, for these qualities are always the first to perish in the horrors of war.

Toward the end of that stay in Managua there was a farewell reception for the sociologists who had come to the Congress. It was a balmy evening at an old nightclub overlooking a clear, still lake. The lake shimmered in the night air, and the music and dancing, rum and talk struck me as a fearsome incongruence. I thought, what is this night, after Corinto and Jalapa? There was a tension, a frantic hilarity, uniforms and strangers, it was a party before the soldiers left for the front, a party of a people at war; I was so aware of the undercurrents, the tensions, the collective awareness under the heat of the music and the night that we were in a time of war, when people so full of life might the next day die. I was suddenly stricken by an overwhelming sense of grief, and the burden of being an American — not guilty, but angry at having to "be an American," and grew withdrawn and distanced from those around me. Even then I was haunted by faces, and leaving in a day, wondered which faces I might never see again.

Now the vibrant, enthusiastic reality of revolutionary Nicaragua must become obscured by the destructiveness of the American terror, the butchers in CIA fatigues, studying a book on guerrilla warfare that teaches them to assassinate teachers, doctors and priests. How can the concentration camp guard empathize with his victims? He only knows how to butcher them. He only knows how to destroy, and makes no distinction between children's schools, hospitals, food warehouses or military outposts. If a revolutionary anti-American Nicaragua exists today, it exists as it does because of the policies of the United States; if the Nicaraguan economy collapses and thus its people suffer, it is also because of the United States, and not any of the doing of the Nicaraguans. When I saw the ruins, I saw the ruins left by U.S. aggression: Somoza ruins and Contra ruins and the ruins of a people's dreams of a better life in their own lifetime. What will stop the murder? Who will stop the ancient murderers in their palaces on the Potomac.

And when I think of Nicaragua, I wonder: is Lucia alive?

About the Permanent Peoples' Tribunal

The Permanent Peoples' Tribunal is a public opinion tribunal that has taken its place in the tradition of similar initiatives in the Western world, beginning with the International Military Tribunal of Nuremburg. This Tribunal was followed by the Tribunal of Tokyo, which judged the Japanese war criminals; the Russell Tribunals on Vietnam (I), on Latin America (II), on the "Berufsverbot" in West Germany (III), and on the indigenous peoples of America (IV); and the Delgado Tribunal that judged the crimes committed by the PIDE in Portugal during the regimes of Salazar and Caetano.

In contrast to these tribunals, which all had certain specific contexts, the Permanent Peoples' Tribunal is a permanent body. It was founded on June 24, 1979, in Bologna, Italy, by the Lelio Basso International Foundation for the Rights and Liberation of the Peoples. The foundation is an organization for study and research, established by Lelio Basso, who was president of Russell Tribunal II on Latin America.

At the closing of that Tribunal, he and his collaborators recognized the need to continue the analysis they had been preparing during the Russell Tribunal's three years of existence. The Tribunal on Latin America had established the violation of human rights in Brazil, Uruguay, Bolivia, Argentina, and Chile, and had begun to arrive at the conclusion that widespread torture, the disappearance of thousands of citizens, and the unpunished murders of members of the opposition to the dictatorial regimes in these countries could not possibly be the result of actions initiated by lone executioners or small groups of killers. Torture, when it is practiced in proportions reaching the point of genocide, becomes a method of government.

This Tribunal was able to demonstrate exactly how multinational economic groups and foreign governments pressure the regimes of these countries to maintain a sociopolitical system that permits exploitation — often to the point of total control — of the countries' natural resources. The conclusion of the Tribunal on Latin America was that there is systematic violation of the fundamental freedoms of entire peoples — the right of every people to self-determination, to their culture, and to the exploitation of their own natural resources. These are basic principles, which have been impressed on the international conscience during recent decades, thanks to the anti-colonialist and national liberation struggles and to activities by the countries of the Third World in the United Nations and other international bodies.

What was missing was the codification of these principles. For this reason, on July 4, 1976 in Algiers, a group of experts on international law who had collaborated in the Russell Tribunal on Latin America formulated the Universal Declaration of the Rights of the Peoples. This statement was to provide a firm basis for the battle to bring international public law up-to-date. The Declaration of Algiers became the political-educational reference point of the Lelio Basso International Foundation, which was established a few weeks later. The Foundation, in turn, created two organizations to plan and organize the practical work with respect to problems that had been dealt with on an individual basis. These organizations are the International League for the Rights and Liberation of Peoples, now established in seven countries, and the Permanent Peoples' Tribunal.

The Permanent Peoples' Tribunal organizes its sessions at the request of groups that are publicly neutral in political matters or political groups united in a common program sufficiently broad to be able to guarantee the greatest possible representation. The Tribunal has its own statutes and carries out its work under the rules contained in these statutes, based on the principles of the Declaration of Algiers, as well as other international agreements and rules of international public law. When the Permanent Peoples' Tribunal sits in session, the accused must be invited to send their representatives or written material to defend their position.

The Permanent Peoples' Tribunal is composed of 56 members chosen from eminent personalities in the fields of culture, art, science, and politics, among them various Nobel Prize winners. For each session, a minimum of seven members are convened. The verdict or judgment of each session is delivered to the International League for the Rights and Liberation of Peoples. As a nongovernmental organization with advisory status to the Economic and Social Council of the U.N., the League guarantees that the maximum amount of information reaches the international organizations and governments represented in the U.N. The verdicts of the Tribunal, thanks to its rigor in judicial matters and its impartiality, are today published and studied at various North American and European universities.

The Permanent Peoples' Tribunal previously held sessions on the Western Sahara, Argentina, Eritrea, the Philippines, Afghanistan (I and II), Armenian genocide, East Timor, El Salvador, Zaire, and Guatemala.

The Permanent Peoples' Tribunal
January, 1983

I
OPENING STATEMENTS

The Charges
Brought by Nicaragua
Against the U. S. Government

Dr. Rafael Chamorro

Dean of the Faculty of Law of the University of Nicaragua, Managua

Honorable Mr. President, honorable members of the Permanent Peoples' Tribunal:

I have the privilege of speaking in the name of the popular organizations of my country which signed the complaint presented to you. They are:

Nicaraguan Committee in Solidarity with the Peoples (CNSP)

Sandinista Workers Central (CST)

Rural Workers Association (ATC)

National Union of Farmers and Cattle Ranchers (UNAG)

National Confederation of Professionals (CONAPRO)

Union of Journalists of Nicaragua (UPN)

July 19th Sandinista Youth (JS 19)

"Luisa Amanda Espinoza" Association of Nicaraguan Women (AMNLAE)

Federation of Health Workers (FETSALUD)

Sandinista Defense Committees (CDS)

National Teachers Association (ANDEN)

Sandinista Cultural Workers Association (ASTC)

Committee of Mothers of Heroes and Martyrs (CMHH)

National Union of Nicaraguan Students (UNEN)

Antimperialist Tribunal of Our America (TANA)

Throughout its history, Nicaragua has experienced political, economic, and military attack and intervention by North American imperialism. In 1821, Nicaragua achieved independence from the Spanish Crown and in 1854, the first North American intervention by the filibusterer William Walker took place. He proclaimed himself President of Nicaragua in 1856, brought slavery into our country, and was officially recognized

This is the formal, verbal presentation of Nicaragua's charges; a written summary complaint was also submitted to the Tribunal.

by the U.S. Department of State. This filibusterer was defeated by the patriotism of the people and the solidarity of the fraternal countries of Latin America.

During the liberal regime of José Santos Zelaya, which started in 1893, military aggression continued. In 1896 and 1899, U.S. troops disembarked in the port of Corinto, San Juan del Norte, and Bluefields to intervene in the internal affairs of Nicaragua. In early 1909, the U.S. Secretary of State sent the Knox Note, asserting that Zelaya's government did not represent the interests and the will of the Nicaraguan people. In October, 1909, opponents of the Zelaya government were organized, financed, and armed by the Taft administration; there was an armed uprising and Zelaya was overthrown with the help of the U.S. Marine Corps.

From that time on, Nicaragua remained politically and economically subject to the government of the U.S. The customs, banks, and railroads of the country were placed in the hands of U.S. financiers, and the meetings of the Central Bank of Nicaragua took place in New York. During that time, those who aspired to the Presidency of the Republic had to be approved by the U.S. Embassy. Elections were supervised by the U.S. Marine Corps and, on the instructions of the State Department, U.S. General Frank McCoy (later, Admiral Woodward of the U.S. Marines) was appointed President of Nicaragua's National Council on Elections.

Against U.S. intervention stood Augusto César Sandino, the General of Free Men, heading an army dedicated to defending national sovereignty until the interventionist forces were expelled. The U.S. forces were replaced by the National Guard, conceived, organized and financed by the government of the United States and having the characteristics of a mercenary army. Anastasio Somoza was put in command of the National Guard, thus beginning the Somocista dictatorship which was maintained by U.S. imperialism until the triumph of the Sandinista Popular Revolution on July 19, 1979.

At the present time, the government of the United States is intervening in the internal affairs of Nicaragua with the manifest purpose of overthrowing our government and regaining hegemonic control over Nicaragua. To that end, it uses economic, military, and ideological aggression, despite the numerous efforts and peace initiatives undertaken by the Sandinista government in the United Nations and other bodies, and in bilateral talks with the United States as well as with neighboring countries.

MILITARY AGGRESSION

Imperialism's current military aggression is the continuation of a long history: 130 years of intervention and aggression by various U.S. administrations. From the moment of the triumph of the Sandinista revolution, the U.S. government has organized, directed, and financed mercenary forces composed, in large part, of former members of Somoza's National Guard. They maintain their base of operations in the Republic of Honduras, where they are trained, paid, and furnished with ammunition, food, and medicines in order to attack human and economic targets inside Nicaragua. President Reagan himself, in public statements, has acknowledged that his government gives direct aid to the counterrevolutionary forces. The attacks against Nicaragua occur constantly and they intensified at the beginning of 1983, especially in the northern region of the country. Incidents in this last period of time have included the following:

A small plane bombed the Augusto César Sandino International Airport, and was shot down by defense forces.

Fuel storage tanks at the port of Corinto were attacked by land and sea, causing a fire of enormous proportions that endangered the population of the port, which had to be evacuated.

The main ports of Nicaragua were mined: Corinto, Sandino, and El Bluff, resulting in damage to merchant ships of different nationalities and leading to the sinking of several Nicaraguan fishing boats.

During the month of August, 1984, a plane provisioning the counterrevolutionary forces was shot down in the northern region; on September 1, a helicopter carrying out an attack near the Honduran border was shot down and the two American mercenaries who manned it were killed.

U.S. support to the counterrevolution is evident. Through the CIA, its forces are provided with transport and war planes, helicopters, speedboats, funds, and all types of provisions. Such facts have been made public through the U.S. mass media.

ECONOMIC AGGRESSION

Economic aggression is manifested particularly in the commercial and financial sectors, and has the clear purpose of maintaining some degree of control over and applying pressure to the Sandinista government.

Initially, the U.S. administration suspended previously approved loans to Nicaragua for financing reconstruction work, economic revival, and purchases of wheat from the U.S. Later, the World Bank and the Interamerican Development Bank were pressured; they suspended their credit programs for Nicaragua.

The United States reduced the Nicaraguan sugar quota sharply (by 90%) and now threatens to stop importing Nicaraguan meat. The United States itself plans attacks on economic targets, which are implemented via the mercenary forces. These include, for example, attacks on granaries and fuel tanks, a maritime blockade to impede exports and imports, and the destruction of construction machinery, health centers, schools, production centers, children's centers, etc., which entail grave damages to the Nicaraguan economy.

IDEOLOGICAL AGGRESSION

Another tactic being used by the Reagan administration in its offensive against the government of Nicaragua is an intensive propaganda campaign to disparage the revolutionary government. The goal is to mislead the world and the people of the United States in order to justify the administration's interventionist and aggressive policies. At the same time, the international news agencies black out information about the reality of Nicaragua. This news blockade is intended to prevent the public from knowing about the achievements of the revolution in terms of health, education, housing, agrarian reform, etc., as well as the process of institutionalizing the revolution based on political pluralism, a mixed economy, and a policy of non-alignment.

Mr. President:

The acts of aggression that I have mentioned in a general manner will be set forth in detail, along with their consequences, in the reports and testimonies which will be presented during this session of the Tribunal.

The U.S. government, through its spokesmen, has presented a series of arguments to justify its interventionist policies. Some of them are as follows:

That Nicaragua provides arms to El Salvador. Using that accusation, the Reagan administration seeks to appear to be "defending" the Salvadoran people by making it impossible for Nicaragua to help the Salvadoran revolutionaries. It is known that the United States has the highest level of technology in the world in all respects, that its spy planes equipped with sophisticated instruments constantly violate the airspace of Nicaragua, that its warships maintain a menacing vigil on our shores, and that, nevertheless, the United States has been unable to offer a single proof of its accusation. The reason is simple: there is no such arms traffic.

That Nicaragua is a danger to the United States and to the countries of Central America. President Reagan's argument has no substantiation. In the real world, pigeons do not shoot at guns! Nicaragua, a small and poor country, cannot be a danger to the most powerful nation in the world, a nation with the ability to put an end to humanity by unleashing a nuclear holocaust. Nicaragua is not a menace to the countries of the region; on the contrary, the Nicaraguan government advocates the peaceful resolution of conflicts, as it has demonstrated before various international organizations to which it has appealed in its search for peace.

That Nicaragua is engaged in an arms race. The people and the government of Nicaragua do not want war; we want peace. We want to reconstruct our country, and we can accomplish this only if we have peace. The arms of the Sandinista army are defensive; they are to defend national sovereignty and territorial integrity. In the U.S. Congress, a North American expert gave testimony demonstrating that our armed forces have no offensive capacity; they are purely defensive.

That the Sandinista government has betrayed the revolution. This argument is used not only by the United States, but also by the counter-revolution, with the goal of establishing Somocismo without Somoza. The Sandinista government, fulfilling the plan of government, has implemented political pluralism, a mixed economy, respect for human rights (as noted by Amnesty International and similar organizations), and the participation of all sectors of society in national affairs, and so forth.

That the problem of Nicaragua is a problem of East-West confrontation. As we indicated, Nicaragua has experienced 130 years of aggression and intervention by the U.S., which started before the existence of the Soviet Union or the Cuban revolution. This means that the aggression is not due to the Soviet or Cuban revolution, but to the interventionist disposition of the U.S. government.

Members of the Permanent Peoples' Tribunal:

Given these facts, which will be expanded upon and detailed in the reports and testimonies to follow, it is evident that the government of the United States has violated norms of international law, the U.N. Charter, the Charter of the Organization of American States, multilateral treaties, and even its own laws, to which I shall not refer because that is an internal affair of the United States.

By the various aggressions and other actions previously mentioned, the U.S. has violated article 2 (4) of the U.N. Charter, which states that "the members of the organization, in their international relations, will refrain from resorting to the threat or use of force against the territorial integrity or the political independence of any state or in any manner inconsistent with the purposes of the United Nations."

The U.S. has not upheld the Declaration on the Inadmissibility of Intervention in the Domestic Affairs of States and the Protection of Their Independence and Sovereignty (Resolution 2131 (XX) of the General Assembly of the United Nations), which states:

1. No State has the right to intervene, directly or indirectly, for any reason whatsoever in the internal or external affairs of any other State. Consequently, armed intervention and all other forms of interference or attempted threats against the personality of the State or against its political, economic and cultural elements are condemned.

2. No State may use or encourage the use of economic, political or

any other type of measure to coerce another State in order to obtain from it the subordination of the exercise of its sovereign rights or to secure from it advantages of any kind. Also, no State shall organize, assist, foment, finance, incite or tolerate subversive, terrorist or armed activities directed towards the violent overthrow of the regime of another State, or interfere in civil strife in another State.

By the interventions and aggressions noted here, the U.S. violates articles 15, 16, and 17 of the Charter of the Organization of American States which declare:

Article 15

No State or group of States has the right to intervene, directly or indirectly, for any reason whatever in the internal or external affairs of any other State. The foregoing principle prohibits not only armed force but also any other form of interference or attempted threat against the personality of the State or against its political, economic and cultural elements.

Article 16

No State may use or encourage the use of coercive measures of an economic or political character in order to force the sovereign will of another State and obtain from it advantages of any kind.

Article 17

The territory of a State is inviolable; it may not be the object, even temporarily, of a military occupation or of other measures of force taken by another State, directly or indirectly, on any grounds whatever. No territorial acquisitions or special advantages obtained either by force or by other means of coercion shall be recognized.

The U.S. has not fulfilled such obligations imposed by international law, customs, and resolutions of the General Assembly of the United Nations as the following:

— The Declaration on the Inadmissibility of Intervention and Interference in the Internal Affairs of States (Resolution 36/103 of the General Assembly).

— The definition of aggression adopted by the General Assembly in Resolution 3314 (XXIX). According to this resolution, the bombing of the territory of another state, the mining of ports, the sending of armed bands or groups, and the sending of irregular or mercenary forces to overthrow the government of another state constitute acts of aggression.

— The principles of international law concerning relations and cooperation among states.

The aggression of the United States constitutes an international crime, a crime against peace. This is why the people of Nicaragua, before the Permanent Peoples' Tribunal, accuse the present government of the United

States, and ask that it be declared responsible before world public opinion for the war it is imposing on our nation and the peoples of Central America, and that it be urged to cease such war and all forms of aggression and intervention in Nicaragua. We also ask that this Tribunal pronounce itself in favor of peace by supporting a people and a government who are struggling to maintain their freedom, sovereignty, and independence, and to attain the peace necessary for reconstructing their country, and forging the future of a free, sovereign, and independent nation.

The Peace Policy of the Revolutionary Government of Nicaragua

Alejandro Serrano Caldera
Ambassador from Nicaragua to France and
Permanent Delegate to UNESCO

In studying the international relations of Nicaragua with both its neighbors and the United States, it is necessary to begin with the following statements.

I. THE AGGRESSIVE POLICIES OF THE REPUBLICAN ADMINISTRATION HEADED BY RONALD REAGAN HAVE CONSTANTLY CREATED OBSTACLES FOR THE PEACE POLICY OF THE NICARAGUAN REVOLUTIONARY GOVERNMENT.

In all conflicts, peace depends on the good will of everyone involved; a unilateral effort is not enough. Nicaragua by herself cannot establish peace, if the United States is unwilling to make its contribution, to accept the revolution as a historical reality, and to seek points of agreement which would permit a solution honorable to all parties.

Nevertheless, leaders of the Republican administration have up to now been unwilling to recognize the reality of the Revolution; on the contrary, they seem compelled to destroy it. For them, the Sandinista Popular Revolution represents a loss of geopolitical space close to U.S. borders and, in the name of national security and defense of strategic borders, they demand the recovery of this territory in the "back yard" of the Empire, where — to use the words of President Reagan before Congress in April, 1983 — fire has broken out.

The aggressions of the U.S. government against the Nicaraguan people are known to all: the mining of ports, terrorist acts, military bases in Honduras, and financial and logistical support to the armed counter-revolution, to cite some examples from a long chain of aggressions. Military, economic, and financial aggression forms part of the strategy and

This is a recapitulation, prepared by the Nicaraguan Embassy in Paris, of Ambassador Serrano's verbal comments before the Tribunal on October 6, 1984.

tactics directed against the Revolution, based on a desire to destroy it.

Efforts are made, planned at the White House and the Pentagon, to give this aggression an ideological basis by invoking the East-West conflict; in reality, the aggression corresponds more correctly to the contradiction between Empire and Nation.

The U.S. has assaulted Latin America, and Nicaragua in particular, ever since it became an empire, and long before the existence of the East/West conflict, before the revolution of October 1917. It was the logic of Empire and not the East-West conflict that led the various governments of the U.S., during their respective terms of office, to take over Cuba in the moment of its independence from Spain; to expropriate immense areas of Mexican land and subsoil; and, with respect to Nicaragua, to defeat Zelaya with the Knox Note in 1909, to assassinate Benjamin Zeledón,* and to intervene in our country in 1912.

It was the Monroe Doctrine, which in 1823 demanded "America for Americans" (meaning America from south of the Rio Grande to Patagonia for the U.S.), that established a policy of aggression, and not the East-West conflict.

This same Monroe Doctrine, revived in different forms — the Manifest Destiny of John Quincy Adams, the Big Stick, Dollar Diplomacy, the national security theory of John Foster Dulles — was also invoked in the Santa Fe Document** during the 1980 Republican Presidential campaign. This same Monroe Doctrine serves as justification for President Reagan's doctrine of the fourth border.

The origins of every liberation movement, every revolution, every struggle for the people's freedom and identity, are not to be found in the East-West conflict, as the Reagan administration claims. According to its point of view, there is an external cause that operates in a mechanical and linear way, which in this case would be the Soviet Union, Cuba, Nicaragua, El Salvador, the rest of Central America. But just as the aggressions against Nicaragua began before the Russian Revolution, so U.S. aggressions against Guatemala and Jacobo Arbenz occurred in 1954, before the Cuban Revolution; and the intervention in the Dominican Republic took place in 1965, before the triumph of the Sandinista Popular Revolution.

Instead of focusing on the domino theory, the United States should consider the exploitation, marginality, and misery in which our people

---

*Through Secretary of State Philander Knox, President Taft sent the infamous Note which in effect told Nicaragua's liberal President Zelaya to step down. Zeledón led the Nicaraguan resistance to Zelaya's overthrow and was killed in a U.S. Marine bombardment — the beginning of direct U.S. military intervention. Knox had close links with U.S. corporate interests and was key in establishing control by U.S. banking monopolies over Nicaragua's economy in the name of helping to "rehabilitate" it. — Ed.

**A policy study commissioned by the Council for Inter-American Security in Washington, D.C., prepared by the Committee of Santa Fe and entitled "A New Inter-American Policy for the Eighties." — Ed.

have lived, subjected to those conditions and repressed by brutal dictatorships and insensitive oligarchies that are supported and even installed by
the U.S. to protect its imperial interests.

II. THIS IS THE HISTORICAL CONTEXT OF THE NICARAGUAN PEACE POLICY, WHOSE SALIENT CHARACTERISTICS HAVE BEEN AND ARE AS FOLLOWS:

— To establish solid bases for peace in Central America through dialogue and negotiation.

— To demand respect for sovereignty and self-determination.

— To insist on the necessary guarantees for the security of all states
affected by this conflict.

— To demand respect for the transformations of Nicaraguan society
accomplished by the Sandinista Popular Revolution.

— To proclaim and put into practice the fundamental democratic principles of elections, pluralism, nonalignment, and the mixed economy.

— To practice a real democracy in which the Nicaraguan people themselves are the protagonists and beneficiaries.

In line with these principles, concrete actions have been taken that
embody the Peace Policy of the Revolutionary Government. A few facts
should serve as evidence of this peace effort:

May 6, 1981: Invitation extended to the Chief of State of Honduras,
General Policarpo Paz, to meet with the Coordinator of the Government
Junta of National Reconstruction, Commander Daniel Ortega Saavedra
(the Guasaule meeting).

November 1981: Visit to Tegucigalpa, Honduras, by Dr. Rafael Córdoba Rivas. Interview with the Chief of State of Honduras and with the
Foreign Minister, Col. Elvir Sierra.

January 27, 1982: Attendance of Commander Daniel Ortega at the
inauguration of President Roberto Suazo Córdoba of Honduras. Conversations with Suazo Córdoba and Mr. Paz Barnica, Minister of Foreign
Affairs of Honduras.

March 15, 1982: Invitation by Foreign Minister D'Escoto of Nicaragua
to Foreign Minister Paz Barnica. Invitation declined on March 17.

April 21, 1982: Since the invitation to meet in Managua was declined,
Foreign Minister D'Escoto visited Tegucigalpa and presented proposals
on the following points:

1. Immediate meeting of the army chiefs of both states;
2. A nonaggression pact;
3. Joint border patrol;
4. Dismantling of counterrevolutionary camps;
5. No installation of foreign naval bases in the Gulf of Fonseca;

6. Bilateral agreements of all types, and repatriation of the Miskitos who wished to return to Nicaragua voluntarily.

May 20, 1982: Meeting at "La Fraternalidad" of army chiefs of staff (from Nicaragua, and from Honduras, Col. José Abdengo Sueso Rosa).

August 24, 1982: New invitation from Foreign Minister D'Escoto to Foreign Minister Paz Barnica to meet in Managua on September 1-3. Invitation declined.

September 4, 1982: New effort by D'Escoto to invite Paz Barnica. Invitation again declined.

October 8, 1982: Meeting of D'Escoto and Paz Barnica.

November 12, 1982: With a new invitation, Mr. Paz Barnica visited Nicaragua and met with Commander Daniel Ortega.

The Contadora Process: On this point, one must note that up to now, Nicaragua has been the only Central American country to explicitly declare its full support, without reservations, for the Peace Act of September 7 and for the Additional Protocol.

This action by Nicaragua has shown, on one hand, its willingness to assume the necessary degree of responsibility for pursuing a true pacification of the area. On the other hand, Nicaragua's action exposed the real intentions of the United States, which developed an entire campaign against the Peace Act and the Additional Protocol.

It would be helpful to mention some of the most important developments in the Contadora Process:

January 8-9, 1983: The Contadora Group met for the first time on the island of Contadora, Panama.

September 1983: The Document of Objectives (21 points). Subsequently, "Norms for the Immediate Implementation of the Document of Objectives."

October 15, 1983: Nicaragua was the only Central American country that offered concrete proposals for the implementation of the Document of Objectives. These consisted of four texts:

1-2. Draft treaty between the Republic of Nicaragua and the United States of America, and draft treaty between the Republics of Honduras and Nicaragua — two bilateral treaties of peace and cooperation.

3. Draft accord concerning El Salvador — a proposal for a bilateral agreement with the U.S. to contribute to the resolution of the Salvadoran conflict.

4. Draft treaty between the Central American republics — a proposal for a treaty of peace, security, and cooperation among the five Central American countries.

These four proposals emphasized the theme of "Regional Security." They were handed over to the U.S. State Department and the countries involved in the Contadora Process. The State Department judged them insufficient and also noted that the State Department wasn't the appropriate recipient of these proposals.

December 1, 1983: The time limit set by Contadora for other countries to present proposals that would lead to implementation of the Document of Objectives expired. No other country offered new proposals. Nicaragua presented three additional documents to meet the supposed "insufficiencies" noted by the U.S.

December 20-21, 1983: The four foreign ministers of Contadora elaborated the "Norms for the Immediate Implementation of the Document of Objectives."

May-June 1984: The Contadora Act for Peace and Cooperation in Central America. Its purpose was to obtain generalized and binding results in the reduction of arms and troops, and in agreements on matters of internal policy and other matters. Nicaragua presented reservations.

September 7, 1984: The new version of the "Contadora Act for Peace and Cooperation in Central America" was presented.

September 21, 1984: Nicaragua announced that it would sign without reservations. The *binding* character of the Act's formulations on matters of internal policy was withdrawn, thus preserving the principles of sovereignty and self-determination which Nicaragua judged to have been impaired by the previous formulation.

III. IN THE FACE OF THE NICARAGUAN PEACE POLICY, THE U.S. INITIATED A POLICY OF AGGRESSION IN CENTRAL AMERICA, CENTERED ON THE NONACCEPTANCE OF A REALITY—THE EXISTENCE OF THE SANDINISTA POPULAR REVOLUTION.

The Santa Fe Document and the Kissinger Report, which are being implemented to a significant degree by the Reagan administration, serve to clarify the true intentions of the Reagan administration in Central America and to integrate the various actions against the people of Nicaragua into a single, logical totality — the logic of aggression.

The Santa Fe Document clearly establishes that the determining factor in the policy and actions of the United States is the protection and advancement of its security, i.e., the strategic and political element. The Document indicates abandonment of the human rights policy, which is seen as a cultural concept that has encouraged certain changes in countries of this hemisphere with negative results for the United States. It is recommended that this policy, basic to the Carter administration, be abandoned as ambiguous and unrealistic. At the same time, it is recommended that any action on any level that could permit changes unfavorable to U.S. interests be opposed. The Santa Fe Document suggests that an economic dependence be established that would facilitate ideological domination by the U.S. through infiltration and economic control of Latin America, and through an inter-American commerce that would not only draw these countries closer to the United States, but also permit a steadily growing identification with U.S. interests.

These positions were incorporated into the Republican platform, which supported a policy of peace through force (on the grounds that weakness provokes aggression); of conditioning American economic aid on acceptance of U.S. foreign policy; and of using American economic aid as a vehicle for exporting U.S. concepts.

In the Santa Fe Document, the Carter administration's economic aid program for Nicaragua was criticized and opposed, even while Carter was still in office. The Document also says that "efforts by the Nicaraguan people to establish free and independent government [sic] should be supported." The Document reiterates that one should return to the principle of treating one's friend as a friend and one's enemy as an enemy, without hesitation.

In its chapter on the new inter-American policy for the 1980s, the Santa Fe Document reaffirms the Monroe Doctrine and recognizes the close relationship between the struggle for power in the old and new worlds. It reserves the right to intervene in an implicit manner and, in a *contrario sensu* it reaffirms that "the U.S. does not desire to pursue a policy of intervention in the foreign and domestic affairs of any Latin American nation unless the Spanish-American states follow policies which aid and abet the intrusive imperialism of extra-continental powers."

Elsewhere, the Santa Fe Document states that a defense system in this hemisphere should consist of three elements or levels. The first and fundamental level, defined by the Rio Pact, makes inter-American intervention possible. The second, a subset of the first, is the regional defense organizations. . .and the third is bilateral accords between members of the first two levels.

The Document also criticizes Carter's policies harshly for abandoning the strategic perspective that shaped Monroe-Doctrine U.S. policy, centered on a conception of national interest and a belief in the moral legitimacy of defending that interest. It reaffirms the lasting nature of the "reasons" for the Monroe Doctrine's emergence 150 years ago.

The criticisms of the Carter administration for inconsistency are based upon what the ideologues of Reaganomics call Carter's moralism and predilection for policies that violate the economic and strategic interests of the U.S.

More recently, there is the Kissinger Commission Report, which is of special importance because of the attention President Reagan's policies should be given. The Kissinger Report situates Central America in the framework of the East-West conflict. It assumes that the Soviet Union has a strategic interest in Central America, which is to use Central America as a pressure point for opposing U.S. actions in Eastern Europe and Afghanistan, and eventually, it follows, as a bargaining chip at the appropriate moment.

The Kissinger Report proposes the thesis of an ongoing U.S.S.R. strategy in the Western Hemisphere, and particularly in Central America and the Caribbean, whereby the establishment of "more Cubas" would enable the U.S.S.R. to distract U.S. attention from other parts of the world that are of greater importance to Moscow. Further, it would enable the Soviet Union to create problems for U.S. relations with Western Europe, which is central to U.S. military and strategic interests.

In this light, Nicaragua is a geopolitical, strategic platform and a bridge to other Central American countries for revolutionary ideas and arms coming from Moscow and Havana.

The Kissinger Report does not dismiss the danger posed to U.S. national security by the establishment of Soviet military bases in Nicaragua. But it rejects the notion that the establishment of a Soviet base in Central America would be the only and most important threat to U.S. interests.

The Report expresses concern about a future threat to the security of Caribbean trade routes, which are needed to supply Europe in case of crisis. Such a threat would require the displacement of U.S. armed forces from other areas to guarantee these routes and defend U.S. interests in this hemisphere.

For these reasons, the Report emphasizes the need to contain what it calls Soviet military activity in this hemisphere. This includes the Soviet-Cuban drive to make Central America part of their strategic challenge and thus a risk to the hemispheric security system and to the U.S.

The Report sees Central America as an important arena of the East-West conflict, and Nicaragua as a center for Soviet-Cuban encouragement of armed insurgency in Central America — a strategic border in terms of U.S. security and a threat to the security of other Central American countries.

Based on these theses, the Kissinger Report elaborates its recommendations for Nicaragua. In general, they consist of maintaining constant military pressure and seeking a general agreement by which the relationship between internal democratization and external security is recognized, with the incentives of development aid and concessions for commercial exchange. In addition, it recommends that the U.S. and other countries be involved in a "regional system for peace," a structure that conforms to U.S. hemispheric and strategic interests, and that an institutionalized mechanism be established in the region to guarantee implementation of such a structure.

Nevertheless, reference is made in several places in the Report to the threat of the use of force. The invasion of Grenada is evoked as an action that, according to the Commission, has made Managua understand that U.S. foreign and domestic policy can change. The need to maintain military pressure and support for the armed counterrevolution is emphasized, without discarding the possibility of direct military intervention by the United States since — in its eyes — Nicaragua ought to know that force is always the ultimate option.

With respect to El Salvador, the line is in essence similar, although applied with specificity. One can perceive that the intention is to equate the situation in El Salvador and that in Nicaragua, tactically and strategically. The two struggles are melded, thus equating a civil war with a war of aggression and tacitly identifying the same solutions for both. These solutions are elections, dialogue, "internal democratization," plans for economic aid (in the case of Nicaragua) conditioned by acceptance of the rules of the political game as established by the U.S., and growing military aid to the Salvadoran army and to the counterrevolution in Nicaragua.

In the case of El Salvador, and specifically in the military arena, the Kissinger Report encourages a substantial increase in military aid that would be based on a budget of $400 million in 1984-1985, and an increase in the ratio of army to revolutionary forces (from a little less than four to one now to a little less than ten to one). This would mean an increase in the Salvadoran army from 35,000 to 120,000 men.

These measures, according to the Kissinger Report, would break the equilibrium of the war, which in the long run favors the revolutionary forces, and should be combined with a political solution by means of holding free elections with all groups participating. However, although a counterinsurgent effort is no substitute for negotiation, such an effort (the sooner the better) is a necessary condition for a political solution. The combination of both elements is the axis of the Kissinger Report and of U.S. policy in Central America.

As is well known, elections have been held in El Salvador without the participation of the revolutionary forces, and the opening of dialogue between President Duarte and the revolution has been announced.

Without precluding tactical changes necessitated by events, the Reagan administration's strategy in Central America rests on three points: 1) *Military*. The increase of financial, human, material, and logistical aid to the Salvadoran army and the counterrevolution, without discarding the use of direct intervention if conditions permit; 2) *Political*. Elections and dialogue that allow — and this is essential — the establishment of domestic conditions that are in the interest of the U.S.; 3) *Economic*. Discriminatory aid, conditioned on acceptance of the rules of the political game that the U.S. seeks to impose.

With respect to Nicaragua, the strategy has another aspect: the use of force by means of the counterrevolution (which does not negate other channels). The use of force has three alternative or complementary objectives: military per se, economic in terms of the effects on the economy of the ravages of war, and political in the sense of using force as a form of pressure throughout the process of difficult negotiations.

Finally, one can also perceive that a fundamental problem remains for the United States that reaches beyond problems of national security, of strategic and geopolitical conditions, and of the internal policies of the Central American countries in general and Nicaragua in particular. This is the fact that a qualitative change such as that produced by the Sandinista Popular Revolution skews the entire, huge mechanism of imperialism. The U.S. is thereby forced to justify and negotiate its military presence in Central America, and to evaluate the possibilities of regional peace in relation to the policies of the Central American nations, with the newly-free countries being able to accept or reject U.S. conduct. All this the system will not tolerate.

Sovereignty and self-determination are foreign bodies in the heart of the Empire, whose logic of domination cannot conceive of peace and co-existence in the region, except in accordance with the imposition of its own interests. At bottom, the Sandinista Popular Revolution introduced to the U.S. the demand that it recognize the historical aliveness of other countries, which before had breathed only because of the Empire, in a vicarious and second-hand existence.

In conclusion, the peace policy of the Revolutionary Government of Nicaragua begins with the recognition of a reality and its contradictions, the reality of Central America and the influence of the U.S., and the contradictions that are being introduced in the area from outside. It is based on a principle: the search for peace through dialogue, as shown in the decision of September 21, 1984 to sign the Contadora Peace Act without reservations. But Nicaragua's peace policy also flows from a legitimate demand: the demand for respect for sovereignty and self-determination, which is at the heart of the search for identity, the search for independence and freedom of Bolívar, and Sandino, and the Sandinista Popular Revolution. This search has meant a fight against two empires, Spain and the United States, and the search for nationhood as an act of historic will, as a concept of identity, as an expression of dignity.

It also means that the U.S. has an obligation to recognize this reality and to accept it, to divest itself of arrogant attitudes and supposed historic, natural rights that derive from its power in the region. For violence does not legitimize any action, not even with time or custom, and aggressions do not make jurisprudence. The United States not only assaults but also seeks to give formal, historical legitimacy to its assaults, deriving right from might instead of basing might on the observance of right. Today, more than ever, it is fitting to observe the wisdom of Benito Juárez and to say with him: "Respect for the rights of others is peace."

Paris
October 6, 1984

Presentation

Richard Falk

Professor of International Law at the
Center of International Studies, Princeton University

It is a great honor and privilege to participate in these proceedings.
The voice of the Permanent Peoples' Tribunal is needed at this historical
moment to lend support to the struggles of peoples throughout the world
on behalf of their sacred rights of self-determination.

The Tribunal has a special responsibility at this stage, when so many
governments are failing to uphold the most elementary rights of international law, especially with respect to smaller states. It is also a time when
international institutions are not able to fulfill the high hopes, which existed
earlier, that the organized international community could protect the liberating movements in their struggles and thereby aid the cause of self-
determination and human rights, both preconditions for political
democracy and independence. We realize that although this Tribunal lacks
police power and operates without the formal sanction of states, it plays
a critical role in defining the conscience of humanity in relation to the
great struggles of our time.

Very recently, a famous historian of Nazi Germany, William Shirer,
wrote that at the time of Nuremberg he had noted the following entry
in his diary on November 19, 1945: "Are we in this shattered old German
town on the eve of a great event in history? Will the trial of the Nazi war
criminals, which starts here tomorrow, establish, as some believe, principles as important to mankind as Magna Charta, the Bill of Rights, and
habeas corpus?" "It is just barely possible," his diary entry went on, "that
this trial may make a greater contribution to the outlawing of war than
all the past pious resolutions of nations and men, than a thousand solemn
treaties, than the Charter and machineries of the new United Nations.
Exciting questions." He ends.

Those questions may have been exciting, as he observed, but what
has happened since that time is that the world has grown understanda-
bly disillusioned with the Nuremberg claim to hold those who act for states
on issues of war and peace accountable for their violations. In other words,
the promise of the powers victorious against fascism to protect in future

Professor Falk also served on the jury of this session.

the rights and aspirations of peoples; to hold accountable the leaders of states when they engage in criminal courses of official conduct; to make governments and their leaders responsible for violations of international law. We can say definitively that those promises made to the peoples of the world in 1945 have not been kept. Those promises have been broken. And that is a serious development, which we as citizens cannot accept passively.

We can not give up the struggle to achieve that kind of accountability for leaders, to achieve the rights of peoples to determine their political, economic, and cultural future free of outside interference. To assure national integrity depends on honoring the aspirations of peoples free from interference by imperial powers operating either directly, through military means, or indirectly, through multinational corporations, banks, and international financial institutions. All these interferences with the rights of people to determine their destiny are the concern of everyone of good will. We live at a time when the borders of countries mean something for governments, but they do not mean something for the people of the world caught up in the dangers and opportunities of a common historical experience. Therefore, the imperative of transnational solidarity has become at this time one of the strongest instruments in the struggle for peace and justice that all of us have. And I think it is as a contribution to that notion of solidarity that Lelio Basso and others conceived of this tribunal, and took the steps that brought it into being, including the issuance of its Algiers Declaration back in 1976 that established a framework within which it has operated.

Let me say as an American that it is a particular cause of sadness that the role of the United States within the world in relation to these kinds of issues has changed so dramatically since the struggle against fascism was waged in World War II. Of course, we need to acknowledge that in the Western Hemisphere, the United States has played an imperial role that goes back to the beginning of its own existence, from the time of the Monroe Doctrine onward. But on the larger world stage, the United States did stand rather firmly against the ideological pretensions of the colonial powers and was a source of inspiration to many independence struggles. It did stand against the notion that world peace could be organized on the basis of power politics and mere geopolitics. It stood for a vision of a much more law-ordered world; it stood for the vision of substituting the collective efforts of nations for the war system; and it stood for the idea that disputes between nations should be solved peacefully, through diplomacy and, if necessary, by submission to courts rather than by the methods of a bully using military superiority to force his will.

All of these ideals, never fully supported in practice, were always caught up in the contradictions of capitalism, caught up in the contradictions of the United States' own expansive search for power and prestige and dominance in international arenas. All these ideals have been abandoned in the post-1945 period — partly in the course of waging the Cold War, partly to fill the vacuum left by the colonial powers in the Third World, and partly to protect the economic dominance of the North against the challenges of Third World nationalism. And the result has been that on an international stage, there is no *normative* leadership at the present time. No one has come, no collective force has come to re-state and to resume the struggle for institutions of peace and justice and procedures to implement these goals. This struggle for a safer, juster world is, in the nuclear age, more critical than it has ever been. One false move can end the entire experience of the human race forever. And that false move depends on the wisdom of the sorts of leaders that now exist in the super-powers, hardly a reassuring feature of our world situation.

For these reasons, it becomes a matter of urgency, it seems to me, for the peoples of the world to understand that law can function as their instrument. It does not belong exclusively to the state. It does not belong to governments if they don't uphold their fundamental, solemn obligations to conduct their affairs in accordance with the law of nations, to conduct their affairs in harmony with fundamental international morality, to act in a manner that is respectful of human rights and of the rights of peoples to seek peace and their own destiny. And it is in relation to this central set of concerns that the Permanent Peoples' Tribunal tries to reinforce this basic claim: that law belongs to all of us, and that we must reclaim it from the destructive forces that are crystallized in imperial power politics at this time. In a deeper political sense, the role of law in the pursuit of *real* democracy needs to be appreciated in a setting in which *formal* democracy has been seriously eroded through the growth of state power.

It is law as performing on behalf of the mission of the weak — weak in terms of technology, weak in terms of weaponry, but strong in terms of the justice that underlies their quest. And it is in this spirit that we take very seriously the opening words of the preamble of the Charter of the United Nations, which speaks of the aspirations of "We the peoples of the United Nations. . ." (not the states of the world — the most fundamental acknowledgement is that of the peoples of the world):

> to save succeeding generations from the scourge of war, which twice in our lifetime has brought untold sorrow to mankind, and
>
> to reaffirm faith in fundamental human rights, in the dignity and worth of the human person, in the equal rights of men and women and of nations large and small, and
>
> to establish conditions under which justice and respect for obligations arising from treaties and other sources of international law can be maintained,

and to promote social progress and better standards of life in larger freedom.

These aspirations of the United Nations Charter, subscribed to by all the members of the organization, that is, by all the leading states, provide the basis for a more just arrangement in the world. But that just arrangement can begin to be realized only to the extent that popular movements within civil society exert sufficient pressure on their own governments and other governments to make the United Nations begin to fulfill the ideas that lay beneath its creation at the end of World War II. It is against that background that the Universal Declaration of the Rights of the Peoples adopted in 1976 at Algiers was drafted to guide this Tribunal. And it took shape on behalf of the hopes that existed in the period of liberation struggles, and it took shape despite the fears and dangers associated with the enormously destructive efforts of domestic and international structures of imperialism to frustrate these popular aspirations.

The question, I think, before all of us now on the eve of this very important session — perhaps the most important session of the Permanent Peoples' Tribunal — is whether we can maintain the kind of commitment that has created the great advances throughout the history of human civilization. The Magna Charta did not come out of the enlightened wisdom of British royalty; it came out of a struggle that was mounted from below by victims of arbitrary and exploitative power. All of the advances of civil society toward justice, the recent advances against colonialism, the civil rights struggle in my own country, represent the outcomes of struggles waged by people who are led and activated by moral passion, including subscription to the view that justice is possible, that its attainment depends on our actions, and that our actions include the right to pass judgment on the illegitimate behavior of governments and statesmen. That is what the Nuremberg Judgment promised us. Nuremberg promised us that in the future all governments and all leaders would be subject to certain minimum conceptions of legality, that no criminal enterprise could be embodied in the political authority of the state and not be held responsible.

And so, as we commence these proceedings, we commence them with a commitment to uphold that vision and to impose responsibility on the most serious forms of criminal enterprise ever known to human experience, namely, the predatory politics of imperial powers being imposed at the expense of peoples who are not adequately armed, or not adequately clothed and fed, in many cases. And it is on behalf of this idea of responsibility for leaders, of accountability for governments, of the possession of law as a resource of the people, that we are dedicated to work as effectively as possible within the framework of the Permanent Peoples' Tribunal, to establish conditions under which justice and respect for obligations arising from treaties and other sources of international law can be maintained. Our mission is to advance the cause of peace and justice everywhere by clarifying the facts and pronouncing a judgment on competing claims as to legal rights. Thank you very much.

Presentation

Freddy Balzán

Executive Secretary of TANA (Antimperialist Tribunal of Our America)

Honorable President of the Tribunal, François Rigaux, Honorable Members of the Jury, Distinguished members of the Nicaraguan Delegation, Ladies and Gentlemen:

First, on behalf of the President and Executive Secretariat of the Antimperialist Tribunal of Our America (Tribunal Antimperialista de Nuestra América, TANA), let me express our appreciation to the Permanent Peoples' Tribunal. We also thank the people and government of Belgium for their hospitality.

This meeting of the Permanent Peoples' Tribunal takes place at a time when humanity finds itself in a recession with respect to rights and justice. Shocking violations seem to be an everyday occurrence, as a result of the current U.S. administration's persistence in placing the world on the brink of total destruction.

As Dr. Rafael Chamorro has pointed out, for more than a century and a half "Our America" — as José Martí used to call it, to differentiate it from the North that exploits and attacks us — has been gathering visions and conducting struggles to overcome the tragic social and economic conditions, the backwardness and underdevelopment, that our people suffer. It would be impossible to mention here more than a few of the many accusations that distinguished personalities from Latin America and the Caribbean have compiled, in numerous books, regarding the crimes and aggressions of all kinds carried out by different U.S. administrations against the freedom, sovereignty, and self-determination of our countries. We need only refer to the so-called Santa Fe Document, which the Reagan administration has applied to the letter, making it unnecessary to recall other doctrines such as that of Manifest Destiny. His goal of political, economic, and military domination is clear.

In this context, on September 21, 1981, the Antimperialist Tribunal was born in Nicaragua as an instrument of the people of our America to defend their legitimate rights. This was at a time when those rights were threatened by the United States: a time when the Reagan administration was organizing the second version of the Halcón Vista or Falcon's Eye military maneuvers to intimidate Nicaragua, a time when Panama was denouncing before the United Nations the violations of the Canal treaty by the U.S.; at a time when two heads of state, Omar Torrijos and Jaime Roldós died, victims of strange airplane accidents. Today, our Tribunal consists of 30 chapters in an equal number of Latin American and Caribbean nations. At present, the Antimperialist Tribunal of Our America seeks to solicit incorporation into the United Nations as a non-governmental organization. We want to express our recognition of the Permanent Peoples' Tribunal as a inspiring example; it has gained international prestige from the moral integrity of its members and its actions.

Like the Permanent Peoples' Tribunal, the Antimperialist Tribunal of Our America is a force of conscience, of public opinion, and a means of constantly denouncing all the Reagan administration's plans for aggression and against peace. This applies in particular to Central America, especially Nicaragua and El Salvador, which are constant victims of the application of the Santa Fe Document. Some of the affirmations in that document, for example, that war and not peace is the norm that rules international affairs, are sufficient for one to understand the constant and repeated violations of international laws and laws of the U.S. itself, violations constantly ignored by the U.S. government.

It was for this reason that TANA, in tribunals held in Panama and Ecuador, and with the support of all the peoples of our America, denounced the war of aggression against the people of Nicaragua — a war to destroy their revolution and their legitimate government. A clear demonstration of that war is the plan executed by the Central Intelligence Agency, on orders from President Reagan, to make the peace talks and efforts of the Contadora Group fail. Meanwhile, the Reagan administration manipulates the international media and information sources to justify its plans to invade Nicaragua; as experts on these matters have said, it is all part of a planned psychological war.

Our America has had serious and painful experiences with this psychological war, as in Guatemala in 1954, when the democratic government of Jacobo Arbenz was removed by a CIA-organized coup d'etat. Seven years later, they tried to repeat it in Cuba but failed at the Bay of Pigs. But the dignity of our America was again humiliated, as former President Juan Bosch said recently, with the invasion of the Dominican Republic in 1965 and again with the bloody events that took place in Chile in 1973, and once again on the little island of Grenada in the Caribbean.

We need only look at the tragedies suffered by the people of Chile, Grenada, Uruguay, Paraguay, Haiti, and Guatemala to fathom the degree of responsibility of various U.S. administrations. But in the case that we are analyzing today in this Tribunal, regarding the aggression against Nicaragua, the situation is much more serious because the peace of the whole Central American region is threatened by the bellicose policies of the current U.S. administration. As with Puerto Rico, colonized by the U.S. in 1898, President Reagan has not hesitated to declare his decision to transform Honduras into a giant military base for aggression against Nicaragua. Thousands of Somocista mercenaries, morally and financially supported by the CIA, are being used as tools in this unjust war being waged by the most economically and militarily powerful capitalist country in the world against a small Central American nation.

Mr. President and Members of the Jury: I believe it is necessary to point out, as Dr. Richard Falk did earlier, that when the International Military Tribunal of Nuremberg was constituted to judge and condemn Nazism and its responsibility for crimes against peace and humanity, a new historical chapter of great importance opened. New crimes and criminals were being judged under international law. Later other tribunals were formed, tribunals such as this, whose integrity earns it credibility among all our people.

I want to inform you that in the hearings conducted by the Antimperialist Tribunal in the two countries that I mentioned before, the Reagan administration was unanimously accused of:

Coercion, by virtue of the facts already cited by Dr. Chamorro, under the U.N. Charter, Article 2, Paragraph 3, and Paragraph 4 which states that members of the organization (the United States being one of them) will refrain from resorting to the threat or use of force against the territorial integrity or political independence of any state, or in any manner inconsistent with the purposes of the United Nations.

Our second accusation against the U.S. government is the flagrant violation of Resolution 3314 of the U.N. dated December 14, 1974. The charges here are:

Militarism, for its efforts to transform Latin America into a giant military base, going to the extreme of violating the Tlatelolco Treaty for the denuclearization of Latin America by placing nuclear bombers in Puerto Rico (information that came from reliable sources in that country).

Economic Discrimination, because of the serious economic crisis that our countries are suffering as a result of the impositions of the International Monetary Fund and the rise in interest rates of American bankers, and the measures taken by the U.S. administration against the weak economies and natural resources of Latin America.

Ideological Aggression, by virtue of the Reagan administration's campaign against international organizations like the U.N., UNESCO, and others, with the excuse that they are influenced by international communism. Also, by its support to counterrevolutionary radio broadcasting financed by the CIA in Honduras and Costa Rica, like the "September 15" and "Voice of Sandino" stations, and the installation of sophisticated equipment to serve the United States in Costa Rican territory.

I would like to end my presentation by stating that other charges against the government of Ronald Reagan are: mercenarism, manipulation of regional organizations, and complicity with genocidal regimes. These charges do not admit discussion; distinguished U.S. personages are in complete disagreement with the illegal activities ordered by the White House.

On behalf of the Antimperialist Tribunal of Our America, let me again express our appreciation of the invitation to be here. Let me also express our hope that all of you will join in the sentiments prevailing in our nations by condemning the interventionist and bellicose policies of the Reagan administration, for the sake of peace in Central America and for the American people. Thank you.

II

TESTIMONY
FROM NICARAGUA

Report on Military Aggression Against Nicaragua by U.S. Imperialism

Captain Rosa Pasos

Sandinista Popular Army

I. INTRODUCTION

Relations between the United States and Nicaragua have traditionally been characterized by the U.S. desire to subject our country to its control. Our country has suffered no fewer than 14 armed U.S. interventions, from that of the filibusterer William Walker in 1856 to the well-known intervention against Sandino in the 1930s. With the triumph of July 19, 1979, Nicaragua began pursuing its own future independently. The current U.S. administration has responded with an unjust and aggressive policy.

The mining of our ports, the indiscriminate bombing of civilian and economic targets, the attacks from the sea, such as the opening of a new front in the Pacific Ocean between Nicaragua and Costa Rica, all form part of the aggressive plans which the CIA has already begun to implement. Among those plans, one of the most relevant is the effort to renew the indiscriminate mining of our waters.

Up to now, the U.S. administration has not altered its policy, despite the overtures toward peace and negotiation by the government and people of Nicaragua and by other forces and governments of the world.

Nicaragua denounces before the world the armed aggression supported by the Reagan administration, an aggression whose accelerating pace brings it closer every day to direct U.S. military intervention and the extension of the war throughout Central America.

*   *   *

The Introduction section has been slightly abbreviated for reasons of space.

II. CHRONOLOGY OF AGGRESSION 1979-1981

In 1979, the ex-Somoza National Guardsmen emigrated from our country, establishing their main camps in the border areas of Nicaragua (El Paraíso, Danlí, and Choluteca, Republic of Honduras). They also established training centers in U.S. territory, principally in Florida and California, in violation of the Neutrality Act by which the U.S. is bound. In 1979, Steadman Fagoth, ex-officer in Somoza's National Security Forces and originally from Puerto Cabezas, department of Zelaya, sent a large number of Miskitos to Honduras to prepare the conditions for creating an organized military force.

Between 1979 and 1981, individuals and armed groups emerged, seeking the military overthrow of the revolution but they were not the principal form of confrontation. Examples are Bernardino Larios, ex-National Guardsman and ex-Minister of Defense in the Government of National Reconstruction, and Jorge Salazar of COSEP (Superior Council for Private Industry), as well as groups of delinquent individuals who operated in the rural sectors of the departments of Jinotega, Matagalpa, and central Zelaya. These were groups of 30 to 40 men, poorly armed.

In 1980, diverse groups of ex-Guardsmen such as the September 15th Legion, the National Liberation Army, and the Nicaraguan Democratic Revolutionary Association (ADREN) began to organize in Guatemala, the United States, and principally in Honduras. They lacked any defined political-military strategy, but the military authorities and government functionaries of Honduras began to offer support to these counterrevolutionaries. There was then an increase in criminal acts against the national literacy campaign; counterrevolutionaries assassinated several young brigade members who were teaching our *campesinos* in the mountains to read and write. Constant attacks, supported by the Honduran Public Security Force, Department of National Investigation, and armed forces were carried out against health outposts and border patrols. At the same time, a political campaign at the international level was initiated with the goals of attracting more Somocistas to the counterrevolutionary ranks and defaming the revolution.

Steadman Fagoth, who had been imprisoned for attempting to organize a movement against the Nicaraguan government, was freed by our authorities. He moved to Honduran territory and, at the behest of the CIA, became head of the MISURA counterrevolutionary forces, which are partially composed of ethnic minority Miskitos whom Fagoth himself had gathered together in Honduran territory.

The MISURA achieved some level of organization and defined a strategy of struggle which was used to carry out the "Red Christmas Plan" in December, 1981. This plan consisted of penetration into the interior of the North Zelaya region by counterrevolutionary elements with the goal of agitating, arming the population, and attempting to take Puerto Cabezas. They were then to call upon the international community to recognize a provisional government, and seek assistance under the Inter-American Treaty of Reciprocal Assistance — assistance that would include military intervention. This plan was completely frustrated by our forces.

In August, 1981, the United States made supposed efforts at mediation, not yet directly imposing a military formula for dealing with the revolution. Thomas Enders, Assistant Secretary of State for Latin American Affairs, arrived in Nicaragua, bringing, on Reagan's behalf, the threat of expanding the counterrevolution and the threat of U.S. military power, if Nicaragua did not cut off relations with the Soviets and the Cubans, stop arming itself, and discontinue the alleged arms flow to El Salvador.

With the failure of this policy, the Reagan administration blocked the diplomatic efforts by the Nicaraguan government to reduce tensions, and attempted to gain U.S. public support for the first $19 million in aid to the contras.

In October-November, 1981, the counterrevolution reached a new stage, which was manifested in new methods. From a contra force of 12-20 groups split by internal conflicts, there emerged a more united counterrevolution, principally in the form of the Nicaraguan Democratic Force (Fuerza Democrática Nicaraguënse, FDN), largely financed and trained by the CIA. It is here that the U.S. government's intention to destroy the revolution through the use of a military strategy — more than through the use of internal and external economic and political tactics — is most clearly visible.

The CIA and the Honduran government worked to develop a more organic structure for the counterrevolution, and in addition the United States began a series of military exercises in Honduran territory. These exercises threatened the security and sovereignty of Nicaragua and at the same time served to provide political and logistical support for the counterrevolutionaries.

From October 7 to 9, shortly before the attempt to carry out the "Red Christmas Plan" on our Atlantic Coast, the U.S.-Honduran exercises called "Halcón Vista — Honduras 1981" or "Falcon's Eye" were begun along the Atlantic Coast of Honduras in the departments of Cortés and Atlantida. The exercises were carried out with U.S. participation, including 757 U.S. military personnel, planes and ships, an amphibious landing craft, and other means of support, making the U.S. leadership of the Honduran armed forces clear. CIA support was evident in 1981, in a December 2 attempt to blow up an Aeronica airliner in Mexico with C-4 explosives. The attempt resulted in injuries to three crew members.

III. THE DEVELOPMENT OF AGGRESSION IN 1982

During 1982, there was a significant increase in counterrevolutionary activity. A political directorate of the FDN emerged, there was a qualitative improvement in its operative structures with the appearance of military units having specific assignments, and the training of commando groups was initiated.

In 1982, the U.S. developed a campaign to compromise Nicaragua in connection with the deepening political crisis in El Salvador. One example of this campaign is the case of Orlando Tardencilla, a Nicaraguan youth whom the U.S. Department of State attempted to force before television cameras in the United States, to prove allegations of Nicaragua's support for the Salvadoran guerrillas. Other examples include the publication of fraudulent photographs in *Le Figaro* of Paris, to justify in the eyes of the world the destruction of the revolution by means of a military intervention. This campaign was uncovered by our revolutionary government, but the U.S. strategy of promoting a counterrevolution continued.

The MISURA forces carried out counterrevolutionary operations in Walpasiksa and Seven Benk, North Zelaya, again with the intention of taking Puerto Cabezas. However, the organization encountered problems and, as a result, a new group led by Brooklyn Rivera took over the leadership.

In 1982, the CIA promoted the counterrevolutionary Democratic Revolutionary Alliance (Alianza Revolucionaria Democrática, ARDE), composed of various counterrevolutionary organizations: the Sandino Revolutionary Front (Frente Revolucionario Sandino, FRS) led by the ex-Sandinista Edén Pastora, the Brooklyn Rivera faction of the MISURA, a group led by Alfonso Robelo Callejas (MDN), and the Nicaraguan Democratic Union of Fernando Chamorro (Unión Democrática Nicaraguënse, UDN). ARDE concentrated its activities in Costa Rican territory, which provided cover for military missions in the department of Río San Juan and South Zelaya.

In 1982, commando groups carried out numerous acts of sabotage against civilian targets. The most important of these acts and targets were:

1. An explosion at the Augusto César Sandino Airport in Managua on February 22, 1982, causing four deaths and three injuries.

2. Río Negro Bridge, in Somotillo, department of Chinandega, March 14, 1982.

3. Río Coco Bridge, in Ocotal, department of Madriz, March 14, 1982.

4. An electrical plant in the department of Chinandega, highway to Somotillo, blown up April 17, 1982.

5. Nawas Bridge in North Zelaya, destroyed by MISURA commandos.

6. At the Iyas construction plant in the department of Matagalpa,

the dynamiting of 31 trucks and all installations, killing the caretaker, on August 29, 1982.

At the end of 1982, "Plan C" was developed. Up to 3,000 counter-revolutionaries (seven units) participated in this plan, which lasted until April 1983. It affected the department of Nueva Segovia (areas adjacent to the town of Jalapa) and to a lesser degree the departments of Jinotega and Matagalpa. The object was to isolate and take over the border area of the town of Jalapa in order to declare it liberated territory.

The counterrevolutionary forces also pursued the following objectives:

1. An urban conspiracy in the departments of León and Chinandega (not successful).

2. The creation of new commando groups of 20-30 men loaded with explosives for sabotaging the means of communication in the rural areas of Chinandega and Estelí.

3. Task forces to carry out military activity in the interior of the country.

4. Finally, the seizure of a garrison in Jalapa as the climax of the plan.

Our armed people aborted the entire plan, leaving a total of 476 counterrevolutionaries dead, 159 wounded, and 113 taken prisoner.

IV. 1983 TO EARLY 1984

In 1983, the policy of aggression toward our country was intensified. Its most significant aspects included:

The Closing of Nicaraguan Consulates

The closing of several Nicaraguan consulates in the U.S. and the expulsion of Nicaraguan diplomats was a vindictive response to the expulsion from Nicaragua of three North Americans who were proven to be CIA agents and who tried to carry out a plan to assassinate the Minister of Foreign Relations, Father Miguel D'Escoto.

Increased Financial Support for Covert CIA Actions

Increased financial support for covert CIA actions resulted in a large increase in terrorist activities, sabotage, and air and naval attacks against our revolution by counterrevolutionary forces based in Honduras and Costa Rica, and with direct CIA involvement; there was also the use of special commando forces, the mining of ports and air attacks, later confirmed by high officials of the U.S. administration.

Some of the principal examples of these actions were as follows:

May 1983. Counterrevolutionary elements infiltrated the state production unit (UPE) at El Amparo, jurisdiction of San Juan del Río Coco, in the department of Nueva Segovia, burning it to the ground and destroying a small airplane and a privately owned truck. Also, commandos

from the MISURA group sabotaged the wharf at Puerto Cabezas, causing partial destruction and damaging some fishing boats.

June 1983. FDN commandos destroyed the Ministry of Construction
(MICONS) plant at La Dalia, situated between the populated areas of
Río Blanco and Siuna, damaging equipment and machinery used in high-
way construction.

July 1983. FDN commandos destroyed the bridge at San Fabián, which
spans the Pan American Highway north of the city of Ocotal. Groups
from ARDE, supported by Push-Pull aircraft, infiltrated from Costa Rica
and destroyed two gasoline storage tanks, burned a sawmill, and damaged
Puerto Isabel in North Zelaya. Counterrevolutionary groups partially destroyed the bridge over the Jigüina River in the department of Jinotega,
as well as the bridge over the Tuma River in the department of Matagalpa.
They also tried to destroy the "Siempre Viva" hydroelectric plant located
at Mina Bonanza. Another counterrevolutionary group partially destroyed
the bridge at Ocote, located in the region of Yaosca, department of
Jinotega.

August 1983. FDN counterrevolutionary forces destroyed the Santa
Elena bridge located in the valley of Pantasma, department of Jinotega.
The Jocote Bridge in the department of Estelí was also destroyed.

September 1983. Among the most significant acts of terrorism were
the following: counterrevolutionary frogmen with high-tech underwater
gear provided by the CIA destroyed signal buoys at Puerto Sandino, the
only port in Nicaragua where fuel can be unloaded; a pirate plane flying
from Honduras fired air-to-ground missiles at the "Nicaragua" electric
plant located at Puerto Sandino, resulting in partial damage; a twin-engine
plane piloted by the counterrevolutionaries Sebastián Müller and Augustín
Román, members of ARDE, bombed installations at the Augusto César
Sandino International Airport in Managua; concurrently, another light
aircraft dropped two bombs on the Central American School of Secondary Education in Managua; a counterrevolutionary airplane fired air-
to-ground missiles at the alcohol processing plant (Induquinsa) located
on the highway between Managua and León; T-28 military aircraft flying from Honduran territory attacked civil installations at Puerto Corinto,
dropping several bombs and unleashing machine-gun fire.

At the end of September, counterrevolutionary elements from Honduran territory attacked the Nicaraguan customs installations at El Espino,
totally destroying them, with the open and unabashed cooperation of the
Honduran government. Finally, ARDE counterrevolutionary elements
attacked the border post of Peñas Blancas, the destruction of which
included Nicaraguan/Costa Rican communication towers.

October 1983. Counterrevolutionary boats using incendiary projec-
tiles attacked fuel storage tanks at Puerto Corinto, destroying several tanks,

causing enormous economic losses, and endangering the lives of thousands of inhabitants of the port. Piranha speedboats attacked the wharf at Puerto Cabezas, causing partial destruction, and leaving one dead and 12 civilians wounded. FDN elements placed explosive charges in the pipeline and signal buoys at Puerto Sandino, damaging the fuel unloading systems.

In addition, a counterrevolutionary group from Honduran territory invaded the village of Pantasma, department of Jinotega, and burned down the MICONS plant, a local branch of Encafé, and the local health center, killing 29 people.

November 1983. Coast Guards of the Honduran Army attacked boats of the Sandinista Navy in the Gulf of Fonseca. Concurrently, counterrevolutionary piranha boats attacked other units at Point Consigüina. Both actions occurred in Nicaraguan waters.

December 1983. The Honduran Coast Guard attacked Nicaraguan fishing boats in national waters at Cape Gracias a Dios. Counterrevolutionary elements attacked and destroyed granaries at Ciudad Antigua, department of Nueva Segovia. Piranha boats supported by Honduran planes attacked units of the Sandinista Navy at Puerto Potosí, department of Chinandega; this action was repeated two days later. Similar actions were carried out in the Gulf of Fonseca, in Nicaraguan waters.

Blackmail and Intimidation

The U.S. policy of blackmail and intimidation was another factor that reflected the intensification of aggression during 1983. The United States initiated military maneuvers — ground, air, and sea — which elevated tension in the region to a dangerous degree.

From 1982 on, the U.S. military presence in Nicaragua has been felt in the periodic flights over Nicaraguan territory of U.S. reconnaissance planes coming from either the continental U.S. or from its southern command post in Panama. This reconnaissance has been systematically directed at discovering the location, composition, and movements of our troops, and in addition has provided intelligence data used to intensify aggression and improve direct counterrevolutionary actions. It was carried out with planes of various types (RC-135s, U2s, C-130s, and F3As, among others). In 1982, 102 flights were detected; this number was tripled in 1983 to some 479 U.S. strategic reconnaissance flights.

The U.S. military presence has also been felt through American naval warships sent to carry out patrols and reconnaissance along our coast, particularly on the Pacific side. To this end, the United States sends one frigate or destroyer — and in some cases even two — on a monthly basis to observe 20-40 miles of coastline. In 1983, we detected 12 American warships involved in these maneuvers and in 1984, as of September, we have detected nine.

The U.S. military presence in Nicaragua increased in magnitude between July and September 1983, when Reagan decided to respond to the peace proposal presented by the Nicaraguan government on July 19, 1983, by carrying out practice maneuvers for a naval blockade along both the Atlantic and Pacific coasts. Three Navy groups participated, composed of warships and 16,484 Marines; over a period of three months, they alternated in controlling the entry and exit of ships at our ports.

These groups were:

1. Aircraft Carrier *Ranger CV-61* and its Battle group

    — July 26-August 12, 1983

    — Location: 100 miles west of the Gulf of Fonseca

    — Patrolled along 20-40 miles of Nicaraguan coast.

    — On July 30, 1983, intercepted by radio and followed the Soviet cargo ship *Alexander Ulianov* coming to unload wheat at Puerto Corinto.

    — An F-14 from the *Ranger* intercepted a C-47 of the Sandinista Armed Forces (Fuerzas Armadas Sandinistas, FAS) some 30 miles south of Corinto on July 31, 1983.

2. Aircraft Carrier *Coral Sea* and its Battle Group

    — August 16-September 10, 1983

    — Location: 125-200 miles from Cape Gracias a Dios in the Caribbean.

    — Conducted joint reconnaissance maneuvers as well as tracking missions and destruction of air objectives with B-52 bombings, September 1-3, 1983.

    — Conducted maneuvers and blockade practice, August 15-September 10, 1983.

3. Navy Battle Group Led by the Battleship *New Jersey*

    — August 26-September 13, 1983

    — Location: 20-40 miles from Nicaraguan coast in the Pacific Ocean.

    — Carried out coastal patrols.

    — Conducted a firepower demonstration with 406-mm cannons 30 miles from El Salvador.

The increased U.S. military presence in the region had already begun by February, 1983, when ground, air, and sea maneuvers called "Big Pine I" [also called "Pino Alto" or by its original Miskito name, "Ahuas Tara I" — Ed.] were officially initiated in Honduran territory. These maneuvers took place in the Honduran departments of Gracias a Dios, Cortés, Comayagua, and Francisco Morazán. Their principal objective was to provide political, moral, and material support to the Honduran Armed Forces and to the counterrevolution, as well as to cover plans to infiltrate our territory. The forces and means used were:

a. U.S. Participation

— Up to 1,600 members of the U.S. Army, Air Force, and Navy

— Two LCM-8 landing craft

— Two landing support ships

— One LST amphibious tank transport ship

— 12 C-130 aircraft

— Three CH-47 Chinook helicopters

— Three 02-A Push-Pull aircraft

— One LKA amphibious craft

— Small communication and engineering units from the 193rd Infantry Brigade stationed in the Southern Command, Panama.

b. Honduran Participation

— Up to 4,000 members of the Army, Air Force, and Navy

— Eight UH-1H-D helicopters

— Four A-37 "Dragonfly" aircraft

— Eight Super Mystère B-2 aircraft

— Four patrol boats

— One Coast Guard boat

— One supply boat

— One LCM-8 landing craft

TOTAL: 5,600 men

In August 1983, new joint Honduran-U.S. military maneuvers called "Big Pine II" or "Ahuas Tara II" were carried out in Honduran territory and lasted through March of 1984. These maneuvers were carried out in the departments of El Valle, Choluteca, Lloro, Colón, Olancho, and Comayagua in Honduras. Their purpose was to create a military situation in Honduras that would permit the Honduran Armed Forces to support the Salvadoran Armed Forces against the Salvadoran national liberation movement. They were also intended to intimidate our revolution through a demonstration of force, and to supply the Honduran Armed Forces and the counterrevolution to an unprecedented degree, strengthening the military, tactical, and training infrastructure in order to fortify the general plan of aggression against Nicaragua.

The forces participating in these maneuvers were as follows:

a. U.S. Participation

— Up to 5,000 members of the ground, sea, and air forces of the U.S. Armed Forces. These included one naval amphibian unit, the 43rd

Ground Force Support Group, the 210th Battalion Air Combat Brigade, and a battalion of engineers from the 20th Brigade of the Army Corps of Engineers from the 82nd Division (Fort Bragg, North Carolina).

b. Honduran Participation

— Up to 6,000 members of the Honduran Armed Forces

— Two infantry brigades

— One airborne battalion

— One tank battalion

— Logistics and security units

TOTAL: 11,000 or twice the number of men involved in Big Pine I.

In connection with these maneuvers, in 1983 and part of 1984, the U.S. constructed the following infrastructure in Honduras:

— 1,000 feet of airstrip expansion at Palmerola, plus radar and communications in the department of Comayagua, with a budget of $13 million.

— 5,000 feet of airstrip expansion at San Lorenzo, department of Valle, on the border with Nicaragua.

— 5,000 feet of airstrip expansion at La Esperanza, department of Intibuca.

— 8,000 feet of airstrip expansion at El Aguacate, department of Olancho.

— 5,000 feet of airstrip expansion at Trujillo, department of Colón.

— Expansion of the air base at Puerto Lempira, department of Gracias a Dios.

— Construction covering 150 hectares and including a communications center, meteorological station, two firing ranges, etc., at the Regional Center for Military Training and Security (CREMS) at Sin Sin, department of Colón.

— Construction of an infantry training camp at San Lorenzo, department of Valle.

— Construction at the U.S. radar base at Cerro El Hule, department of Francisco Morazán, with a budget of $5 million.

— Remodeling and expansion of the highway that connects Dulce Nombre del Culmí, department of Olancho, and Ahuasbila and Mokorón, on the Nicaraguan border, with a budget of $7 million.

— 5,000-foot airstrip expansion at Comayagua, department of Copán.

— 5,000-foot expansion of the drainage system and a 1,000-foot park at the airstrip of El Paraíso, department of El Paraíso, bordering on Nicaragua.

The plans that the counterrevolutionaries tried to carry out in early 1983 formed part of the original "Plan C" with some modifications, since urban and suburban commandos in the Pacific region had been ineffective and were almost totally neutralized by our security forces. For this reason, new task forces were introduced in February. After the frustrated attempt by the "El Suicida" counterrevolutionaries in Jalapa, "Plan Siembra" ("Seeding Plan") was put into action. This plan involved the introduction of forces with air support deep into the country in several areas, principally in the departments of Matagalpa and Jinotega; it always included the possibility of seizing Jalapa with forces stationed in Honduran territory along the border. Revolutionary resistance to the plan resulted in 409 counterrevolutionary casualties: 226 dead, 159 wounded, and 24 prisoners.

In mid-1983, the U.S. government met with difficulties in providing "covert" support to the counterrevolution. As a result, it needed to carry out actions against our country that would give credibility to the FDN. The FDN had been discredited by its misuse of funds, and there was opposition in the U.S. Congress to providing aid. The leadership of the FDN was changed; the CIA came to exercise more direct control over its funds, and/or to direct its actions more closely, as well as to reactivate air supply.

The CIA initiated the "Marathon Plan" at the beginning of September, in which it regrouped about 1,300 counterrevolutionary forces at Somoto and Ocotal, in the Nicaraguan departments of Madriz and Nueva Segovia. Because of the terrain, the CIA believed that it was possible to carry out a quick operation to seize Ocotal and Monoto to serve as garrisons in liberated territory, and to bring in Honduran forces supported by task forces operating in the departments of Jinotega and Matagalpa.

This new plan was aborted, leaving 188 counterrevolutionaries dead, 40 wounded and 12 prisoners, for a total of 240 enemy losses. After the Marathon Plan, the CIA rapidly organized a new counterrevolutionary offensive for November and December, bringing in task forces with 3,000 counterrevolutionaries. This new offensive was called the "Sierra Plan" and consisted, once again, of trying to take Jalapa, as the seat of the offensive, and Murra, Ciudad Sandino, Santa Clara, and San Fernando in the departments of Madriz and Nueva Segovia, utilizing the support of forces still operating in the departments of Matagalpa and Jinotega. As a complement to this plan, the counterrevolutionary forces were to carry out major actions at Point Consigüina in the Gulf of Fonseca with the objective of making us disperse our military efforts, thereby weakening the Jalapa command center.

The counterrevolutionary Sierra Plan lasted through January, 1984, when our people again responded to the aggression by breaking up the plan. The result was 256 enemy casualties: 154 dead, 85 wounded, and 17 captured.

This last offensive in 1983 coincided with the U.S. invasion of Grenada in November. The invasion created a very tense situation because of the imminent danger of intervention in Nicaragua, as well, given that the "Big Pine II" maneuvers climaxed on November 15 with the landing of the 28th Amphibian Infantry on the Atlantic coast of Honduras.

V. DEVELOPMENT OF MILITARY AGGRESSION IN 1984

In February, 1984, the Sierra Plan was aborted, leaving only a small group of armed men in the north of Cerro Kilambe in the department of Jinotega, and in the region to the east of the department of Matagalpa. The bulk of those forces were concentrated in Honduran territory. The CIA strengthened the FDN in particular, which was organized more efficiently with the adoption of a structure of regional commands having two or three task forces in each command. Nevertheless, the military strengthening of mercenary forces did not include an organic political strengthening, basically because of the contradictions within the FDN and those between it and the other counterrevolutionary organizations.

Beginning in February and March of 1984, the counterrevolution began once again to infiltrate from Honduran territory, with the goal of reaching various areas of Nicaragua. It was at this time that the CIA succeeded in having the FDN structured with five regional commands as follows:

a. Regional Command Nicaráo, led by ex-general Benito Bravo, who had his principal base at La Lodoza, in Honduran territory.

b. Regional Command Segovia, led by ex-general Manuel Rugama, with support bases at Quebrada de Oro, Las Mercedes, and La Estrella, in Honduran territory.

c. Regional Command Diriangén, led by ex-general Luis Moreno Payán, alias "Mikelima," with a primary operational base in Las Vegas, also in Honduran territory.

d. Regional Command Rafael Herrera, led by Encarnación Valdivia, whose main base of operations was at Banco Grande, in Honduran territory.

e. Regional Command Jorge Salazar, led by ex-general Juan Ramón Rivas, alias "El Quiché."

At the beginning of April, FDN counterrevolutionary forces launched a new offensive with forces numbering 6,000 counterrevolutionaries in all the operational areas of the regional commands. This offensive was characterized by the deployment of counterrevolutionary forces to multiple locations, and the use of new tactical/strategic concepts of military action. The prime objective was to develop a general offensive in the rural and mountainous regions of the departments of Jinotega and Matagalpa, which would permit the counterrevolutionaries to reach populated areas of relative importance and attain economic objectives, thus creating the conditions for an easy, direct intervention by the U.S. armed forces.

This offensive continued to develop during May, despite the fact that forces employed in the main command were defeated and exposed as being on the defensive. Due to the continued and effective response of our troops, it became impossible to carry out major actions; activity was limited to acts of sabotage and attacks aimed at centers of agricultural production, and small villages. At the beginning of June, these counterrevolutionary forces continued their effort to create a "general offensive" but toward the end of the second week, they abandoned the idea as a result of the defense effort of our troops that practically dismembered the regional commands headed by Diriangén and Segovia.

This victory of our revolutionary troops forced the main counterrevolutionary forces to retreat toward Honduran territory. In the central region of Nicaragua and in the north of Matagalpa and Jinotega, some counterrevolutionary forces remained in order to expand their social base, and to create logistical and support structures that would facilitate their presence there. Nevertheless, the retreat of the principal counterrevolutionary groups to Honduran territory, as well as the response of our people, considerably weakened the operational capacity of the small groups of dispersed forces that remained in Nicaragua.

Simultaneously, with the retreat of those main groups to Honduran territory, groups operated in the central region in the department of Jinotega. Following a CIA plan called "Operation Puente" ("Operation Bridge"), counterrevolutionary forces were infiltrated into the department of Matagalpa, where enemy activity increased; the main goal of the plan was to aid counterrevolutionary detachments that tried to reach the departments of Boaco and Chontales in order to join the ARDE forces infiltrating into the south from Costa Rica. All this activity was supported by counterrevolutionary forces that infiltrated the department of Nueva Segovia and maintained constant pressure on the border to the north of San Fernando, as well as by ongoing provocations and movements by the Honduran Army.

In the middle of July, infiltration into Nicaraguan territory by major FDN groups from the regional commands of Segovia and Diriangén began, with the objective of reactivating their operational areas and launching a new offensive similar to that of the recently thwarted "general offensive." At the beginning of August, and with the same objective, there was increased counterrevolutionary activity characterized by minor actions intended to give the impression of a generalized war across a wide expanse of territory.

Meanwhile, ARDE had kept its main groups operating inside the country during April and May. It had other counterrevolutionary bases concentrated in Costa Rican territory, bases from which it attacked the village of San Juan del Norte in May. The goal was to carry out a propagandistic action and distract attention from the victories of the Sandinista forces, who were beating back counterrevolutionary groups in the interior of the country. Those groups sought to establish themselves in areas adjacent to the farms and to Nueva Guinea in South Zelaya. ARDE's plans to attack the village of Nueva Guinea, to dominate the agricultural settlements and the Juigalpa El Rama highway, to attack the villages of Acoyapa and San Carlos, and to initiate action in the Isthmus of Rivas, were frustrated by the energetic response of our people and their army.

During this period, MISURA was obliged to continue acting in accordance with the "Black Cloud Plan" ("Plan Nube Negra"), which paralleled FDN actions, in the village of Tronquera, in the Miskito settlements and at the Siuna, Rosita, and Bonanza mines. The latter were attacked in April with the objective of creating the conditions for kidnappings from Miskito settlements, an action that ARDE also tried to carry out with attacks on Sumubila and Sandy Bay Norte. The main counterrevolutionary forces remained in Honduran territory, with small groups dispersed in our territory. ARDE did not succeed in defining its tactics, which in practice led to a stagnation of its operations, although it continued to kidnap some Miskitos. At the beginning of August, the existence of the so-called "Rigoberto Cabezas Plan" was discovered, which consisted of joint actions by the FDN/MISURA to take over areas near the mines. This plan has never been implemented.

Throughout 1984, the CIA increased military and logistical aid through air supply shipments. It also tried to assassinate Edén Pastora in an attempt to achieve total unity of the counterrevolutionary forces with which Pastora was not in agreement. The CIA pressured MISURA to accept unification, supposedly having obtained in September the ratification of a unity document constituting the Integrated Nicaraguan Revolution Unity (Unidad Revolucionaria Integrada Nicaragüense, UNIR).

Terrorist actions and sabotage continued; the following incidents are the most significant:

January 1984
- Piranha boats and Honduran planes bombed the installations at Puerto Potosí, department of Chinandega, killing one person.
- Two aircraft belonging to the FDN attacked the "Montelimar" sugar installations in the department of Managua.
- Piranha boats attacked a fishing boat, the *San Albino*, in Nicaraguan waters in the Gulf of Fonseca.
- A twin-engine boat armed with high-caliber machine guns attacked Puerto Costero de Tola, department of Rivas.

February 1984
- Six A-37 and Push-Pull aircraft flying from Honduran territory bombed communication towers at Volcán Casita, department of Chinandega, on the west side of the country; concurrently, the border town of

Manzanillo on the Pacific coast of Nicaragua was attacked.

March 1984

The following counterrevolutionary actions — among others — occurred:

- Counterrevolutionary commandos destroyed electric towers at San Francisco del Norte, Chinandega, affecting electrical communications with Honduras.
- In Puerto Corinto, the ship *Los Caribes,* flying the Panamanian flag, was damaged by a mine explosion. In this same port, the ship *Geopontes VI* suffered damage from the explosion of another mine.
- In Puerto Sandino, the Soviet ship *Lugansk* was damaged by a mine explosion.
- Speedboats attacked civilian motorboats and installations in the port of El Bluff on the Nicaraguan Atlantic coast. The port was also mined.
- Speedboats attacked the port of San Juan del Sur on the Pacific coast of our country and the coast of Montelimar, attempting to sabotage fuel storage installations.
- In Puerto Corinto, the Liberian merchant ship *Iber Fhases* sustained damages from a mine explosion.
- In Puerto Sandino, piranhas attacked the merchant ship *Omin No. 7,* sailing under the Panamanian flag.
- Counterrevolutionaries from the MISURA group, coming from Honduran territory, sabotaged the hydroelectric dam "Salto Grande" in the department of Zelaya.
- In Puerto Corinto, a Nicaraguan fishing vessel sustained damage from a mine explosion.

April 1984

- On April 1, a naval unit coming from Costa Rican territory attacked a fishing vessel for 20 minutes, leaving it with 20 bullet marks.
- On April 3, piranha-type speedboats coming from Honduran territory attacked the post of Potosí with machine-gun fire.
- On April 8, 350 counterrevolutionaries coming from Costa Rican territory attacked the border post of San Juan del Norte on the Atlantic coast with mortars, machine guns, and rifles.
- On April 11, 13, and 14, counterrevolutionaries stationed across from the coast of San Juan del Norte attacked fishing vessels No. 2 and No. 20, as well as Coast Guard boats No. 231 and No. 233.
- On April 17, mercenary forces coming from Honduran territory attacked the Miskito settlement of Sumubila, department of Zelaya, destroying the installations of the Agrarian Reform Institute of Nicaragua, a health center, and the cocoa warehouse.

— On April 26, 400 counterrevolutionaries coming from Costa Rican territory attacked the post of El Castillo on the southern border of our country with mortar and rifle fire.

— On April 28, two piranha-type speedboats coming from Honduran territory attacked the port of Potosí with machine-gun fire.

— A total of 13 attacks by members of the Honduran Army have been
recorded, involving mortar fire and riflemen, on April 1, 5, 6, 10, 11, 13,
14, 15, 17, 22, 23, and 24 at the border posts of Poza Larga, Las Minitas,
Vado Ancho, El Naranjo, and La Ceiba, all in the department of
Chinandega.

— There was a total of 10 sabotage actions against state farms (destroyed)
by CIA mercenaries on April 4, 8, 11, 12, 16, 17, 19, 23, and 27 in the
departments of Jinotega, Matagalpa, and Nueva Segovia.

May-September 1984

— On May 2, a fishing boat was sunk at Puerto Corinto when it hit a water
mine.

— On May 7, CIA mercenaries from Honduran territory sabotaged a bridge
on the Mancotal River in the department of Jinotega.

— On May 2, 3, and 16, CIA mercenaries from Costa Rican territory attacked
the customs post at Peñas Blancas with 81-mm mortars.

— On June 1, CIA mercenary forces based in Honduran territory attacked
the city of Ocotal, department of Madriz; there were 52 enemy casualties.

— On June 1, CIA mercenary forces from Honduran territory attacked the
city of Somoto, department of Madriz, with mortar fire.

— On June 1, CIA mercenaries from Honduran territory attacked the Miskito settlement of Sumubito, department of Zelaya.

— June 25, a special group of CIA mercenaries from Honduran territory
sabotaged El Granero, located nine miles southeast of Ocotal.

— On August 7, CIA mercenaries attacked the border outpost of Cárdenas
with rifle and L/G M-79 fire from Costa Rican territory.

— On August 27, CIA mercenaries from Costa Rican territory attacked the
border town of San Juan del Norte with 81-mm mortars.

— On August 13, 80 counterrevolutionaries destroyed the El Paraíso Cooperative, four miles west of San Rafael del Norte, department of Jinotega.

— On August 24, groups of counterrevolutionaries detonated explosive
charges in Valle Jinocuabo, department of Jinotega, where there were
trucks from the Ministry of Construction (MICONS).

— On August 26, counterrevolutionary groups sabotaged Radio "Poder Popular" in Puerto Cabezas, department of Zelaya, injuring two *compañeros*
and partially damaging the station.

— On August 27, a C-47 airplane was shot down while taking supplies to the Diriangén Regional Command in Zapote, 10 miles southeast of Quilalí, Nueva Segovia.

— On September 1, a UH-500 helicopter was brought down in Apalí, one mile east of Santa Clara, Nueva Segovia, after bombing military installations; two U.S. mercenaries died in the crash.

— On September 19, two electric poles were sabotaged two miles northeast of Somotillo, department of Chinandega.

Despite the fact that Reagan's re-election campaign has made his foreign policy even more of a public issue because of criticism by the opposition, he has not decreased his aggressive actions against Nicaragua in 1984. Reagan's unconditional support of the counterrevolutionaries has isolated our revolution internationally, and caused economic destabilization and internal crisis. Aspects of the U.S. government's campaign related to the situation in Central America can be summarized as follows:

A. Support for Counterrevolutionary Groups

On three occasions in 1984, the House of Representatives has voted against the request made by the President to give more financial support to the counterrevolutionary forces. In August, Congress resumed discussion about allocating $21 million to the counterrevolutionaries for fiscal year 1985.

In spite of the opposition to contra aid encountered by the Reagan administration, it has sought alternative funding; some sources estimate that $17 million have been channeled through "private organizations."

B. Political-Diplomatic Campaign

Since the beginning of June, 1984, the Reagan administration has promoted a huge campaign which promises to continue even after the November elections, to discredit the Sandinista Popular Revolution. Some of the manifestations of this campaign have been:

— Publication on July 18, 1984, of a new White Paper by the State Department and the Department of Defense entitled "Background Paper: Nicaragua's Military Build-up and Support for Central American Subversion."

— Attacks against Nicaragua in the Organization of American States (OAS) on the violation of alleged commitments made to that organization in July 1979.

— Campaign to discredit the electoral process, including the utilization of counterrevolutionary group leaders and politicians outside the country.

— Refusal to support the Contadora Act.

C. Additional Military Maneuvers

U.S. military maneuvers in Central America continued. Some of these are:

1. Granadero Maneuvers. From April to June 1984, the Granadero
maneuvers have taken place in two phases with the participation of forces
from Honduras, El Salvador, and the United States, in the departments
of Copán, Lempira, Ocotepeque, Santa Bárbara, Cortés, Olancho,
Choluteca, and El Paraíso. The primary objectives of these maneuvers
are: to improve the capacity and technical expertise necessary for carrying out multinational operations; to lend continuity to the process of stan-
dardizing the joint operational procedures of the participating armed
forces (with special attention to the amphibious landing and air transport of troops); and to prepare the physical, political, and military conditions for the development of an invasion of El Salvador and/or
Nicaragua, taking advantage of the arms build-up of Honduran forces
and the counterrevolution.

Participants in the first phase of these maneuvers were:

United States

- The 864th Infantry Battalion from Fort Lewis, Washington.
- One Company of the 82nd Airborne from Fort Bragg, North Carolina.
- One Company of the 18th Airborne Army Corps.
- 224th Battalion of Military Intelligence.
- 43rd Support Group, U.S. Army.
- 101st Battalion of the Air Force.
- Company of the 3rd Battalion of the 7th Group, Special Forces.
- Destroyer *US-DEYO* DD 984.
- Frigate *US DEID* FFG 30.

Honduras

- One anti-tank battalion.
- Two Companies of the 1st Battalion of the Corps of Engineers.
- 75 Marines from the Amapala Naval Base.
- One battalion from the Infantry.
- Unknown number of ships and planes.

El Salvador

- 100 Marines from La Unión Naval Base.
- Unknown number of naval units from La Unión Naval Base.

The second phase involved the following participants:

United States

- 625 troops from the 227th Air Force Battalion of the 1st Cavalry Division.
- 160 troops detached from a battalion of Special Forces from Fort Bragg.

— 100 troops from the McDill, Florida Air Base.

— 100 troops from the 193rd Infantry Brigade, Southern Command.

— Total: 985 troops.

Honduras

— One infantry brigade, 3,000 to 3,600 men.

— One anti-tank battalion, 600 men.

— Total: 3,600 to 4,200 troops.

El Salvador

— "Atonal" Battalion, 1,200 irregulars.

— Company of 100 parachutists.

— Total: 1,300.

2. Emergency Alert Exercise. This exercise was carried out between March 22-30 in Honduras with the participation of 500 North Americans composed of Green Berets and parachutists from the 82nd Division, air-transported for anti-guerrilla activities.

3. "Guardians of the Gulf." This exercise was carried out between May 30-June 26 in the Gulf of Fonseca, with the participation of two U.S. naval units from the frigate FFG-30 *Reid* and the destroyer DD-989 *DEYO*. It had the objective of detecting the so-called arms traffic from Nicaragua to El Salvador.

4. Air-Sea Maneuvers. The aircraft carrier CV-67 *John F. Kennedy* and a battle group (one submarine and three warships) carried out air-sea maneuvers from July 15-23 in waters off the Atlantic coast of Nicaragua. Between July 19-21, 21 combat planes of the types F-14, A-7, A-6, and S3 from the aircraft carrier *Kennedy* carried out exercises with live rockets and bombs in areas next to the San Andrés and Providencia Islands.

5. "Operation Lempira." This operation was carried out in Honduran territory between July 23-August 5, with the participation of 500 U.S. troops and 1,200 Hondurans in combined anti-guerrilla, survival, and air transport actions, in the departments of La Paz, Comayagua, and Francisco Morazán.

6. Ground Actions. Ground action groups from the battleship BB-61 *Iowa,* the rocket-launching frigate FFG-29 *Stephen W. Groves,* the rocket destroyer DAG-17 *Connyham,* and small aircraft carriers PHM-2 *Hercules* and PCM-S *Aries* carried out shows of force in the Pacific Ocean off the coasts of Guatemala, Costa Rica, and Honduras. On August 29, they passed through the Panama Canal, heading toward Florida and Puerto Rico.

The U.S. military presence in Honduras is now:

— 200 Green Berets from Fort Bragg, North Carolina, who participated in joint counterinsurgency maneuvers in the area of Marcala, bordering on El Salvador.

— 250 members of the 224th Battalion of military intelligence from Hunter Army Airfield (Fort Stuart), Georgia, stationed at the Palmerola Air Base, operating 10 "Mohawk" OV-1 airplanes with the objective of reconnaissance operations in El Salvador.

— 200 troops from Fort Hood, Texas, who arrived at Palmerola together with the Huey and Chinook helicopters.

— 150 Marines assigned to man and protect the radar station at Isla del Tigre.

— 150 troops operating the radar station at the El Hule hilltop, southeast of Tegucigalpa.

— 400 troops at Palmerola, coordinating center for military operations of the High Military Command in Honduras and the base for the Bravo task force.

— 150 Special Forces military personnel assigned to the Regional Military Training Center (Centro Regional de Entrenamiento Militar, CREM) of Puerto Castilla.

— 75 Green Berets in San Lorenzo carrying out counterinsurgency training.

TOTAL: approximately 1,575 U.S. military personnel.

U.S. projections for military involvement in Central America in 1985:

— Construction of permanent campaign hospitals at Palmerola, Department of Comayagua, and a hangar for aircraft maintenance, at a cost of $6 million.

— Construction of fuel storage tanks, plus two highways and an ammunition warehouse for airplanes, at the La Ceiba Air Base, Department of Atlantida, at a cost of $8 million.

— Construction of warehouses, ammunition depots, and fuel tanks in San Lorenzo, department of Valle, at a cost of several million dollars.

— Construction of a naval air base and other facilities in Puerto Castilla, department of Colón, with a budget of many hundreds of millions of dollars. The Honduran government has initiated the construction of 450 feet of docks, which will be expanded to 1350 feet, as well as fuel storage tanks.

VI. CONCLUSIONS

1. A civil war does not exist in Nicaragua.

2. There does exist a war of aggression by the U.S. It follows a global interventionist plan utilizing a mercenary army known as "counterrevolutionary forces," which operate, thanks to the support the U.S. has guaranteed them, from neighboring territories, especially Honduras.

3. Along with the material and economic damage that the armed inter-

vention is causing to the country, the interventionist strategy attempts to use the mercenary army to exhaust and destabilize Nicaragua's capacity for military defense. The goal is to then introduce the superior interventionist forces of the United States and overthrow the revolution.

4. The U.S. is currently planning to develop a military offensive throughout the country, utilizing its mercenary troops. Its purposes include obstructing the electoral process and the agricultural production efforts at the end of the year, while simultaneously developing the conditions for future military attacks against the revolutionary government.

Prepared by the Department of Public and
Foreign Relations of the Ministry of Defense.

Managua, Free Nicaragua
October 1984

On the following pages are four of the charts which accompanied the presentation of Capt. Pasos; a video, photographs, maps and other material were also entered in evidence. — Ed.

Table 1: COUNTERREVOLUTIONARY ACTIONS
ON NICARAGUAN TERRITORY

Year	Combats	Ambushes	Attacks	Acts of Sabotage	Kidnappings	Assaults on Towns	Assassinations	Provocations	Infiltrations	TOTAL
1981	15	5	19	2	3	1	4	79	47	175
1982	20	6	16	6	1	1	8	155	70	283
1983	553	125	184	52	40	40	10	108	93	1,205
1984 to 9/12	334	104	126	38	20	—	8	103	79	812
Grand Total	992	240	345	98	64	42	30	445	289	2,475

Table 2: AERIAL VIOLATIONS

From Costa Rican Territory

Year	Number	Type of Aircraft
1981	50	Helicopters, small planes
1982	23	Helicopters, small planes
1983	130	Helicopters, small planes
1984 (to 9/12)	1,046	Helicopters, small planes
TOTAL	1,259	

From Honduran Territory

Year	Number	Type of Aircraft
1981	139	Super-Mystère planes, B-2, A-37, T-33, T28
1982	173	Push-Pull, C-47, DC-6, C-130, Cessna small planes
1983	229	UH-IH Helicopters, HWY, unidentified planes
1984 (to 9/12)	780	(Information not yet available.)
TOTAL	1,381	

GRAND TOTAL   2,640

Table 3: NAVAL VIOLATIONS

From Costa Rican Territory

Year	Number	Type of Vessel
1981	6	Fishing boats
1982	4	Fishing boats
1983	10	Speedboats, Coast Guard and a variety of vessels ("Cayucos," "Pangas," and unidentified)
1984 (to 9/12)	25	(Information not yet available.)
TOTAL	45	

From Honduran Territory

Year	Number	Type of Vessel
1981	14	Patrol Boats
1982	18	Piranha speedboats
1983	51	Coast Guard and fishing boats
1984 (to 9/12)	320	Coast Guard and fishing boats
TOTAL	115	
GRAND TOTAL	160	

Table 4: U.S. INTELLIGENCE FLIGHTS

Year	Number	Type of Aircraft
1981	29	RC-135
1982	102	RC-135, U-2/TR-1
1983	479	107 RC-135, and 372 U-2, C-130, EC-13 C, and E-3A combined
1984 (to 9/12)	165	(Information not yet available.)
TOTAL	775	

Economic Aggression:
A Policy of State Terrorism

Magda Henríquez
Augusto César Sandino Foundation

A. INTRODUCTION

On July 19, 1979, the Somoza dictatorship, which was supported from the beginning by the U. S. government, left us with a foreign debt that reached $1.6 billion. The Sandinista National Liberation Front took on the hunger, desolation, adversity, and death left by the war of liberation with only $3 million, all that the lackeys of Washington had not been able to take with them. After that date, the more reactionary sectors of the U.S. government began to elaborate their strategies and tactics for destroying the hope of the Nicaraguan people (and other peoples of the world) by economic suffocation, financial embargo, and a commercial blockade — strategies linked to military and ideological aggression and a campaign of international disparagement.

But U.S. economic aggression did not begin after the revolutionary triumph in 1979; it was simply a matter of aggression taking on another form. From 1856 to 1979, Washington's ambitious plans took diverse forms: from the filibusterer William Walker, an American who proclaimed himself President of the Republic of Nicaragua and was received in the United States with the honors of a "Head of State," to plans for the construction of an inter-oceanic canal in response to North American greed and gold fever. [The discovery of gold in California intensified the need for a waterway that would facilitate transport between the East and West Coasts of the U.S. — Ed.] Those forms included financial support for governments that catered to U.S. interests and the overthrow of those that did not; the full-fledged application of Dollar Diplomacy at the same time as the Big Stick policy, with military forces under U.S. control installed in order to guarantee the presence of the United States in Nicaragua militarily as well as financially. Thus, Nicaragua, with its long experience of economic and financial aggression, took on a great challenge in 1979. To take on that challenge is, in itself, an inalienable right of all peoples: the right to free dom, development, and sovereignty.

Confronted by the vast task of reconstructing the country in a period of world economic crisis that weighs even more heavily on developing countries, the Nicaraguan economy needed a considerable flow of foreign resources. The World Bank, for example, estimated that need at $300 million for 1982 and 1983, of which $125 million should have come from multilateral sources. But foreign resources have been blocked by the aggressive policy of the Reagan administration, which has used its political influence on financial institutions to that end. As a result, transactions with multilateral entities dropped from being 32.3% of Nicaragua's foreign financing in 1980 to 15.6% in 1983.

In and of itself, the commercial aggression was intended to cut off channels of exchange that, for a country like Nicaragua, continue to be important economically. Some examples are: the virtual elimination of our sugar quota and the reduction of our meat quota, the suspension of credit for the import of wheat and oil, the closing of our consulates in the U.S., and finally the mining of our harbors, a material expression of the commercial blockade.

B. CHRONOLOGICAL ACCOUNT

A few days after taking office, the Reagan administration decided to suspend an initial $15 million from a loan of $75 million previously approved by the Carter administration for the financing of reconstruction work and revival of the economy.

In March of that same year, the United States suspended a previous loan agreement of $9.8 million for the purchase of wheat from the United States under the P.L.-480 program.

The suspension of another $11.4 million affected rural development projects, improvements in education, and the expansion of various health programs.

The Latin American Council, highest body of the Latin American Economic System (Sistema Económico Latinoamericano, SELA), in its Decision No. 90, "Solidarity with Nicaragua," expressed "its profound distress at the decision of the government of the United States of America to suspend the credit that they had agreed to give the government of Nicaragua for the purpose of buying wheat, as well as the repercussions that such a measure will have for the people and the economy of Nicaragua."

In April 1981, the government of the United States decreed the suspension of all subsequent, official, bilateral aid to Nicaragua. In the same vein, the government of the U.S., the Export-Import Bank of the U.S., and the Overseas Private Investment Corporation withdrew their promissory notes for the financing of commercial activity directed toward and within Nicaragua. That decision caused critical damage to the supply of spare parts and the repair of manufacturing equipment. In December 1981, the U.S. representative in the Interamerican Development Bank vetoed a proposal presented to the bank's Special Operations Fund to provide $500 million for the development of cooperatives in the farming sector of Nicaragua.

After February 1982, American pressure in the World Bank caused that organization to take unilateral action against Nicaragua, which included suspension of its loan program and the requirement of an economic stabilization program. In 1982, the United States threatened not to import Nicaraguan meat if our country bought breeding studs from Cuba, using as a pretext the possible spread of aphtha even though numerous international organizations affirmed that this disease does not exist in Cuba. Recently, the quota of Nicaraguan meat was in fact reduced.

The policy being promoted through the International Development Bank at the end of the first trimester of 1983 meant losses for Nicaragua of $35.4 million in funds that were going to be channeled through the Interamerican Bank of Economic Integration.

In May 1983, the United States announced a 90% reduction in the sugar which the U.S. bought from Nicaragua, citing exclusively political reasons. Our quota had been 58,800 metric tons; with the cut it became 5,880 metric tons. The Government of National Reconstruction considered this a violation of the rules and principles that guide international commerce, and presented a formal complaint to the Secretariat of the General Agreement on Tariffs and Trade (GATT). On June 8, 1983, Nicaragua met with the United States in the context of GATT mechanisms for the solution of differences, with the hope of finding a mutually satisfactory arrangement.

Confronted by the negative attitude of the United States, the Government of National Reconstruction requested the establishment of a GATT committee of arbitration charged with examining the complaint presented by Nicaragua. In its report, the committee of arbitration concluded that by reducing the Nicaraguan sugar quota, the United States had violated its contractual obligations as a GATT member. On March 13, 1984, the Council of Representatives of GATT unanimously approved the report of the arbitration committee, and requested that the U.S. quickly re-establish Nicaragua's sugar quota (61,900 tons for 1984). The Council of GATT was put in charge of monitoring compliance with this recommendation.

However, the White House spokesman announced that the United States would not re-establish its Nicaraguan sugar quota. In a special, urgent session on May 27, 1983, the Latin American Council of SELA decided "To repudiate the step taken by the government of the United States of America against Nicaragua, which affects the autonomy and threatens the economic security of this member," and "to urge the government of the United States to revoke said measure."

In June, 1983, the government of the United States ordered the closing of all the Nicaraguan consulates in that country (leaving only one embassy), thus affecting the flow of commerce between the two countries.

Once again, Latin American solidarity was manifested, this time in the decision of the Latin American Council of SELA on September 21, 1983. Its reasoning and disposition read as follows:

Considering:

> That in spite of the request of the Latin American Council of SELA in its Decision 148, the Government of the United States of America has continued to apply economic measures of a restrictive nature that affect the people and the Government of Nicaragua, some of which are the cancellation of cargo flights by the Nicaraguan airline, AERONICA; the closing of the Nicaraguan consulates; the unjustifiable veto of a request for resources from the Special Operations Fund of the Inter-American Development Bank; and the statement by the U.S. Treasury Department announcing the decision to oppose all requests for loans that Nicaragua might make to multilateral financial entities in which the U.S. participates;

> That the application of such measures does not contribute to the creation of a peaceful climate in Central America nor does it support the effort being made by the Latin American countries to achieve peace in that region.

> ARTICLE 1: To reiterate its repudiation of the new restrictive economic measures adopted by the Government of the United States of America against Nicaragua which, besides being illegal and arbitrary, affect the autonomy and threaten the economic security of said Member State, as stipulated in Article 3 of Decision 148.

> ARTICLE 2: To urge the Government of the United States of America to revoke said measures and all other actions that might constitute acts of economic coercion against a Member State.

> ARTICLE 3: To note with approval the manifestations of solidarity with Nicaragua that have been expressed in the present situation.

C. MILITARY AGGRESSION AND ITS SOCIOECONOMIC CONSEQUENCES

The replacement of buildings, machinery, materials, and natural resources, necessitated by the devastation wrought by the Somoza dictatorship during the Nicaraguan people's war of liberation, was estimated at the time to cost about $300 million.

As a result of the military aggression of the United States, Nicaragua has suffered the destruction of ports, damage to production, and destruction of vehicles used in construction, health clinics, schools, production centers, and childcare centers. These losses total some $300 million, which represents one fourth of our annual investments.

From January to March 1984, damages reached 149.9 million córdobas. [The official exchange rate has ranged from 10-28 córdobas to $1.00 — Ed.] In 1983, material damages were valued at 1,280.9 córdobas, or 77% of all damages.

Another $38 million represents the cost of resettling the population of the border zones who are victims of the terrorist policy of the American government. In foreign exchange, the total material damages in 1983 equalled $128.1 million. This represented 31% of our exports, which in national currency equaled 3% of our gross national product; 20% of investments; and 6% of the total domestic consumption.

1. Destruction and Blockade of Our Ports

Blockading the transport of commodities, through the criminal mining of Nicaraguan ports by the Central Intelligence Agency, has affected the supply of perishable consumer goods and Nicaraguan exports. Daniel Ortega Saavedra, Coordinator of the Government Junta of National Reconstruction and Commander of the Revolution, pointed out in his speech before the 5th Legislative Session of Nicaragua's Council of State: "The same U.S. administration that has blockaded our access to long-term multilateral funds has, by mining our ports, forced us to confront not only a financial blockade but also a physical one, aimed at closing off our access to trade."

In 1983, the present U.S. administration participated with agents of the CIA in sabotaging a number of oil tanks in Puerto Corinto (as was later confirmed by high-level officials of the U.S. administration). They destroyed, among other things, more than 600 metric tons of foodstuffs donated by the United Nations, and provoked a fire of extremely dangerous proportions, with damages calculated at more than $380 million. That fire was successfully controlled, thanks to the cooperation of sister countries such as Cuba, Mexico, and Colombia, the latter two nations being members of the Contadora Group.

To the general policy of aggression has been added the mining of the principal ports of Nicaragua in open violation of the law and international maritime transport. On May 10, 1984, the International Court of Justice unanimously indicated that the United States should immediately cease and refrain from any action that restricts, blocks, or endangers access to or from Nicaraguan ports, particularly through the placing of mines.* This contemptible action has, to date, caused damages totaling more than 10% of our exports.

In a special session on April 28, 1984, the SELA denounced and con-

*This was the Court's provisional measure, pending its final decision; the term "indicate" is the Court's language in that measure. See the Appendix for excerpts from the Court's order. — Ed.

demned the mining of Nicaragua's ports. In his speech of May 4, 1984 to the 5th Legislative Session of the Council of State, Commander Daniel Ortega Saavedra gave an up-to-date account of the effects of imperialist aggression. He stated:

> The ongoing military aggression by U.S. imperialism against the Sandinista Popular Revolution has been accentuated by new forms of aggression against our people. It is a dirty war, directed and controlled by the CIA operating against Nicaragua, using its air force to attack economic and defense targets — as in the attacks against "Volcán Casita," Potosí, and San Juan del Sur. Naval forces have also been used to attack economic installations with speedboats carrying cannons and mortars, attacking ports and fuel storage tanks along the Nicaraguan coast.
>
> There is also the more direct use of American ships and destroyers as support for the speedboats. To all this add the CIA's criminal act of placing mines in the main ports of our country, an act which represents the development of a more direct military and commercial blockade. Thus, new elements are introduced into the Central American conflict: an aspect of the global nature of the conflict in the area.

Damages from the mining of our ports have thus far reached some $9.1 million and are composed of $2.2 million in partial damages to foreign ships and $4.1 million in loss of investments, mainly due to a drop in production from fishing as a result of the sinking of five boats.

The imperialists' economic boycott has affected the arrival of raw material, consumer goods, and replacement parts for industry. As a result, there have been fluctuations and stoppages in the production of consumer goods which, at certain times, have provoked crises in the supply of such necessities as oil, soap, toilet paper, powdered milk, and toothpaste. Small industry has also been affected by the scarcities, with negative consequences for the sustenance of thousands of humble families.

In 1984, as a result of the mining of our ports and the actions of CIA mercenaries, our exports of coffee, sesame seed, and meat have been delayed, costing us some $9.2 million. Also, ships carrying powdered milk and butter oil have been forced off course to ports in Costa Rica; this delayed their arrival in our country, affecting the well-being of our infant population.

2. Destruction of the Productive Capacity

Our productive capacity is another favorite target of the counterrevolution. By attacking it, the U.S. government aims to weaken our defense potential and lower the people's morale. There has been 298.4 million córdobas-worth of damage inflicted on the infrastructure of the productive sector. Production is the sector that has suffered the most from terrorist activity, up to a total of 875.1 million córdobas, which constitutes more than 40% of all damage. One must also keep in mind the unquantifiable effects of the damage to production on the cultivation of corn and beans, the delivery of meat and milk, the harvesting of coffee, fishing, and the extraction of wood and minerals. As is to be expected, all of this negatively affects the recovery of production, investment efforts, and raising the people's standard of living.

In the northern and Atlantic zones of the country, counterrevolutionary activity has caused much damage in the agricultural and livestock sectors, since agricultural activity has diminished due to the relocation of peasants who had to be moved to more secure areas. Basic grain production has been one of the most affected areas because of counterrevolutionary attacks on the cooperatives located in these zones; their damages reach 192 million córdobas. To this must be added large, although not quantified, losses to small individual producers.

Damage to the production of coffee, tobacco, and other crops amounts to 168 million córdobas, and livestock production has suffered losses up to 29 million córdobas, mainly through the theft of herds by mercenary groups moving across our borders. This affects not only the consumption of milk and meat by our population but exports as well. Agroindustrial production has also been affected by the scarcity of foreign currency, which causes a lack of spare parts and makes equipment maintenance more difficult, with negative effects on the production of milk, rice, sugar, and other essential products.

Fishing has been one of the industries most affected by counterrevolutionary military actions. In 1983, we had a 116-vessel fleet, but only 41% was functional; the rest was not, either because of the lack of maintenance and repairs or because vessels were being used for defense-related purposes. In the present period, 13 boats have been lost (six stolen, two set on fire, and five sunk by the mines) whose replacement value is approximately $6 million. To this should be added the loss of $10 million in prawns and lobster which could not be exported because of the destruction of vessels in which to ship these products.

Our gold and silver mines have been affected by economic difficulties in replacing obsolete equipment and the lack of spare parts as well as other goods, which result from the scarcity of foreign currency aggravated by imperialist aggression. This has contributed to the diminishing of industrial gold production at a rate of 11% (compared to 1982). The energy problems in the Siuna and Bonanza mines, which result from the partial destruction by CIA mercenaries of the "El Salto" dam at a cost of 15 million córdobas, will lead to an even greater drop in industrial gold production in 1984.

The actions of the CIA mercenaries have also appreciably affected the timber industry in the war zones, making it unable this year to produce and export 19 million board feet, worth some $6 million. They also impeded the implementation of numerous development projects in the forestry sector. The criminal actions of the mercenaries have caused the destruction of three of the people's agricultural storehouses, reducing our capacity for gathering and storing basic grains by 8%; the closing of five of the people's stores; and the destruction of transportation equipment, thus diminishing our distribution capacity in the war zone as well as increasing the difficulty of transporting crops to consumer centers.

The infrastructure of the economy as a whole has also been attacked, with 174 million córdobas in damages of which the most important are:

— The destruction of storage tanks of flammables and the blowing up of energy and telecommunication transmission towers, as well as bridges, dams, and storage sites. The destruction of the Corinto storage tanks alone meant a loss of $8 million.

— The blowing up of construction equipment and its storage sites.

— The blocking of communication routes by the mining and destruction of bridges, as well as by attacks on the Augusto C. Sandino Airport and the customs offices at Peñas Blancas and "Las Manos."

Setbacks in infrastructural projects have caused an additional estimated loss of 259.6 million córdobas. Taking all factors into account, the effects of terrorist activity on the general economic infrastructure add up to a loss of 517 million córdobas, or one fourth of all damages.

3. The Cost of Defense—46 Months of Aggression

For 46 months, Nicaragua has been the object of aggression by the United States of America. Nicaragua, a small country with barely three million inhabitants, is being attacked by a world power, a nuclear power, which spends millions of dollars to destroy it with the complicity of traitors. And for 46 months, Nicaragua has been defeating the aggression.

This means that, in addition to the economic damage inflicted by the aggression, defense of the country necessarily imposes a considerable economic burden. In 1983, we found ourselves forced to dedicate 20% of the total budget to defense and security, compared to 18% in 1982. In 1984, it has been necessary once again to raise this proportion — to 25% — because of the magnitude of the imperialist aggression. The financial cost of defending the country has made necessary the raising of taxes, restrictions on extending good health care and education, and inflationary pressures that affect, above all, the workers.

In material terms, defense requires a quota of food supplies, construction, fuel, and industrial products. The productive sectors have lent their own means of production, such as boats and trucks, to support our Sandinista Popular Army. Defense also requires the cooperation of workers, peasants, technicians, leaders of the people's organizations and youth, who have joined in, giving to this historical task the best cadres of our labor force — our principal productive force. All these brothers, the best of our heroic people, could be planning the economy, designing projects, building silos and harvesting crops, instead of suffering and dying on our borders to defend the country against an inhuman and immoral aggression.

From May 4, 1983 until today, we have found ourselves obliged to mobilize extraordinary resources to head off a criminal intensification of imperialist aggression and destruction in all its forms. As a result, we have had to address serious difficulties in bettering our people's standard of living.

The aggression has obliged us to halt the advancement of health care projects, forcing us to close many primary care units while impeding the construction and opening of others. Some vaccination schedules have been suspended, and it has been impossible to maintain the level desired in our anti-malaria programs. The economic effects of war have considerably diminished the funding of all health services; the total cost of the aggression in the area of health has been 25 million córdobas. They have destroyed 17 health centers and 15 health workers have died, among them one doctor, while 11 have been wounded and 13 kidnapped, including three nurse's aides.

The social security and the well-being of the people of Nicaragua have suffered dramatic setbacks as a result of the necessity to divert funds to care for people relocated from the war zones, who comprise more than 114,000 Nicaraguans. It has been necessary to locate them in new settlements, where food, medicines, utensils, and housing are needed. This one aspect of the aggression has meant the need to spend $53 million on an emergency plan for the next six months.

Our children in the countryside have been deprived of their centers of Rural Infant Services (SIR), which have been damaged and destroyed at a cost of 9 million córdobas. Also, large sums have had to be set aside as special pensions for the families of heroic combatants fallen in the defense of their country. Supplying basic consumer products to the population has been seriously affected by the aggression. The cultivation of corn and beans in the battle zones as well as the provision of essential imported articles have been made very difficult, necessarily leading to diminished supply. Also, the destruction of the means of transportation and storage, and their priority use for defense, have disorganized the networks of commerce.

Under these circumstances of general scarcity, it was necessary, during the last months of 1983, to favor the combat zones in terms of supply quotas. Thus a serious lack of supplies developed in regions III and IV which provoked unscrupulous speculating activities. The situation was complicated by ideological diversions aimed at creating confusion about the true cause of these problems: the U.S. war of aggression.

The financial consequences of the war situation, combined with supply problems, raised the rate of inflation in the prices of basic necessities by 40% in 1983. This had a serious impact on the standard of living of the common people, who continue putting up with shortages in a spirit of heroism and sacrifice.

Employment, above all in fishing and mining, has also been seriously affected by destruction of the productive capacity. The scarcity of foreign exchange, also a result of the economic aggression, has hurt the manufacturing industry above all and caused an additional loss of jobs. If these sectors could work to full capacity, at least 10,000 more jobs would be generated. Also, as we have mentioned, the aggression has accelerated inflation and hurt workers' buying power.

Furthermore, workers have felt the aggression directly. In terms of human lives, on which no value can be put, there were 88 civilian victims in 1982 and 1,550 in 1983, of whom 605 were killed, 102 wounded, and 843 kidnapped. These figures include only government workers and victims in the farming cooperatives. From January to March of this year, there have been 249 victims, of whom 54 were killed, 23 wounded, and 172 kidnapped. The total between 1982 and March 1984 is 1,887 victims, of whom 747 were killed, 125 wounded, and 1,015 kidnapped. They are all victims of the policy of state terrorism that the Reagan administration has unleashed on our heroic people.

Imperialism does not want the Nicaraguan people to enjoy the right to education, which the people won on July 19, 1979. Its criminal actions have semi-destroyed rural schools, interrupted the construction of 27 more, and forced the closing of 138 primary schools. Several thousand children have been left with no primary instruction. The number of primary school teachers killed has risen to 23. Adult education programs have been the target of criminal attacks, with 647 grass-roots adult education collectives forced to shut down. Reagan's terrorism has assassinated 135 *compañeros* whose only crime was to dedicate their free time to liberating the rural people from illiteracy and ignorance. Such are the dividends from past aid to the counterrevolution; such would be the dividends from the appropriation of $21 million that the Reagan administration is asking from the U.S. Congress!

But while in Washington they are debating aid to the assassins of school teachers, 1,800 of these grass-roots teachers have been mobilized in the Infantry Reserve Battalions to pursue those who assassinated their brothers, and to defend the gains that the people have achieved through the Sandinista Popular Revolution.

Cultural programs have also been affected, and three cultural workers have been killed.

Programs to extend electrification have been affected by counterrevolutionary sabotage of transmission and electrical towers.

The construction of more than 2,000 homes has had to be suspended because the material resources had to be diverted for the displaced people in the resettlement zones.

The programs to provide potable water in Nueva Segovia and Madriz, and sewerage pipelines in Puerto Corinto have been suspended, affecting sanitation in those areas.

In sum, the standard of living of all Nicaraguans, to a greater or lesser extent, has been affected in many ways by the state terrorism policy of the U.S. administration. All that has just been said can be verified by photographs that show the truth of this sad reality. You can verify it by visiting Nicaragua. This is not a scary novel or a hypothetical case of what *genocide* could be, nor much less a script for a cowboy movie. It is the bitter reality that the U.S. government is imposing on us, a bitter reality that can be assessed in terms of destruction, material damage, economic slowdown, loss of profits, and hunger. What we cannot measure is the human cost: the dead, the mutilated, the orphans, the pain of mothers and wives before the cadavers of their sons and husbands assassinated by bullets bought with U.S. dollars.

It is the sad reality of an economy under attack, of a people willing to die but never to give up.

Managua, Free Nicaragua
September 30, 1984

The Ideological Offensive
Lilly Soto
President, Union of Journalists of Nicaragua

INTRODUCTION

The ideological offensive against Nicaragua by the present administration of the United States needs to be seen in historical perspective, in the context of U.S. foreign policy toward Latin America generally and toward Nicaragua in particular.

The design for a global Latin American strategy was set forth in the well-known Santa Fe Document, a program of action calling for measures of varying types but primarily military, and aimed at re-establishing the political-military domination of the U.S. over Latin America and the Caribbean. It is a secret to no one that Ronald Reagan achieved the Presidency by proposing to re-establish the military strength of the United States.

Let me reiterate before this Tribunal that Nicaragua is suffering from a war of organized aggression, financed and directed by the U.S. through the Central Intelligence Agency (CIA), which directs the armed counterrevolutionary groups. The development of this war is not limited to the counterrevolutionary war, whose content and scope have been substantially elaborated by military specialists of the Pentagon. However, that aspect must be noted in order to correctly understand the ideological offensive unleashed against Nicaragua. The "information war," a basic component of the counterrevolutionary war, is intended to create currents of public opinion adverse to the Nicaraguan revolutionary process.

I. THE U.S. AS INSTIGATOR OF THE IDEOLOGICAL OFFENSIVE AGAINST NICARAGUA

1. Beginnings of the Offensive

In October 1979, only three months after the triumph of the Sandinista Popular Revolution, this information war was begun. Propaganda operations originated with the Interamerican Press Association (Sociedad Inter-

The full title of this presentation was "The Ideological Offensive: A Base for the Military Aggression of the United States Against Nicaragua."

americana de Prensa, SIP), a private institution registered in the state
of Delaware, and were launched at the 35th annual meeting of SIP in
Toronto, Canada. There have been repeated denunciations of this organization for its role in the manipulation of information, in open collaboration with the CIA; these denunciations also refer to the involvement of
this group of high-ranking media executives in the plans of the U.S.
military-industrial complex.

In the face of the disinformation campaigns directed against Nicaragua
and their increasing slander, organizations of Latin American journalists
met in Nicaragua between April 28 and May 2, 1981. They characterized the campaigns as a transnational offensive against Free Nicaragua.
The World Assembly of Journalists, under the auspices of the International Organization of Journalists, made public the conclusions of that
meeting so that the peoples of the world would be aware of events in
Nicaragua and the deliberate distortion of those events by international
press agencies and by some CIA-financed news media.

The Reagan administration, through its main spokesmen, has undertaken an intense campaign designed to justify U.S. foreign policy toward
Central America, especially Nicaragua, and to ameliorate the growing
dissatisfaction of world public opinion with that policy. The President
of the United States would have the world believe the following regarding Nicaragua:

— In Central America and particularly in Nicaragua, the United States
is trying to stop Soviet expansionism, which uses Cuba and Nicaragua
as its puppets. The Soviets aim to create instability in El Salvador.

— The democratic countries of Central America, including
Guatemala, Honduras, El Salvador, and Costa Rica, are threatened by
this expansionism, and it is crucial to offer them material and military
resources for their defense.

— The Sandinistas did not comply with their original program and
they have embarked on the road to totalitarianism, attempting to undermine the principles of Western democracy.

— The government of Nicaragua is hostile to the government of the
United States, and for that reason all economic aid to Nicaragua has been
curtailed.

— The situation in Central America threatens the security of the United
States, which must be defended.

— The United States stands for liberty, and for this reason has given
aid to the counterrevolutionaries fighting the Nicaraguan government
(who are seen as "freedom fighters" by the Reagan administration).

— Nicaragua violates basic human rights, and in particular commits
genocide against the indigenous peoples.

2. Official Positions of the Reagan Administration

Personal positions of President Reagan have been converted into his administration's public policy. The following excerpts from recent speeches by Reagan corroborate the statements made above concerning his policy toward Nicaragua and Central America.

a. On Central America

"Shortly after taking power, the Sandinistas — in partnership with Cuba and the Soviet Union, began supporting aggression and terrorism against El Salvador, Honduras, Costa Rica, and Guatemala. They opened training camps for guerrillas from El Salvador, so they could return to their country and attack its government. These camps still operate. Nicaragua is still the headquarters for Communist guerrilla movements. And Nicaraguan agents and diplomats have been caught in Costa Rica and Honduras, supervising attacks carried out by Communist terrorists."[1]

b. On the Nicaraguan Military Build-Up and Nicaraguan Subversion in Central America

"The mines were planted in response to a flood of new arms shipments," said the President.[2]

The Sandinistas have "no honor, no honesty," said the President in an interview for Irish television, and intend "further revolutions throughout all of Latin America."[3]

The present government of Nicaragua has not lived up to any of its promises regarding human rights, free elections, freedom of religion and the press, Reagan has said. He characterized the contras as "freedom fighters," who took part in the revolution against Somoza in 1979 until they were forced into exile by the Sandinistas, the totalitarian and communist element of the revolution.[4]

"Those were homemade mines that couldn't sink a ship." He dismissed the debate over the mines, as "much ado about nothing."[5]

The following are excerpts of the most important points in a document on the military build-up in Nicaragua and support for subversion in Central America, published by the U.S. Department of State and the Department of Defense on July 18, 1984 in Washington, D.C.[6]

"The subversive system that seeks to destabilize neighboring democratic governments includes communication centers for Salvadoran guerrillas, safe houses, arms depots, vehicle shops, training camps for guerrillas, and assistance in transporting military supplies to Salvadoran guerrillas via air, land, and sea. El Salvador has been the principal target of guerrillas and Nicaragua-sponsored subversion, but Costa Rica and Honduras have also been subjected to armed attacks, bombings, attempted assassinations and other violent activity."

"The threat from Nicaragua to the democratic governments of Central America and the support system Nicaragua maintains for guerrillas are all the more formidable because behind Nicaragua, providing support, are Cuba and the Soviet Union."

In his radio broadcast of April 14, 1984, the President observed that:[7]

— "Central America has become the stage for a bold attempt by the Soviet Union, Cuba, and Nicaragua to install communism by force throughout the hemisphere."

— "Costa Rica, Honduras, and El Salvador are being threatened by the Nicaraguan army and security forces, backed by a Soviet bloc and Cuban supported Sandinista army and security force in Nicaragua that has grown from about 10,000 under the previous government to more than 100,000 in less than five years."

— In 1983, "The Soviet bloc delivered over $100 million in military hardware. The Sandinistas have established a powerful force of artillery, multiple rocket launchers, and tanks in an arsenal which exceeds that of all other countries in the region put together."

And another example of President Reagan's statements about Nicaragua's subversion:

— "Our friends in the region must also face the export of subversion across their borders that undermines democratic development, polarizes institutions, and wrecks their economies. This terrorist violence has been felt by all of Nicaragua's neighbors. . ."[8]

d. The Lack of Personal Freedom in Nicaragua

"Nowhere is this threat more pressing than in Nicaragua, a country which today marks the fifth year of Sandinista dictatorship. The Sandinista revolution, like Castro's revolution, is a revolution betrayed."[9]

"Faced with mounting internal pressures and disillusionment abroad, the Sandinistas have announced an election for November of this year. We would wholeheartedly welcome a genuine democratic election in Nicaragua. But no person committed to democracy will be taken in by a Soviet-style sham election."[10]

There is much "less personal freedom" in Nicaragua today than during the Somoza dictatorship, declared President Reagan on July 18, 1984.

"The Sandinista revolution is a revolution betrayed, a revolution that has left in its wake a trail of broken promises, broken hearts and broken dreams," said President Reagan to the White House Outreach Working Group on Central America, a group of American citizens who were invited to the White House on July 18, 1984, to hear information regarding administration policies in the region.[11]

e. Responsibility of the OAS to Observe Nicaragua

"Given the unprecedented involvement of all of us in the process that brought the Sandinista regime to power," the OAS declared, "the member nations have a continuing interest — indeed a responsibility — in monitoring the situation in Nicaragua to see whether or not the Sandinista government has, indeed, carried out the commitments it so solemnly made to us in 1979."[12]

Since its inception, the Reagan administration has followed a program of ideological aggression against Nicaragua with the following stages of implementation:

a) Preparation of internal conditions in the U.S., under the pretext of the "Soviet threat" to the region and the possibility that the Nicaraguan example would be followed by other countries in the area. The White Paper played an important role in this regard.[13]

b) Involvement of other Central American governments in escalated aggression against Nicaragua, a task carried out through the so-called "Central American Democratic Community" in order to coordinate armies and ideological apparatuses.

c) The creation and open support of counterrevolutionary communication media in neighboring countries.

d) The coordination of this program of ideological aggression with groups inside Nicaragua that support the fall of the Sandinista Popular Revolution, and finally, the aggravation of internal contradictions in support of civilian groups representing the counterrevolutionaries, leaving a military resolution as the principal alternative.

These plans have been manifested in various stages, first, by use of the ancient principle of lying and distorting reality and second, by manipulating dichotomies between ideological concepts (democracy vs. totalitarianism, freedom vs. repression, etc.) in order to associate the Sandinista Revolution with all those concepts characterized as negative.

II. COMMUNICATION STRATEGIES OF THE U.S. IN CENTRAL AMERICA

The manipulation of information by international communication monopolies has been widely denounced. Their use of lies, inaccuracies, and silence has impeded the people's struggle in Nicaragua, as in all parts of the world, to break the chains of domination and exploitation. This is what happened in Grenada, and this is what is happening today with the struggle in El Salvador, as well as with the Sandinista Revolution, which is seen as an example by many Central American and Latin American peoples.

1. Growth in the Communication Structure

a. The Voice of America

A new aspect of the campaign is the direct enlistment of the Voice of America, the official radio station of the U.S. government, through the installation of equipment in Costa Rica to transmit radio programs to Nicaragua. The U.S. Information Agency (USIA) is another official entity participating in this operation, which violates international legal norms. Involvement of the USIA implies an even greater degree of participation by the United States in destabilizing the Nicaraguan government.

Certain aspects of the decision to launch this operation must be pointed out. It is U.S. military policy to try to break Costa Rica's neutrality in the regional conflict. The French evening newspaper *La Croix,* citing official Costa Rican sources, stated in its September 16, 1984 edition that "the government of Costa Rica has accused the United States of wanting it to compromise (its neutrality) in its fight against Nicaragua through the installation of a transmitter for the Voice of America in northern Costa Rica."

The terms of the agreement between the U.S. government and the radio station have been kept secret because of laws restricting foreigners from operating radio stations in Costa Rica. The installation cost more than $3.3 million.

b. Counterrevolutionary Radio Transmitters

The installation of radio transmitters in areas of Costa Rica and Honduras bordering on Nicaragua signals a new stage of development of U.S. communications strategies. For the last two years, both countries have operated radio stations with transmitters directed toward Nicaragua. The clandestine station called "September 15th," organ of the so-called Nicaraguan Democratic Forces, broadcasts from Honduras; the radio station "Voice of Sandino," organ of Democratic Revolutionary Action (ARDE), is based in Costa Rican territory. Another radio station transmits in the Miskito language, attempting to induce a negative attitude toward the revolutionary government among the Miskitos and encouraging separatism.

Radio station IMPACTO also operates from Costa Rica. It was installed at the urging of the CIA, as logistical support for the political and military activities of the counterrevolutionary forces. Radio IMPACTO represents the most highly developed effort of the CIA to provide a single, coherent voice for the politico-ideological positions of the groups fighting the Sandinista government. For this reason, it is important to outline briefly the main positions put forward by Radio IMPACTO; we can then see how they are similar to those of the United States. They are:

— The Revolution was betrayed.
— The FSLN is a totalitarian government.
— The FSLN violates human rights.
— The mass media are censored in Nicaragua.

— The FSLN wants to destroy traditional Christian values.

— The government and the FSLN are incapable of solving the country's economic problems.

— Basic necessities will be in short supply.

— The FSLN exports revolution and wants to take over Central America.

— The government is becoming militarized and it makes secret pacts with the Soviet Union and the communist bloc.

It is important to point out that the ideological basis of Radio IMPACTO aligns with that of the newspaper *La Prensa*. The content is basically identical, but presented in a different manner. IMPACTO puts forth concrete positions on specific problems; however, it is propelled by the same ideological concepts as *La Prensa's*, like the defense of "Christian values" and "democracy." Its role is one of correlating politico-military positions with ideological objectives espoused by opposition political parties, through means of communication like *La Prensa*. Radio IMPACTO operates in the south of Honduras in much the same way as in Costa Rica, installing radio stations with the support of the Honduran government.

Together these stations endangered the April 1980 agreements reached in Buenos Aires at a meeting in which all Latin American countries as well as the U.S. and Canada participated. The goal of that meeting was to coordinate technically and avoid situations such as those created by the United States in Central America and the Caribbean.

In its eagerness to destroy the Nicaraguan Revolution, the Reagan administration has violated various international laws and has ignored agreements made under the jurisdiction of the International Communications Union (Unión Internacional de Comunicaciones).

2. Other Methods Used in the Ideological Offensive

To these developments in the area of radio, we must add campaigns carried out by North American news agencies, news bulletins distributed locally and overseas by the U.S. Information Agency through U.S. embassies, international newspapers and magazines which are strongly influenced by U.S. foreign policy, and bulletins of the Interamerican Press Association and the International Broadcasting Association (AIR) — all critical elements in the propaganda offensive against Nicaragua.

The origins of these tactics against Nicaragua can be found in the propaganda campaign initiated by the U.S. between 1970 and 1973 against the Popular Unity government of Salvador Allende in Chile, where the media in the service of imperialism played a basic role in the overthrow of the Allende government. The number of articles, commentaries, editorials, chronicles, columns, essays, reports, and interviews against the Nicaraguan Revolution which have been published and distributed in different countries and languages surpasses to date the quantity of similar propaganda disseminated throughout the world against Chile.

Official documents of the Committee for the Study of Governmental Intelligence Operations, published in English in 1975 and in Spanish in 1976, reveal the magnitude of CIA involvement in propaganda operations, and demonstrate many common features with the current campaign against Nicaragua.

In the same way that the economic collapse of Chile was predicted, the daily newspaper *La Prensa*, organ of the opposition, has in recent times maintained the nonviability of the Nicaraguan economy and the theme of freedom of the press. "Freedom of the press" is a central theme used against the Nicaraguan process which was also used to discredit the popular government of Chile, according to the document mentioned above. It has been difficult to reproduce this scenario in Nicaragua, due to the consolidation and strength of the Revolution, although they have tried to carry it out by other means. This implies that the campaign in Nicaragua is conditioned by the historical particularities of the country.

Key aspects of the internal offensive have rested with *La Prensa,* certain sectors of the Catholic hierarchy, the creation of religious sects, and a news bulletin of the U.S. government, which is similar in format to a magazine. In Nicaragua, the U.S. embassy circulates more than 2,000 copies of this bulletin, which is openly hostile to the Revolution.

3. The Role of *La Prensa* in Domestic Disinformation

If we analyze the daily newspaper *La Prensa,* we can clearly see how it coincides with policies of the Reagan administration.

a. *Description of* La Prensa

A study of this newspaper during April-May 1984 shows beyond a doubt that it has clear political goals. An analysis of the scope and content of the editorial page and the national news section reveals the following:

i) The editorial page is basically composed of three types of articles: those on politics and religion and those critical of state management. Only 3% is devoted to articles on cultural matters. The basis for ideological conflict can be found in the paper's criticism of the state's conduct of national affairs. *La Prensa's* positions are of a political nature, drawing on the moral authority of the Catholic religion for support.

ii) On the editorial page, articles of a political nature (which constitute more than 50% of the total and close to 45% of the space used) are primarily devoted to anticommunist themes and criticisms of state management.

Various positions are clearly manifested: a pro-North American tendency, support of dialogue with the opposition (including the counterrevolutionaries), an identification between the Sandinistas and Somocismo, and unconditional support for any position of the Episcopal Conference, whether theological or political.

iii) In the national news section, the correlation is somewhat different in terms of the type of message conveyed and the less explicit style. 29% of the news is of a political nature, and opposition news — criticism of the elections and of the projected Law of the Means of Communication that was presented by the Patriotic Revolutionary Front (Frente Patriótico Revolucionario, FPR) to the Council of State — clearly predominates. There are three main kinds of religious coverage: religious ritual (articles on popular festivals and gatherings of the hierarchy) usually with many photographs; unconditional support for the Catholic hierarchy; and articles specific to church doctrine and the hierarchy.

iv) There is a total absence of news about social and economic advances of the Revolution, which is clear evidence of *La Prensa's* partiality.

b. Characterization of the Contents of La Prensa

The main tactics used by *La Prensa* — and through it, by the opposition political parties — to attack the Sandinista Popular Revolution can be summarized as follows:

— To characterize the Revolution as aligned with the Soviet bloc.

— To present the revolutionary government as opposed to political solutions and to the development of dialogue with the counterrevolutionaries.

— To characterize the Revolution as violating human rights, especially freedom of expression, religion, and organization.

— To portray the FSLN as persecuting the Catholic Church.

— To characterize the Sandinista state as incapable of managing and reviving the economy.

— To maintain that the FSLN has imposed a totalitarian state.

III. ONE PLAN—VARIOUS EXECUTORS

The ideological aggression follows a Reagan administration plan whereby CIA agents, counterrevolutionary groups, domestic means of communication, and political groups representing the counterrevolutionaries utilize the same rhetoric and the same points of attack with the objective of overthrowing Nicaragua's revolutionary government.

1. Obvious Similarities

The Reagan administration, armed counterrevolutionaries, and internal dissidents share the following, main positions:

a) That the present upheaval in Central America has its origin in the East-West conflict. All national liberation movements are machinations of Moscow.

b) That "a favorable political climate" must exist before elections can take place.

c) That government should return to the first government of national unity, permitting representatives of the bourgeoisie to assume key positions in the provisional revolutionary government. These actions are considered necessary in order for the U.S., the armed counterrevolutionaries, and some political parties to set aside their present opposition to the FSLN.

d) That the only way to come to grips with the crisis is to have a national dialogue that includes the former Somoza National Guardsmen and mercenaries who are fighting against the Nicaraguan government.

In order to demonstrate clearly these points of coincidence (of content), we refer to statements by those involved in this campaign of ideological aggression against Nicaragua:

President Reagan

Regarding the FSLN, "There was an outright refusal to hold genuine elections coupled with the continual promise to do so. Their latest promise is for elections by November 1984." Since the Sandinistas took power, "Internal repression of democratic groups, trade unions and civic groups began. Right to dissent was denied. Freedom of the press and freedom of assembly became virtually nonexistent." "The contras, the freedom fighters in Nicaragua, have offered to lay down their weapons and take part in democratic elections; but there the Communist Sandinista government has refused" to allow their participation. (Reagan then cited the Kissinger Commission's conclusion that it was necessary to fortify the U.S. position in Central America, providing financial and military aid to its friends.)[14]

Armed Counterrevolutionaries

We are fighting to return the revolution to its original principles. . . ."We would agree to a cease-fire in exchange for guarantees that would facilitate our participation in truly democratic elections" (counterrevolutionary statements on Radio IMPACTO).

Domestic Opposition

Political parties of the Ramiro Sacasa Democratic Coordinate: "The Sandinistas must fulfill their original agreement with the OAS. . . .We need a national dialogue with all parties, including those who have taken up arms."

Superior Council for Private Industry (Consejo Superior de la Empresa Privada, COSEP): The FSLN has "deviated from its original objectives, which explains the external aggression against Nicaragua by those who are compelling a dialogue between all parties involved, including the armed opposition. . ." (statement by Enrique Bolaños, from a pamphlet containing the text of his comments on the radio program "Línea Directa").

The Catholic hierarchy: For there to be a "true peace between Nicaraguans, it must proceed from an understanding between all parties, including those who have taken up arms" (Pastoral Letter).

La Prensa: "By setting aside its original program, the FSLN has provoked the democratic sectors. Not finding a means of expression, these sectors opted for armed struggle. For this reason, any resolution that might lead to national reconciliation must include the armed opposition in a dialogue encompassing all of the nation's forces."

Although *La Prensa* has not voiced an opinion on a series of important topics, among them U.S. intervention, its stands on many basic issues coincide with those of the U.S. and the FDN and ARDE mercenary forces.

In the same vein, *La Prensa* has coincided politically with the counterrevolutionary forces in calling for a series of conditions to be met, the main one being to have the national elections monitored. Thus it endorses open involvement by the United States in the internal affairs of Nicaragua — a position also reiterated by some reactionary parties in the country.

2. Positions on the Aggression

The position of the reactionary domestic sectors on the aggression has been one of partial silence, with these sectors implicitly justifying the aggression by affirming their differences with the FSLN and other parties of the Revolution.

During the same period that the dailies *La Prensa* and *Barricada* were analyzed as described above, the first dedicated barely 2% of its news to counterrevolutionary aggression, whereas *Barricada* dedicated 80% of its total space to that subject.

While the reactionary sectors are silent, international organizations such as the World Court in The Hague have declared their opposition to continued financing of CIA and counterrevolutionary aggression; they have also called for ceasing the mining of Nicaraguan ports, for a political solution to the situation in Central America, and for peaceful coexistence in the region. It is ironic that church hierarchies in other countries also condemn the imperialist actions — especially churches in the U.S., which thereby condemn their own government — while Nicaraguan bishops support and justify the escalation of aggression.

3. Exposing the Truth

The avalanche of slander has been disproved by the clear, unequivocal position taken by Nicaragua in various world forums and, fundamentally, by its seriousness in looking for peaceful, negotiated solutions to the region's problems.

One can clearly see that the purpose of deceiving world public opinion is to "create proper conditions" for a direct U.S. military intervention against Nicaragua. The objective of all the military maneuvers in recent years has clearly been to prepare the armed forces of Honduras, El Salvador, and Guatemala militarily, as well as to prepare the peoples of those same countries psychologically.

In the Central American region, the misery that exists by itself disproves the U.S. theory that the present situation there is a result of East-West conflict — an argument not accepted by most capitalist countries, including those of Latin America.

The "favorable climate" that the U.S. demands in Nicaragua would, in fact, mean the repression of the mass organizations, stopping the agrarian reform process, and restraining the mobilization of the people for the defense of their homeland. The total effect would be to impede all the measures taken — in accordance with the people's demands — to overcome Nicaragua's problems. The "return to the original principles of the revolution" championed by the opposition is nothing more than a strategy to justify positions that harm our sovereignty. Demands for initiating a national dialogue with all parties, "including the counterrevolutionary forces," have as their only purpose the establishment of a regime of Somocismo without Somoza.

In conclusion, the ideological campaign has two principal objectives which are shared by imperialism, the armed counterrevolution, and internal dissent: a) to create favorable psychological conditions leading to the overthrow of the National Government of Reconstruction (and with it the direction set by the FSLN) through an armed U.S. intervention, under the pretext of restoring order and security to the region; and b) to institutionalize the right to carry out the counterrevolution, which coincides in essence with U.S. strategy in the region.

IV. PLURALISM IN THE FACE OF AGGRESSION

In spite of the military aggression that the country has faced since 1980, ideological room has been made for all sectors of the population within the Sandinista Popular Revolution, based on its principles of political pluralism and a mixed economy. Major mechanisms exist for pluralistic participation in ideological debate and democratic political struggle: the media, the Council of State, political debates, and the election campaign.

1. Access to the Media

In addition to legal access, there is real access to the media by diverse sectors of the population. At present, there are 34 radio stations, four dailies, 22 magazines, two television stations, seven periodicals, and numerous booklets and documents edited by mass and party organizations of different persuasions, state institutions, and private economic, social, or religious organizations. Ownership of the major media is distributed in such a way as to guarantee access by diverse political and economic sectors.

Ownership is distributed as follows: 19 radio stations, two television channels, one daily newspaper, and a magazine are government-owned; two dailies and four magazines are in private hands; one daily, six periodicals, and 17 magazines are owned collectively.

Conservative sectors control 10 radio stations, four party journals, and one trade-union publication. The centrists possess three radio stations and one magazine. Progressive and revolutionary sectors control a party radio station, three party periodicals, and four party magazines, two magazines and two periodicals controlled by trade unions, and one periodical and three magazines that are independent.

Both privately owned and state-run radio stations have a nationwide range, although in most cases such a range is attained only by linking up with the regional stations.

The radio stations with the greatest range are La Voz de Nicaragua (The Voice of Nicaragua, state-owned), Radio Sandino (controlled by the FSLN), Radio Mundial (World Radio, private), and La Corporación (The Corporation, private), with a range extending to approximately 70% of the nation. The regions of Nicaragua that are reached by these stations include the Central Pacific and part of the Atlantic Coast regions.

It is important to note that the state has allocated significant resources for the purpose of integrating the Atlantic Coast with the rest of the country. There are two radio stations that broadcast exclusively in the Miskito language, for listeners in the Atlantic Coast region. In spite of this, one must acknowledge that relative isolation from national news still exists in the region.

The main print media are: *Barricada, La Prensa,* and *El Nuevo Diario.* The first is a party publication and the others are independent or privately controlled. These three dailies, which have the greatest circulation in the country, constitute almost the totality of the written press.

While the physical existence of various types of media demonstrates respect for pluralism, it is the variety in content which genuinely confirms that ample space exists for the dissemination of diverse ideological positions.

Radio stations, dailies, magazines, and the rest of the media have varied audiences and their pages are exceedingly diverse; they include articles of an informative, religious, political, and cultural nature, approached from different angles. That is to say, there exist sufficient means to exercise one's influence on Nicaraguan society, to such a degree that all sectors of the population can find a direct channel for expressing their opinions through the media.

2. Access to Power Through a Legislative Body, the Council of State

In order to guarantee the pluralistic participation of different forces, the Council of State was formed on May 4, 1980, involving eight political parties and three trade-union and social organizations with institutions representative of the economic and religious sectors. Since then, the Council of State has become a forum for discussion in connection with its task of legislating on the most diverse aspects of national life.

3. Uncensored Political Debates

It is important to emphasize that the debates which take place in this forum are not subject to censure of any kind. The media, including the state-controlled or FSLN radio stations, report the political positions of the opposition on special programs such as "Línea Directa." Through these programs, the people of Nicaragua can hear, ask questions about, and respond to the positions articulated by the various political and labor organizations of the country.

4. Elections

Another manifestation of Nicaraguan pluralism can be seen in the national elections for President and Vice President of the Republic, as well as for members of the National Legislative Assembly, scheduled to take place November 4, 1984. The elections have been organized within the context of military aggression; the Government Junta of National Reconstruction has declared that only direct, large-scale, military intervention would cause the elections to be suspended.

In order to create favorable conditions for the elections, the Law of Political Parties was discussed and approved; through this law, political parties with diverse ideologies become institutionalized.

On August 4, 1984, an amnesty was granted to those who had left the country after the Revolution as a result of confusion or being deceived, to encourage their participation in the electoral process. Not included were counterrevolutionary leaders who committed crimes against the Nicaraguan people.

The Election Law was approved, which regulates the standards, participation, and rules of the electoral process through the Supreme Electoral Council.

The national elections encountered obstacles as a result of Reagan administration policy. Reagan intensified his aggression through the involvement of more than 8,000 mercenaries in the region, in order to upset the elections and depict a military solution as the only alternative.

The Ramiro Sacasa Democratic Coordinate (which involves three parties and trade-union centrals) has attempted to promote abstention from the electoral process, at the same time demanding super-monitored elections and a national dialogue with the counterrevolutionaries.

Thanks to the flexibility of the Revolution, the period of registration for the elections has been extended until September 30, in order that parties which have not yet registered can do so. Thus the contention of the parties of the Coordinate, that the only alternative is military, stands refuted in the face of the process of institutionalizing the Revolution.

V. WE WANT PEACE

It is our belief that international solidarity is one of the forces capable of exposing in detail the bellicose foreign policy and militarism pursued by the Reagan administration.

It is through international solidarity that one can demand respect for one's borders, eradicate the use of threats in international relations and the state terrorism encouraged by the government of Ronald Reagan, and recover the people's right to determine their own destiny without outside interference. It is international solidarity which strengthens us in our struggle for peace and for disarmament. Moreover, it supports us in the struggle to break through systematic disinformation regarding Central America and the Caribbean, especially Nicaragua, El Salvador, and Guatemala, and to denounce the posture assumed by reactionary sectors of the United States that constitute an open threat to the security of the peoples of the world.

Honorable Tribunal:

We have come to denounce the government of the United States and its escalating, aggressive actions against Nicaragua. The United States is determined to destroy the Sandinista Popular Revolution. To that end it is conducting an ideological offensive designed to confuse and disinform the peoples of the world. It seeks to create psychological conditions which, together with the naval warships off our coasts and Yankee troops permanently established in the region through joint military exercises and military maneuvers, will allow the United States to invade Nicaragua directly.

We have come to denounce the use and abuse of the media by the United States in order to carry out campaigns of confusion and lies against our people, and our desire to build a sovereign and free nation after centuries in which our rights and freedoms were denied.

From Nicaragua, we have brought convincing proof of United States actions against our country. We trust that the wisdom of honorable and progressive men and women will not permit this new genocide. It rests in your hands and on your awareness to alert the world to this crime against humanity.

Honorable Tribunal:

In the tenacious spirit of Nicaragua's people, who arise in the face of aggression, we have revealed the truth today before you. We reiterate to the world that the people of Nicaragua want PEACE.

October 1984

Notes

The following are provided in order to offer readers sources in English for statements originally made in English; these are the sole responsibility of the editor. The author's sources were various Spanish publications including Boletín de Noticias (News Bulletin), *in which these statements were translated into Spanish.*

1. *The New York Times,* May 10, 1984.
2. *The Washington Post,* May 30, 1984.
3. Ibid.
4. *The New York Times,* May 10, 1984.
5. *The Washington Post,* May 30, 1984.
6. The title of this document was "Background Paper: Nicaragua's Military Build-up and Support for Central American Subversion."
7. All citations from this radio broadcast are found in the *Department of State Bulletin,* September 1984.
8. *Department of State Bulletin,* June 1984.
9. *Department of State Bulletin,* September 1984.
10. Ibid.
11. *The Washington Post,* July 19, 1984.
12. *Department of State Bulletin,* September 1984.
13. An apparent reference to the State Department White Papers of February 1981 and May 1983.
14. *Department of State Bulletin,* June 1984.

Presentation

Ernesto Cardenal

Priest, writer, and Minister of Culture of Nicaragua

President Reagan has maintained that the problem of Nicaragua is part of the East-West confrontation. Nothing is further from the truth. What has really happened is that the U.S. has intervened in Nicaragua for more than a century, long before the existence of East and West. We have been victims of the United States since the doctrine of Manifest Destiny emerged in the middle of the last century, declaring that the United States was designated by Providence to control Latin America. That doctrine is still in effect, with more strength than ever.

In the middle of the last century, we saw the United States bomb, set afire and destroy San Juan del Norte Harbor on the Atlantic Coast of Nicaragua, to serve its interests. Next came the freebooters Henry L. Kinney, U.S. Army Colonel, and Joseph Faber, a U.S. government trading agent, who tried to take over an extensive area of our Atlantic coast and even established a government there. Later the filibusterer William Walker seized the country militarily, declared himself President of Nicaragua, and was recognized and accepted by the U.S. government. He decreed slavery in Nicaragua and tried to annex Nicaragua as well as the rest of Central America for the United States, until he was defeated in our National War with the help of the other Central American countries. In the years that followed, the United States shifted from military to political and diplomatic aggression, its sights set on assuring an interoceanic canal route through Nicaragua.

Toward the end of the last century, a liberal nationalistic government emerged in Nicaragua and tried its best to break away from North American impositions, which were those of monopoly capitalism. In response, U.S. troops landed at the harbor of Corinto on the Pacific coast. Later, at the beginning of this century, the U.S. armed and financed a rebellion of the Conservative Party, which it put in power and thereby took over the country's entire economy — customs, railroad, and National Bank. The center of power was no longer to be found in the government of Nicaragua but in the United States and its Embassy. Nicaragua became practically a North American protectorate and its sovereignty was sold for $3 million in the Chamorro-Bryan Treaty. Elections were held according

to the laws of the United States and oversighted by the U.S. Marine Corps.
U.S. troops occupied Nicaragua for over 25 years: first, from 1912 to 1925
and later from 1926 to 1933.

   When the Bertrand Russell Tribunal met in Rome in 1976 to judge
the Latin American dictatorships, I attended as a witness for Nicaragua,
sent by the Sandinista Front (Frente Sandinista). On that occasion, along
with a large number of documents which I presented about the atrocious
violations of human rights by the Somoza dictatorship, I also read a poem
of mine, telling the Tribunal that I thought poetry could be as valid as
prose in making this accusation. In the same way, I want to present before
this court today a fragment of a poem of mine which I think illustrates
the meaning of that first intervention in 1912.

It happened that another country needed those riches.
By the loan agreements of 1911 Nicaragua ceded her customs houses
and the management of the National Bank to the moneylenders.
The bankers reserved for themselves the right
to acquire the National Bank. By the agreements of 1912
the railroad was also compromised. On February 2, 1911,
the banking group Brown Brothers & Co.
took an interest in us. In order to pay a loan
we would have recourse to another, and so on
forever. (Once begun, there is no way out.)
The bankers came like barracudas.
The marines landed to reestablish order
and remained in Nicaragua for 13 years. Not enough
to control the customs houses, the banks, the railroads.
Nicaragua sold its land as well.
Adolfo Díaz, a $35-a-week employee of the Angeles Mining Co.,
was the "capitalist"
of the "revolution," loaning the movement $600,000.
The payment of the loan to Brown Brothers
was to be guaranteed by the revenues of the customs houses.
Corruption, corruption of the nation, the banquet of the bankers
was a banquet of vultures
gentlemen in black tails hovering like vultures.
And the politicos: like blind bats that shit upon us
hanging there in the dark crapping and pissing on us
shit and piss of abyss-colored bats
black wings fluttering in the black air.
Another $500,000 loaned for the stabilization of the currency
but — the banquet of the bankers —
the money doesn't come out of the pockets of the bankers in

New York either.
The collateral was that the country would be turned over to
the moneylenders.
The money from the loan of 1911 was to found the National Bank
but it left the National Bank in the hands of the bankers.
The bankers Brown Brothers bought all the paper that they wanted
or rather, all the paper money that they wanted, at 20 to the
dollar
and they sold it at 12.50 to the dollar, all the paper they wanted
or rather to buy 20 pesos cost a dollar (and they were able to buy
as much as they wanted) and when sold (whenever they wanted),
they were worth a dollar sixty. That is to say
they bought money cheap in order to sell dear
they bought it from the country to sell it back to the country and
by doing so increased the price of corn, houses, education,
dances, train tickets.
That was the plunder of the mafia of the bankers.
Like stickup men they held up the national currency.
Afterwards the moneylenders loaned back the country the
country's money
at 6% interest.
The revenue of the nation collected by the foreign bankers
deposited in a National Bank controlled by those foreign bankers
and distributed by the foreign bankers
linked to the United States Secretary of State
(who owned shares in the Angeles Mining Co.)
Just as the Honduran taxes were collected by Morgan
Morgan the ferocious
like when the wild boar comes shrieking down
or the smell of puma is in the air
Afterwards the nation's land was sold for 3 million
dollars (Chamorro-Bryan Agreement)
which also went directly into the hands of the bankers
(The U.S. acquires a canal zone without limitations
2 Caribbean islands
and a naval base
the country for 3 million — and the money to the bankers —
and the customs houses continue to be controlled by the moneylenders for
an indeterminate period — until the total cancellation of the debts —
and the moneylenders have acquired the National Bank, and
the railroad, buying 51% of the shares for a
million dollars, and all that remains of the nation is its flag)

The night dark and no kerosene in the farmhouse.
An owl sings over the nation.
The have silenced the song of the little *pijul*.
No need to annex the land
but enough for the U.S. to control the country (through Díaz
and every president since) with
all the advantages of annexation but neither its risks nor expenses
"unless one wishes to play with words"
— a professor, circa 1928, to the *Paris Daily News* —
"it is perfectly clear that Nicaraguan independence doesn't exist"
To invest capital in Nicaragua, and to protect it once
invested, was the job of the State Department.
Political expansion with an eye to economic expansion:
and economic expansion because capital didn't have sufficient
yield in the U.S. or yielded less
than it did in Nicaragua
that is: imperialism
interventions for investment or vice versa
Diplomacy operating through the bankers to subjugate the nation
the bankers operating through diplomacy to extract the money
Together, in impeccable formality, the funereal vultures.
Hovering about the Gross National Product.
— Or like sharks about the smell of blood.
Internal chaos and corruption set the stage for foreign intervention
which in turn encouraged further chaos and corruption
(clear as the *piche's* eye — clear as daylight)
From here then:
imperialism like an obstructing destabilizing element, etc.
factor of backwardness, of corruption in Nicaragua: has violated
treaties, constitutions, judicial decisions
provoked civil war stolen elections bribed
covered up corruption prostituted politics impoverished the people
impeded unity kept their agents in power against
the will of the people jacked up prices defended
oppression unleashed death
Nicaragua found itself (when Sandino appeared) with
part of its territory already in foreign hands, the foreign debt
increased, its financial life subjected to
the New York Banking Syndicate, and completely stultified.
The whole country
what Cabo Gracias a Dios looks like today: a row
of huts, with a single street on which, a few steps from the sea,
a vulture and a dog wrangle over the guts of a fish.

As I said, the first intervention in this century was from 1912 to 1925 and the next from 1926 to 1933. General Benjamín Zeledón, a patriot who rebelled in 1912 against the first intervention, was defeated and assassinated by the North Americans. His body was dragged through the streets by a horse, to terrorize the people. This spectacle was witnessed by a child of humble origin named Augusto César Sandino, who would later rebel against the second intervention. After six years he succeeded in defeating the U.S. occupation forces, and in 1933 he drove them out of the country. But before leaving, the North American troops created an occupation army called the National Guard and installed Anastasio Somoza as its unconditional chief.

As is well known, Somoza and the United States government treacherously killed Sandino. Next, the United States government put Somoza in power. And for almost half a century, the Somoza family (three Somozas) governed Nicaragua — which was in reality a nation occupied by the United States during that entire period, not by its troops but through the Somozas and the occupation army, the National Guard.

This continued until Somoza, the National Guard, and U.S. imperialism were expelled by the Sandinista National Liberation Front. Two decades earlier, the Sandinista Front had taken up Sandino's struggle and, after a long war with great problems at first but then with the support of all the people, it triumphed on July 19, 1979. When the Sandinista troops triumphantly entered Managua, to the greatest popular acclaim ever seen in our history, Nicaragua became totally independent of U.S. imperialism. It is the first country on the American continent to become independent from the United States, and that is the reason for the war being waged against us. The reason we are suffering is not the East-West conflict.

That is why Comandante Daniel Ortega was right when he said at the United Nations, three years ago:

> . . . *why were our countries raped, invaded, humiliated on more than 200 occasions from 1840 to 1917? With what excuse, if at that time there was not a single socialist state in the world and the Czar reigned over all the Russias? Treaties were imposed on us, loans were imposed, we were invaded, the status of "protectorate" was granted by force, all under the same guise of U.S. "National Security" as was first invoked in the Monroe Doctrine, later called Manifest Destiny, and afterwards the Big Stick, then Dollar Diplomacy. . . .*
>
> *Border expansion, safe maritime routes, military bases in the Caribbean, governments that were bought off, and docile governments: a liberal ideal that became unabashed expansionism.*
>
> *. . . . How to explain the multiple aggressions, interferences, and landings between 1917 and 1954 in Latin America, when no Cuban Revolution existed and it was not possible to accuse Cuba of "interference," an accusation that would be reserved for the future?*
>
> *The United States did not snatch Cuba and Puerto Rico in 1898, and*

could not have imposed the Platt Amendment, in order to save the Caribbean territories from the influence of the Soviet Union — because it did not exist yet.

The United States did not land its Marines at Veracruz, Haiti, and Nicaragua, nor did it, starting in 1903, build the most formidable naval force ever seen in Caribbean waters, in order to be the victor of the East-West conflict. It was simply protecting its territorial expansionism, the interests of its financiers and bankers, of its big businessmen, who were then beginning to pillage Latin America.

Those were Comandante Ortega's words. As I said before, we have been victims of the United States since the declaration of Manifest Destiny, which is more than ever in effect under President Reagan. But why is the United States interested in us? Let me delve into a boring subject called statistics.

Economically, Central America represents 2½% of the total Latin American product. Its potential as a market is $472 per capita, whereas the Latin American mean is $1,964 (almost $2,000 per capita). North American investment in Central America is 2½% of its total investments in Latin America, with one of the smallest rates of return in the whole world. The economic growth of Central America in recent years has been negative. In 1982 the negative trade balance was $2,355 million. On the other hand, the aid that the United States granted to Central America between 1981 and 1982 was 70% of the total economic aid given to Latin America during the same period. This indicates that Central America is not a source of economic accumulation for the United States, but instead costs it a lot of money. Nicaragua is a fiscal deficit, combining a low rate of return with a low trade level, and a high financial risk. Therefore, Central America is an economic burden for the United States.

What, then, is the interest they have in us? Naturally, it is a geopolitical interest. Our bad luck has been our geography. Hundreds of kilometers from the United States, we are considered by that country as its border. They have recently called us, shamelessly, their fourth border. In 1982, 15% of the United States military budget was allocated for the Caribbean Basin only. The Monroe Doctrine is not a dusty document of the past, nor is Manifest Destiny.

Central America and the Caribbean have been considered the United States' "back yard." Every tension in the region has produced an intervention. And it is the region that has had the most military interventions in the world. This means that U.S. interests are incompatible with the existence in the area of genuine nations, independent of the United States. The United States has presented its interests as the interest of the entire West. This explains U.S. actions in relation to Arbenz's Guatemala in 1954, Cuba in 1959, Panama in 1964, Nicaragua in 1979, Grenada in 1983, and in El Salvador, Honduras, and Guatemala today. It is not that they wish to prevent another economic, social, and even political model from emerging in the region, but rather that they do not want their imperialist geopolitics to be questioned. Thus our beautiful geography has been our curse, and this has been the case since the last century.

The United States currently describes Nicaragua as part of its new cold war between West and East. But it is not the loss of control by the United States over the region that creates instability; it is the presence of the United States in the region that creates instability — for the region, and for the United States itself. It is not a "National Security" problem, but rather a "National Insecurity" problem, of the U.S. not wanting to recognize that our people reject being prisoners of its geopolitics. Our anti-imperialism is not an ideological product, infiltrated from the East, but the logical product of our history of foreign domination. The social revolution in the region is a geopolitical revolution, and this geopolitical revolution is naturally a social revolution. U.S. domination has made democracy impossible in our countries. In order to achieve a genuine democracy, the first requisite is to free ourselves of that geopolitical curse.

And so it happens that U.S. hegemony at a world level is being questioned in the Central American crisis. The same thing happened in Vietnam, where economic interests were also secondary. The conflict with us is growing worse because the Reagan administration has involved us in its global confrontation with the Soviet Union, in its new cold war. And thus the danger of a regional war endangers world peace. The great danger, for us and for the world, is expressed in the fact that President Reagan has said before the Congress of the United States that there is no area of the world more closely integrated into the political and economical system of the United States, and none more vital to North American security, than Central America. And, as Mrs. Kirkpatrick has said at the United Nations, for the United States the most important region in the world today is Central America.

The tragedy for us is that they do not see us as a reality, but rather we are a ghost in the mind of a psychopath. And for the United States, Nicaragua is only a symbol — but a symbol that must be destroyed.

Testimony of
Orlando Wayland Waldimar

Miskito teacher

My name is Orlando Wayland Waldimar, Miskito Indian, native to Ulwas, Río Coco, Atlantic Coast of Nicaragua. I am 25 years old and single. I got my bachelor's and master's degrees at the "11 de Septiembre" (Sept. 11) National Institute, Waspam, Río Coco.

In 1983, I was working with the adult educational program in Francia Sirpi. On November 19, some time in the afternoon, a white jeep arrived in the community. In the jeep were Bishop Schlaefer and three other religious leaders. Supposedly they came to offer Mass. That same night I went to sleep — early, as I always do, about seven o'clock. I slept until around eleven o'clock at night, when I heard some shooting and I got up. The contras had the area around Francia Sirpi surrounded. They were shooting like crazy. Their goal was to scare the people, force them out of their beds, and then take them to Honduras.

Most of the people hid underneath their beds or in other parts of their houses, or in the mountains. When the contras realized that the people were not coming out, they started a house-by-house search, forcing people out at gunpoint, kicking and slapping them. Five contras came toward me. They grabbed me, and tied my hands, and called me "communist spy," because they consider all who work with the government to be "communist spies." We are collaborators. That is how they think of us. I remember that the old people were crying, as well as the children and the women — the whole town was crying. The contras were shouting, "Let's go! Let's go!"

There was a young man working with the adult educational program named Richard Thomas, who didn't want to leave with the contras. They shot him in the back, right in front of me. He was killed. I had my hands tied, and from that moment I thought I was lost. They had already killed one person who worked with me. Then I saw a group of contras ransacking José Zúñiga's store.

Compañeros, the nine of us were taken because we were government workers. We walked, we walked a whole day. The contras took three stolen cows with them. On the way, they started to drink some liquor; they got drunk and they went crazy, shooting and scaring the people. The old people and the poor children were trembling, crying "Don't kill me." The contras shouted back, "Don't talk, let's go."

The road was muddy and the old people couldn't walk fast enough. The contras were saying, "Walk fast, walk fast, we have to get to Honduras." The old people were crying. They took us to a hill where they concentrated all the civilians, and left us there, surrounded. The commander was Juan Solórzano, whose nickname was "León Blanco" (White Lion), and the sub-commander was Orlando McLean, nicknamed "Boa Negra" (Black Boa). The commander said they were going to kill the animals and give the meat to the people to eat. They slaughtered the cows and gave the meat to the people. But it wasn't enough, because there were about 1,200 of us, so everyone got only a small piece and stayed hungry.

We slept there that night, and the next day we left around five in the morning. The contras were stealing money, watches, and wallets from the civilians. They were hitting the children and the rest of us. I also noticed that there were several pregnant women. I don't know if it was because of the terror, but two of them delivered their babies. The umbilical cords were cut with a knife. The women tied the babies around their waists with bandages.

After a day and a half of walking, we heard sounds which indicated that the army was coming, and that there was a battle going on with the rear guard of the contras. The commander told us, the civilians: "You have to walk fast, because what is coming behind us isn't confetti, you better walk fast." We ran and ran. Nothing happened to the civilians. They took us to Honduras, running day and night.

We arrived at the Río Coco. When we got there, Steadman Fagoth Müller, who had worked as a security guard for Somoza, was waiting for us. (Yesterday you saw him in the magazine *Seminario* that Compañera Rosa Pasos was showing to you.) He was waiting with his guards to receive the people. Commander Solárzano took me to him and said, "These are not workers, these are spies." Müller said, "So you work with the Sandinistas, but now you are going to see what will happen to you in Honduras." Müller then handed me over to a commander whose nickname was Cara de Malo ("Evil Face").

Commander Cara de Malo was the torturer, the one who murdered the people. He took me to the bank of the river and pushed me down a hill. I almost fainted, and then he took me to the water, and pushed my head beneath the surface to drown me. How did they do it? I was tied down, and one of the contras held my neck, like this, and pushed me into the water. I was almost unconscious, it was as if I were dead, and he was hitting me. The water was coming into my mouth and nose. Sometimes when I think about what he did, I feel that I don't exist in this world, because it was so painful.

Then a big boat approached us, towed by two people from Honduras who helped the people cross the river. When we crossed, Steadman Fagoth gathered all the people together. He said, "All the men have to be recruited to the MISURA [a counterrevolutionary organization that included indigenous people and whose name represented the Miskitos, Sumos, and Ramas — Ed.] to support the struggle." They recruited 40 youths. Afterwards, we walked an hour from the river bank into Honduras. We came to a road that detoured north, the road to Mocorón. Most of the civilians were taken down that road to a concentration camp called the Juan Pocirpe camp. After that, there was another detour toward Auasbila. They took the nine of us there. The other 40 were taken to a training camp.

My group was brought to a counterrevolutionary camp. I was hoping that they would put me in a cell with a roof and a floor. When I arrived, I saw a sign that read P.C., but I didn't know what P.C. stood for until later. There was a kind of pen, where people raised pigs, with a fence about waist high. It had a hole and they told me, "O.K., communist spy, get in." They forced the nine of us through the hole, so we were crawling toward the fence. They closed the hole and we could not stand up, we could only stay in a sitting position. They had taken my shirt, pants, and shoes, so I was left only in my underwear. It was raining and the rain was soaking me. The earth underneath us was turning to mud. We were trembling, trembling, and the contras were watching us. "Nobody can speak here," they said.

We slept that night. The next day came the torture, the worst torture, the most horrible that the contras applied. There were three torturers. I do not know the name of one of them, but I know the other two. One was Manuel Escobar. He was a Miskito Indian from Asang. The other was a woman, Gredel Domingo, a Miskito Indian, too. They started to torture me. First they took me to the water, threatening to drown me in order to extract military information about Nicaragua. They told us, "You people have a good command of military information. That is why we are torturing you. To get that information." But what kind of information did I have? I am an ordinary worker. They pushed me into the water constantly, fifteen times, twenty times. It was such an experience that sometimes when I talk here, I know I am alive, but I feel that I am dead.

Then they put big ants that bite inside my underpants. They were biting me and I was jumping. "Give us the information. If you give it to us, we will not send you to the ant hill," they said. They sent me to the ant hill to extract information from me. How did they do it? I was tied like this, and they put the ants on my chest. I was jumping and crying, and they were laughing. They are not human, they are irrational. I say irrational because to treat a brother like this is possible only for people who do not have a human mentality.

At night, they put me in the ditch and I spent all night there. I was trembling, I was dying. They told me "If you will give us the information, we will take you out." Every night they would put me in the ditch. The next day they would put me in the ditch again, to clean it out. There were leaves in the ditch, and those leaves had to be cleaned out. After that, they would cut pieces of branches from the *suita,* a tree whose leaves are used to make roofs for houses — on the coast, we used to do that. They would beat me with a stick from head to toe. They would leave me bruised, bruised as if the blood would soon come rushing out through my skin. They would inject me, the so-called paramedics, and when I was getting better, they would hit me again. They did this to me every day for a month and a half.

I could not take it any more. Then Steadman Fagoth came and told us: "We will spare your life, on the condition that you join the struggle. We can still kill you, but we are leaving you alive so you can support the struggle." I accepted because I was dying, and because I was in their hands. What else could I have done? I had to accept.

They took me from the camp to politicize me. They told me that under Somoza you could buy a lot of pills with 20 córdobas, but now, under communism, you could not buy anything with 20 córdobas. I told them "Yes, yes." What else could I have said? If I contradicted them, they would have killed me on the spot and decapitated me. Slowly, they were coming to trust me more. I had to change my attitude, I had to line myself up in their ranks. They gave me a pair of blue pants, a blue shirt, a blue cap, and a pair of American jungle boots.

For the second time Steadman Fagoth talked to us. He said: "By 1983 the CIA was giving us 150,000 lempiras [Honduran currency — Ed.], but with 150,000 lempiras the struggle cannot be won. We need more money." So he wrote to the CIA, he said, soliciting an increase in financial aid. The CIA approved the request, and by 1984 it was providing 250,000 lempiras every month.

When I was leaving, I understood the sign P.C. It meant Command Post, and the commander was the brother of Steadman Fagoth, Hilton Fagoth Müller. (He is in the magazine, along with his brother.) Hilton was the one who gave orders for my torture. They appear as anti-Sandinista guerrilla fighters. They are not guerrilla fighters, they are counterrevolutionaries who are killing the indigenous people and the people of Nicaragua, day after day. They are the people who bring terrorism, financed by the CIA.

Afterwards, Hilton Fagoth told me, "You have to go to a military training camp." I answered, "Yes." They took me to a training camp, where I found three of Somoza's Guards. They used only nicknames, not their real names there. One of them was called Chan. He was an ex-Guard of Somoza's from Masaya. Another was Samba, and the other was Mercenario. There I was trained. Because I was alive and not dead, my greatest anguish was my mother and father. My parents depended on me, and now I was kidnapped. What did my mother think? I felt a deep pain, a pain that I think I will never feel again. I would prefer to die.

I was trained. Chan was the instructor who taught us how to shoot and how to disarm the enemy. Mercenario was in charge of teaching us about mines, the things that destroy bridges and are planted in roads to kill civilians. Samba was in charge of teaching us how to kidnap people and to set up ambushes.

At the camp I saw an olive green helicopter with the letters USA and three pilots. They were blond Americans, North American gringos. They came to leave weapons at the camp because it had the sign. Next to the sign, there was a tent where two American gringos were staying. Chan, the ex-Guard, told us that they were military veterans who had fought against Vietnam. The helicopter brought all kinds of weapons. I can tell you what kinds: RPG-7 M-79 grenade launchers, carbines, M-50 and M-60 machine guns, mines, and other weapons. Who received those weapons? The gringos received the weapons and then gave them to Hilton. At Hilton's camp, there was an arsenal where they stored the weapons from the helicopter. All the weapons were made in the U.S.

A big, olive green plane with two engines came, too. That plane could not land, so it parachuted canned food. I went to get the food from the parachutes. The food was marked USA, and we turned it over to the gringos. The food was only for the commanders and the gringos. They told us that because we were guerrilla fighters, we did not have to eat well. They said they would give us a corn drink, which was badly prepared, and beans.

The letters CIMM on our camp stood for MISURA Military Instruction Camp. There was another camp that I had a chance to visit, about 10 minutes away. Six Chinese men in black uniforms were there; I did not know where they came from. Fagoth told us they were South Koreans. Close to that camp was another training center, where there were 10 North Americans. A sign there said TEA — Special Air Troops. The gringos offered special air training to the contras, who infiltrated Nicaraguan airspace every day.

During the training, the Somocista Guard named Mercenario taught us how to work with explosives. Some were anti-personnel mines, called Claymore, which are used to kill people. The other kind of mine was an anti-tank mine, which is placed on the roads. When a truck comes down the road, it is blown apart and all the people are killed. Another explosive they had was TNT. Later, he showed us white phosphorus and C-4s. Those are the explosives that the ex-Guard named Mercenario taught us how to use. He said he was trained in Argentina.

After our training, they took us back to Nicaragua and sent one group to kidnap the people of Sumubila. Another group was sent to blow up Salto Grande in Bonanza. Still another group went to set up ambushes in the community of Wiskonsin. Five people stayed in La Esperanza.

I was in the group that was sent to set up ambushes in Wiskonsin, an area I know very well. Around 3:30 in the afternoon, I was in the front line, and I asked permission from the person in charge to get some oranges. I told him, "I am hungry," and he gave me permission. . . .Then I went to cut the oranges and I escaped, because I knew the area.

I ran, ran, ran, always looking back, because if they had captured me, they would have killed me. I went through the community of Francia Sirpi, the place where I was kidnapped. I slept near a bridge called Ocampo. I heard a noise and thought that the contras were after me, so I started shooting. Then I saw that it was a rat.

In the morning, I went to give myself up to the Sandinistas in La Tronquera. They took me to see my mother. My mother was wearing black, and when she saw me she fainted. It was a pain that I will always have. My mother and my father started crying, and the whole town was there to welcome me.

In the name of the Indian race and the people of Nicaragua, I accuse the Reagan government. It is the government that leads, finances, and provides weapons to the counterrevolutionaries who are attacking Nicaragua. That kills and murders the people of Nicaragua and the Indian race. That commits acts of terror against them. Thank you.

Testimony of Digna Barrera

Civilian from the city of Estelí

My name is Digna Barrera, 29 years old, mother of two children and from the heroic city of Estelí, in Nicaragua. To begin my story, I can tell you that I was kidnapped in the El Zapote community of the Department of Nueva Segovia of Region One, when my husband and I were going to a little farm that the Agrarian Reform gave us.

At about 4 p.m., we arrived at the house of Amadeo Fajardo, my uncle, and were offered a meal. After we ate dinner, at about 7 p.m., I went out of the kitchen to the corral, to get a cigarette from my husband who was talking with my uncle. Only my uncle was there, so I asked him where my husband was, and he answered that he was over there, under the tree talking with some *"compas" (compañeros)*.

Very confidently, I went toward them. Two men answered my greetings very aggressively, and told me that the boss had ordered me to go with them. The man in charge was tall and dark, and wearing a black cap. He ordered me to give up all that I had, and they took my jewelry. I was asked to give up my guns, but I answered that I didn't have any, that we had just come to our farm nearby. At that moment, I saw my husband coming with his hands tied. He had been brutally beaten, and they told me: "We came from the Ministry of the Interior in Managua to arrest the two of you because you are contra supporters." I answered, "You are crazy, we are not contras, we are Sandinistas." A man who was traveling with us told them, "I came with this couple and I have three sons who are in the army in Managua." And they answered: "Then you'll come with us, too, that might help them." They took him and tied his hands. There were five of them altogether.

Two of the kidnappers stood with my husband and me under the tree, while the other three talked in secret with my uncle. After that, we all started walking, while the last man erased the footprints with a tree branch. After walking a while, we arrived at a place where about 50 men were waiting. There I was brutally raped many times, in my rectum and my vagina. I was forced down on my knees and raped at the same time that my husband was cruelly beaten. They kept asking us what the plans of the contras were, but we knew that they were the contras and they confirmed that to us, saying they were from the Nicaraguan Democratic Front (Frente Democrático Nicaragüense, FDN).

Later a group of five arrived with two peasants tied up. One was called Juan Valladares, the other I know was a campesino, but I didn't know his name. Meanwhile, I was repeatedly raped in front of my husband. When they had all the prisoners together, we started walking again toward Planes del Cedro, Amores del Sol. There we waited for 30 minutes, and then they took us on a truck to a place called Las Cucharas, still in Nueva Segovia. Nearby they had a safe house, where they got some food and cigarettes. When they finished eating, we continued walking and were given only a few pieces of fruit to eat. We stopped to rest from 1 a.m. until 5 a.m.; it was May 4. Later we arrived at a place where they had made a camp with tents — these were waterproof, dark green, and had the U.S. brand stamped on them. The backpacks, canteens, everything the men carried was from the United States.

Some supporters came down to the camp with chickens, food, and pigs. The contras gave these people money to bring them liquor, pills, and drugs. These same supporters signaled when the army was in the area. They kept raping me in front of my husband, I was in great pain and wanted to scream, but they covered my mouth very tightly with a hand-kerchief.

After almost four days, I asked them what their struggle was for, and they answered that they were fighting against communism, for freedom of the press, and free expression. I asked them why I was kidnapped for being a Sandinista when they were letting the traitor Pastora live, who always said that he was a true Sandinista. The answer was: "That's none of your business, bitch, you'll see what is going to happen to the two of you in Honduras. We are going to kill you, we are going to cut off your ears."

Afterward, by a river, and while more troops were coming, I told them that I had decided to cooperate with them, as my Uncle Amadeo Fajardo was doing. I told them that I would be very loyal. In other words, I was acting, while inside me I was dying, because we do not sell ourselves, nor do we surrender.

They answered that they were going to talk to the three commanders, who were called "El Veneno" (the poison), "El Buitre" (the vulture), and "El Barbita" (the little beard). Finally, they said that a message was going to be sent to my uncle to ask if I should be set free. He must have pointed out that they had to make sure I wasn't lying, that if they thought I was going to be a traitor, it would be better to kill me. But my deep love of life, of our revolution, and of our brothers gave me the strength to con-vince them that I was really sincere.

Then they let me go. But before that, they asked Juan Valladares, who had also been kidnapped, if he was with the revolution. Juan answered: "Yes, I love the revolution because under Somoza I never had any land. The revolution gave me land to work and live." They made him lie face up on the ground, and with a spoon they tore out his eyes. After that they shot him. He said only: "Oh, my mother!" Those were his last words.

When they told me to go, I asked them to untie my husband and to let me kiss him, because he was going to die anyway. They agreed, and while I kissed him, I told him out loud: "*Viejo,* I'm leaving to fight together with these people. If you behave with them, everything will be well," and I winked one eye at him. He answered, "Yes, I'm going to fight for my people." With that, I knew he would escape alive. I trusted God, that man, and the revolution, and I knew he was going to come back to me, and so he did.

They sent me back, guarded by a contra. This man raped me by the trail. He threatened to kill me with his gun on my chest. I was bleeding a lot and my feet were swollen, I was in great pain and starving, but my love for life and for the people gave me strength to go through this humiliation once again.

When I got back to my uncle's house, he wasn't there but a peasant told me that he wanted me to go to the house of Rosario Vellorín. I went and found him. He asked me if my husband Agustín had been killed, and I said yes. He told me that I was to be given 20,000 córdobas to inform State Security that he, Rosario, had also been kidnapped. I agreed and told him that he was to bring the money the next day to my home in Estelí. But as I had said before, we don't sell ourselves, nor do we surrender. I told everything to the authorities and Amadeo Fajardo was detained. He is my mother's brother, but I don't feel any remorse because he is a traitor and he almost got us killed. We'll never forget his betrayal and we owe all this to Ronald Reagan. That is all, *compañeros.* Thank you.

Testimony of Rev. Norman Bent

Moravian pastor from the Atlantic Coast

My name is Norman Bent, a colonialist name, originally from the Nicaraguan Atlantic Coast, from the indigenous community of Tasbapauni, "Red Earth." I was born of a father of Afro-Caribbean slave origin and a Miskito mother from the Atlantic Coast. I am married and with my wife we have procreated five children.

I am a Protestant pastor, from a church that originated in the 14th century in Czechoslovakia. In Nicaragua, it is known as the Moravian Church. I have studied at the University of Costa Rica, in the Latin American Bible Seminar, and I have been parson of the Moravian Church in the capital city of Managua for two and a half years. Nevertheless, I maintain relations and direct contact with the Atlantic Coast, through my brothers and sisters who come to visit, today more than ever. I also maintain contact through the leaders of my church. They work daily in the reconstruction of a destroyed nation, together with the indigenous people who form the church to which I belong.

I will not tell you about my experience from a juridical point of view, nor from a theological one, but I will tell you about the living experience of a Nicaraguan native.

The Atlantic Coast of Nicaragua was known under British colonialism as the Miskito Coast, and under the regime of José Santos Zelaya as the Department of Zelaya, named for him. It covers more than half of Nicaragua, but only about 300,000 Nicaraguans live there, who belong to different ethnic groups: Miskitos, Sumos, Ramas, Creoles, and Mestizos.

It was occupied by Great Britain until 1894, when reincorporation treaties — which never came to be reality — were signed with the neocolonialist government of Nicaragua.* Years later, after these treaties of reincorporation, the multinationals continued their occupation with the single purpose of extracting the abundant natural resources of our beloved country. Companies like Coca Company, Bragman's Bluff, United Fruit Company, Standard Fruit and Steamship Company, Bonanza Mines, Neptune Mining Company, Rosario Mining of Nicaragua, La Luz Mines, etc. They took our resources to help develop the countries that today are supposedly developed. These companies used the labor of my indigenous

---

*See Appendix, "The Miskitos: Interview With Two Priests," for historical background on Zelaya and reincorporation. — Ed.

brothers, whom they kept isolated for many years because the indigenous were cheap labor, allowing the companies to enjoy the rich resources of Nicaragua.

As indigenous people, we suffered isolation not only under the colonial system of Great Britain but also during the occupations of the transnationals, until 1979. In the last decades, the Miskitos, Sumos, and Ramas and my fellow descendants from Afro-Caribbean slaves served only as instruments of the big powers, which very much includes the United States.

In 1972, an indigenous pastor discovered, through his limited nationalist conscience, the exploitation of his people along the coast of the Río Coco — specifically in the community of Waspam — by traders and representatives of the Somoza dictatorship. He saw the systematic exploitation of his people, not only of their labor but also of their limited, basic grain products. He tried to organize an indigenous cooperative. It was oppressed and politically persecuted by the Somoza dictatorship, which accused it of being a racist, separatist, and communist movement.

But the Indians, directed by some of those pastors, continued the struggle to organize themselves for their defense and for the cultural development of the people of the Atlantic Coast. They formed the organization called ALPROMISO [also spelled ALPROMISU, Alliance for Progress of the Miskitu and Sumu — Ed.]. Later, Somoza cleverly bought off their representatives and their leaders, and transferred them to Managua, giving them houses in the aristocratic zones of the city and separating them from their people. The few leaders left in the Atlantic Coast region continued to struggle underground because Somoza did not tolerate this organization.

The year 1979 gave a new opening to the indigenous struggle, with the victory of the Sandinista Popular Revolution in Nicaragua. For the first time, the indigenous struggle was publicly recognized — by the Revolutionary Government of Nicaragua, which authorized the incorporation of the Ramas into the organization. Later the Creoles were also invited as observers.

MISURASATA [the name indicates the participation of Miskito, Sumo, and Rama Indians — Ed.] was organized with the total support of the Revolutionary Government of Nicaragua. The government wanted to use it as a vehicle to carry out the revolutionary programs of social reform for the benefit of my indigenous and Creole brothers and sisters from the Atlantic Coast, who had been forgotten, pushed aside, systematically isolated, and left only to the goodness of the Protestant and Catholic missionaries and to God's blessing. However, the Miskito leaders did not use the opportunity given them in a correct way. They could have worked for the reincorporation of the Moskitia territory or the Department of Zelaya into the rest of the nation, so that our indigenous and Creole brothers could benefit from the social, economic, cultural, and political reforms that the Revolutionary Government of Nicaragua is carrying out for them today. [By 1982, most of MISURASATA's leaders had joined counterrevolutionary forces in Honduras, and the organization was renamed MISURA. — Ed.]

I would only like to mention Steadman Fagoth Müller. He was not only discovered to be an agent of Somoza's state security, who betrayed many people fighting Somoza. He also fought for the separation of the Atlantic Coast from the rest of the nation, to create an independent state where he would be nominated as Prime Minister of the Mosquitia or perhaps, to return this area to the British Crown. He was captured and forgiven by the Revolution and allowed to return to work with his people.

Nevertheless, he escaped to Honduras, betraying his people, taking with him approximately 300 Miskito youngsters, and joining the Somoza National Guardsmen. Using the "September 15" clandestine radio station, and under the direction of the CIA, he invited young Miskitos to go to Honduras, to form an "Indigenous People's Liberation Army." As of May 1981, under the direction of Steadman Fagoth, young Miskitos have been recruited, trained, armed and supervised with funds given by the CIA, to carry out military activities along the river that forms the border with Honduras. The Indians have always lived on both sides of this river, and know it perfectly.

They started to carry out sabotage actions, assassinations of Indians by Indians, kidnappings of Indians by Indians, simply because they were indigenous teachers; simply because they were indigenous health workers; simply because they were indigenous agricultural technicians, now in the service of their brothers who need them to help develop themselves. In December 1981, again under the direction of Steadman Fagoth, a counterrevolutionary indigenous band attacked the villages of Asang, Santa Isabel, Raza, and San Carlos, especially the community of San Carlos. They killed approximately 60 persons, indigenous soldiers, and civilians.

With the purpose of providing security to those communities, which were constantly being attacked by the indigenous counterrevolutionaries across the river, the Revolutionary Government started evacuating people inland. This was not only to give them physical security, but also in the hope of improving their social and economic life. When the evacuations started, the counterrevolution — through its radio — told the indigenous people that the Sandinistas were putting Indians in concentration camps to burn them alive and give their land to Cubans and Vietnamese. The Indians, my brothers, were frightened by such stories and crossed the river in great numbers. Not only did the counterrevolutionaries create a situation of terror among my indigenous brothers, but they also caused many deaths.

The reality of the Atlantic Coast today is that the indigenous family is totally divided. There are approximately 23,500 in Honduras, 5,500 in Costa Rica, 15,000 in camps — in settlements that our Revolutionary Government had to build. There are 3,000 in Managua and 7,000 in the urban zones in South Zelaya. These people fled from the war because their own brothers were killing them. In many of the cases that I have mentioned of displaced indigenous Miskitos, Sumos, Ramas, and Creoles, especially those who are in Honduras, Costa Rica, and Nicaragua, their children have remained alone and they are without their children.

As happens naturally to every human being, our government — in its struggle for integration and for offering participation to the indigenous people, for the first time in the history of the Atlantic Coast — has made some mistakes. We have always pointed out those mistakes and the government has accepted this. But they have tried to correct those mistakes, and they did so by declaring an amnesty for all the indigenous people involved in counterrevolutionary activities. And, as of December, the government has maintained a policy of reunification of the indigenous family, of repatriation of my brothers in Costa Rica and Honduras, even promising that they can return to their communities on the Río Coco when the unjust war imposed upon Nicaragua is stopped.

The Moravian Church to which I belong is member of an international committee of repatriation formed by different offices of our government, the International Red Cross, and the United Nations High Commission on Refugees. The government has also invited the Organization of American States (OAS) to participate, but it never replied. A European organization for refugee migration participates in this committee. However, our work since December has been very difficult. One week after the amnesty was declared in the struggle for repatriation, I accompanied others to Costa Rica — representing our church — to explain the amnesty to my brothers in the camps in Tilarán and Puerto Limón, and to invite them to return to their land, because only in their own land can they sing new songs to Jehovah.

But the government of Costa Rica, in spite of its neutrality, did not cooperate with the team that went there. When we arrived at the camp at Puerto Limón in the Atlantic Coast area of Costa Rica, our indigenous brothers told us, "You are our pastors; we love you, even in exile, but we do not want anything to happen to you. There is a counterrevolutionary plot against your lives. You will be ambushed and assassinated if you do not try to get out of these camps as soon as possible." We have clear proof of this aggression against the team that traveled to Costa Rica in December because after we left the camp, on the road between Puerto Limón and San José, Costa Rica, two Toyota vehicles, without license plates and carrying approximately five armed persons each, started to follow us. We escaped because it is a heavily traveled road.

Our work was, and still is, difficult. In January, our Bishop and a member of this Tribunal, Compañero Adolfo Pérez Esquivel, Nobel Peace Prize winner, obtained for the first time permission to visit our Miskito brothers in the camps in Honduras. Although the Honduran government promised cooperation, it never kept its promise.

The hope of my people is Peace. The hope of my people is the right to life. The hope of my people is to return to the Río Coco, which means life to them. The hope of my people is to reunite with their sons, today dispersed.

The U.S. administration, through the CIA, continues to arm my indigenous brothers in Honduras and Costa Rican territories, sending them back along the Atlantic. They send them to continue attacking their own brothers, also indigenous, who today participate in the popular militia in order to defend their own future — their own education, their right to health and housing, their right to live, their right to land, which means life to the Indian. Because of the participation of the CIA of the most powerful government on earth, there is the danger of the extinction of an ethnic group — the indigenous people of the Atlantic Coast.

Members of the jury, all those here present:

> In the name of the indigenous people of Nicaragua,
> of all the people of Nicaragua,
> in the name of all the Indians of the world,
> in the name of the poor —
> for love of justice, peace, and the right to life,
> in light of all the legality that exists in the world, all the
> international law books,
> I accuse the government of the United States
> of the suffering of all the Indians in Nicaragua today.
> And I ask your cooperation,
> in raising your voices to demand
> for the love of God and in the name of God,
> that the United States, which never likes Indians
> (because it never liked the Indians of North America),
> cease to put its hands into the affairs
> of the Miskitos,
> Sumos, and Ramas
> of the Atlantic Coast of Nicaragua.

Thank you.

Testimony of Brenda Rocha

Member of the Militia

It was around the time of July 19 [anniversary of the overthrow of Somoza — Ed.], and it was our job to guard the hydroelectric plant; the contras always look for times when the people are celebrating in order to attack, destroy, and kill thousands of people — children, husbands, brothers, girlfriends. On July 24, 1982, at around 5:30 p.m., a *campesino* came to tell us that the contras had had him tied up. They had told him that they would be attacking that night, and interrogated him about how many militia there were, how many women, how many men, what weapons we had. He came to alert us.

I came out of our guard-house quite at ease, since I did not know what was happening. I picked up some ammunition as I walked out. Most of the people had been evacuated and taken to the church nearby. When I arrived at the trench, I asked the other woman (there were only two of us) what was happening. She was just beginning to tell me about the *campesino* when we heard the first shot, which almost hit a *campesina* with her two-month-old baby. Luckily, it missed her. We all then became very alert. It was the first time we had to fight the contras.

The contras began to fire and yell obscenities. We began to return their fire; they became more aggressive, firing more and yelling more to lower our morale, but we never became demoralized. We knew that we had to defend our people, our children, and a plant which provided electricity. That plant cost the people of Nicaragua millions of dollars.

The combat lasted for 45 minutes. It was very painful when we lost our first *compañero*; we had never seen a *compañero* die before. But we decided to continue fighting. They began to kill us, one by one. I saw how they fell. Then the *compañera* next to me fell — we had been together since I first began in the militia. She told me to jump to the other side of the trench because she was going to die and did not want me to die. So I jumped to the other side with another *compañero*.

When I got ready to fire (the contras were above us in the hills), I was wounded in the right arm. I did not pay attention to the wound and attempted to fire with my left arm, but it was impossible because by then, I was wounded in both legs. I was hit about five centimeters from my ovaries, and it was very painful. The *compañero* next to me was killed. Then I heard a grenade hit, which killed the other two *compañeros*.

The contras started to come down out of the hills, thinking we were all dead. I was almost dead. There was one other *compañero*, also 15 years old, who was still alive. The contras went into the house where we used to live and I could hear them destroying things. I pretended to be dead. The contras went up to the dead bodies and cut their throats open. They came up to the 15-year-old *compañero* and began to slit his throat while he was still alive. Then they made him get down on his hands and knees and shoved a bayonet up his anus, which is what finally killed him.

They proceeded to cut the throats of the other two *compañeros* next to me. They were going to do the same to me, but then one of them yelled that our back-up forces were coming — the militia — so they only took my rifle, kicked me, and started running.

They were wearing nice new shoes, uniforms, new backpacks, and had automatic rifles. They were well dressed, while we wore our humble uniforms and boots. But we knew why we are fighting, and why we were there, we are conscious. We knew we were not there to kill, but to defend our sovereignty, our country, our children, and their dreams.

The contras left and I was lying there almost dead. A *campesino* found me and took me to the church. I was there until the combat was over. After midnight, I was taken from the church to the hospital at Bonanza, where I received emergency care. In the morning, I was transferred to Managua, where doctors tried to save my arm, but it was impossible because too much time had elapsed. They had to amputate it.

That is how seven *compañeros* died, and how thousands of *compañeros* continue to die. And it is all because of Reagan, who is always attacking us, financing the counterrevolution, so that they kill young people and leave orphans. But we have to continue and we will go forward.

Testimony of Ramón Sanábria

Member of the Christian Base Communities

My name is Ramón Sanábria, and I was born in a village called Jalapa, department of Nueva Segovia, in the north of Nicaragua right by the border with Honduras. My parents were peasants by birth, and because of that, it was very difficult for me to get an education under the Somoza dictatorship.

I am a member of the Christian Base Communities that were organized because of the aggressions of Somocismo. That hateful regime created a need for the people to come together, to grow stronger, and to fight back against it. Those of us who were a little more aware went to faraway places in Nicaragua, to communities like Quilalí, Tastaslí, Sololí, Los Tlatanales, close to Limay, on the border with Honduras. At that point, the Somoza regime realized that the base for something new — the revolution — was being created in those places.

So they began to repress us in a criminal way. Delegates of the Word found carrying out their activities were jailed, tortured, and many times thrown from helicopters. There were *compañeros* that died while carrying out their responsibilities. Persecution was the fate of all who were dedicated to raising consciousness among the peasants. Our people had always been told that they were poor because God wanted them to be poor, but they were never told that others were getting richer while they were becoming poorer every day.

This work of raising consciousness took us to many places, to various mountains in Nicaragua. We accomplished our task, and the peasants were ready to help in the struggle of the Sandinista Front, a struggle for our true freedom.

And so the month of September came for the Delegates of the Word and the Base Communities, when the insurrections began among our people. In September, during the first insurrection in Estelí, *compañeros* like José Norberto Briones, Francisco Luis Espinoza, Nordi Esther González, and Paulita Ubeda were killed while carrying out their sacred duty — carrying out charitable missions. Luis Espinoza and *Compañero* Briones were taking a woman about to give birth to a safer place when they were both assassinated, along with the woman, who was minutes away from bringing a new child into the world. In the village of Condega, where the killing took place, it is said that a terrible scream was heard when this happened — and now it is said that it was the cry of Nicaragua, giving birth to the new man.

That was the commitment that we Christians had made during the repressive period of Somocismo.

When we got to July 19, 1979, we were very happy, for we had won, we had won the struggle against Somocismo. Now our job is even harder; they tell us our work has just begun. We have to strengthen the Christian Base Communities because they are precisely the foundations of the revolution. [The base or "grass-roots" Christian communities frequently distinguish themselves from the Church hierarchy by their active support for the Nicaraguan revolutionary process. — Ed.] So we joined the struggle and went to work in the marginalized villages, the villages destroyed by the war, to form our Christian Base Communities. And we do it very differently, perhaps, from the way it is done in other countries.

I once wrote a letter to one of the villages, saying,

> I wanted to bring you a present, but I didn't know what to bring. Then I had the chance to send you a good present, although it means I myself will not be with you. And that is the opportunity to harvest coffee for the next 10 days. I am writing this letter to tell you that this will be my offering. The little coffee that I pick will be turned into health, housing, roads, repairs, and food, which is why I am doing this with all the love and enthusiasm that I feel. And you should know that in every grain of coffee that I harvest will be all your faces, the faces of your children, and of the children I still don't know. And for all the love that I feel for you, Our Lord will multiply every grain of coffee that we pick.
>
> I want to ask that you also make the Lord a present with a smile this Christmas by taking better care of each other, of all the *compañeros, compañeras,* and children. Wherever I may be, I'll always be thinking of you. A merry Christmas to all of you and a big hug, I love you very much.

This letter is like a testament in that village, and because of it, the people make a greater commitment.

This is why we are here in this Tribunal. Mr. Reagan might smile when the Judgment is given, as he did at the sentence of the World Court in The Hague. But perhaps that smile will change into a tragic expression when the finger of history points to him as the worst killer of the people, and our God, who is a God of life, asks him one day: "Mr. Reagan, what have you done to your brother?"

Testimony of Tomás Alvarado

Student and member of a Reserve Infantry Battalion

My family is of a proletarian background. In 1981, I was studying to be a teacher when I read in a newspaper of my country, in *Barricada,* that residual elements from the Somoza National Guard, who had been expelled after the triumph of the revolution in 1979, were in training camps in Miami, Florida, with others in Honduras. These Somocista groups were being financed, advised, and directed by the Reagan administration. I discussed this with my *compañeros* at school, and in my neighborhood, and then we continued our daily lives as students, just as you all do here. But subsequently, there were incursions from Honduran territory by Somocista counterrevolutionary groups who attacked the border guardposts. In another issue of the paper, I read about a genocidal Somocista Guard who said, from a training camp in Miami, that he was going to return to liberate us from communism — from exploitation — and install a democratic government.

We quickly recalled that when these "liberators of democracy" — liberators from exploitation, as they call themselves — were in Nicaragua before the triumph, they repressed me and my classmates when we had strikes at our schools. Some of us were captured and taken to prison; some were released, others — we don't know to this day what happened to them.

We also recalled the infamous cleanup operations that the Somocista Guardsmen used to carry out. I'm not speaking about cleaning up garbage, but young people. We had to leave our mothers, fathers, brothers, and sisters, and flee to the mountains outside of Managua. From the mountains we could see how Somoza's Air Force attacked our neighborhoods with 500-pound bombs, rockets, and machine-gun fire. Those assassins didn't care where the bombs fell, they didn't care if there were women, children, or elderly people in those areas. They just cared about maintaining the dictator Somoza in power. And in that article in *Barricada* they said they were going to come and free us from the yoke of exploitation, from communism!

This is why I decided, with eight of my *compañeros,* to join a reserve infantry battalion, as the only way of not returning to the past. Upon joining the battalion, we first received military training at an army school,

The above is an excerpt from this witness's testimony.

where the importance of defense and our army's norms of combat were explained to us. We also received instruction in the weapons we were going to use, and other kinds of training.

Then my *compañeros* and I were mobilized and sent along with others to the border sector near Honduras called Jalapa, Nueva Segovia. During a battle against a contra group, I was able to see how the contras use Honduran territory to direct attacks against economic and military targets. I was in this sector for four months. Then we were replaced by another reserve infantry battalion. (I belong to Reserve Infantry Battalion No. 5010.) These *compañeros* had also made the decision to defend our country. We returned to Managua to be with our families and go back to our studies or workplaces. But we continued to belong to the battalion and thus were able to see how the counterrevolutionary aggression, which is supported and guided by Mr. Reagan and the CIA, continues.

In mid-1982, counterrevolutionary groups which had been trained in Miami returned to Honduras and formed what they called task forces. These task forces enter our territory, victimizing the peasants and attacking economic targets — above all, attacking the people of Nicaragua. I learned of this while I was in Managua, because other battalions were mobilized and sent from there to areas affected by these counterrevolutionary forces. In 1983, we were mobilized to Chinandega, which is also a border area.

During an attack there, I was able to witness the logistical support that the Reagan administration gives the contras. Our commanders told us that on a hill about 1,200 meters away, there was a contra camp. We climbed to the camp and engaged them in combat. There were about 80 contras. They opened fire on us in a disorderly way, and then retreated to Honduras. Characteristically, they left behind backpacks, canteens, belts, clothes, food, hammocks, coats. These things all had "Made in USA" labels.

After five months, I was assigned to the Nueva Segovia sector again. On July 28, 1983, we were informed that remnants of one of those task forces was in Quilalí, a town in the municipality of Nueva Segovia. Our commanders decided to confront this group in order to force them back to Honduras. The march there was difficult, because we had to walk seven kilometers through an area where there are no roads. During one of our rest periods, I began to think of my family and friends and how I would see them after this, and how I would be able to play football again, after we drove the contra forces from our territory.

The march resumed, and we arrived at an area where the population had been evacuated to places deep inside our territory. At about 5 a.m., an unequal battle began. There were some 300 contras against 60 of us. The combat was disorganized on their part, since they fired without apparent targets. At around 9 a.m., they began to shout insults at us. They called us son-of-a-bitch, communist, "Little children — did your mom give you permission to go out?" One of our *compañeros* yelled back that if we were children, then why were they unable to defeat us? They just continued to yell: "Hurray for imperialism, down with Sandinismo."

At around 10:15 a.m., I was in a secure spot with other *compañeros* — a farmer and a student — when we were assigned to climb to a higher position. If we could get there, it would help a lot in winning this battle. We were to proceed in a quiet manner. One of the contras saw us climbing, and a rain of bullets descended upon us. We did not fire back, but instead lay flat and hugged the ground. When the fire stopped, we stayed quiet. The contras thought we were dead. We knew, though, that we had to carry on with our mission. *Compañero* Raúl had the idea that we should get up and fire without stopping as we ran toward the hill. That is what we did, and it was effective. . .

Testimony of
Rev. James Lloyd Miguel Mena

Baptist pastor from the North Atlantic region

Honorable gentlemen of the jury of the Permanent Peoples' Tribunal, ladies and gentlemen, and my colleagues in the delegation from Nicaragua:

I intend to be very brief in my presentation this afternoon because I realize that our time is extremely limited. However, there are certain facts that need to be shared.

Humanity is living today in the darkness of an arms race more intense than before, and it is living under much greater injustice than before. The injustices are much more dangerous, of a magnitude unknown in the world until now. Never before has the human race been so near to its utter destruction as at this moment, and many people are living under deprivation and oppression. The countries of the world lack peace and justice.

But peace is not merely the absence of war. Peace cannot be built upon injustice. Therefore, a new international order is required, based upon justice for all nations, including Nicaragua. Based upon a respect for the dignity, human dignity, with which God has imbued all persons.

In the face of new levels of aggression, funded and financed by the United States government, the Ecumenical Commission for Peace represents the Evangelical Community of the North Atlantic regions of Nicaragua from where I come, which are greatly affected. We therefore accuse the Reagan administration of the aggressions taking place in our country. The United States feels that we are the big brother of the Latin American countries, and that we will shape the destiny of these smaller nations. However, we do not feel this way. There was never a reason for us to be treated as though we were anyone's back yard, but now we have reached the place where we can make our own decisions — with our own determination — and finally shape our own destiny.

As we said, we accuse the Reagan administration of the aggressions which have taken place in our country. For example, I, as a Baptist pastor who lives in that region along with many church members, many families, have had to disperse to different places because of the aggression. The potential of the churches has suffered. The aggression by imperialism has created an uncertain future for the rest of the members of the church, on the national and also the regional level. A certain percentage of our church members remains, because we are endeavoring in our country to reconstruct our social, our political, our religious, and our cultural destiny. But the intensity of the aggressions has caused tremendous problems for our religious institutions because we have so very little.

With the few minutes that I have, I would like to try to give a brief description of North America's policy of aggression in Central America. An aggressive North American policy has been unleashed in Honduras and has created tensions and the threat of war in Central America. The United States government is accused of violent actions in response to changes taking place in Central America. The United States government is accused of provoking the destruction of economic installations and the infrastructure in our country. The United States government is accused of sustaining a military dictatorship in Honduras. The United States government is accused of converting Honduras into a military base in the region. The United States government is accused of provoking constant counterrevolutionary hostilities against Nicaragua from Honduras. United States policy pretends to work for peace, but instead, it sets other governments against Nicaragua, and has revitalized a movement by the name of CONDECA* to bring us into opposition with each other, for its own interests. Nicaragua has been making every effort to achieve peace and stability, even when we are called communists and victimizers of other countries in Central America, and are accused of aggression.

I will mention a few examples of imperialist aggression, and the disrespect for human dignity which makes us angry. But let me also say that these indignations shall be converted into heroism and patriotism, until our enemies, the imperialists, are defeated. I need to quote here the words of the late Martin Luther King, Jr., "We shall overcome, we shall overcome some day. Deep in our hearts, we do believe, we shall overcome some day."

From July 15, 1983 to July 19, 1984, there have been approximately six attacks and kidnappings in the region where I live. For example, in Sumubila, about 1,000 persons were kidnapped. In Sukatpín, some 800 people were kidnapped. And the installation that provides jobs for over 700 men and families was burned down.

Gentlemen of the jury, picture the counterrevolutionary who is trying to destroy the infrastructure and the industrial base of our labor force.

---

*CONDECA is the Central American Defense Council, a regional alliance for "mutual assistance" of the pro-U.S. military establishments of Central America's most repressive governments. It was originally initiated in 1964 by the Pentagon and the CIA; the speaker is referring to Reagan administration efforts to reactivate it, a very disturbing prospect since CONDECA has obvious potential for serving as a regional cover (and excuse) for a U.S. invasion of Nicaragua. — Ed.

Families are poor, people have to give their families something to eat and somewhere to live — and the counterrevolutionary burns down the sawmill. Work ceases, there is nothing to do; we fold our hands. It must be understood that this is a very painful condition.

In Columbus, around that same time, 50 persons were kidnapped and one person died, a soul brother by the name of José de Cupertino. There had been an earlier kidnapping of about 1,200 persons. In Sumubila some 60 persons were kidnapped, and the health center was burned. There was also one death. There were ambushes between August 15, 1983, and July 19, 1984. On August 14, 1983, counterrevolutionaries financed by the CIA and the United States government ambushed and killed Lt. José Rusland and two others. On July 12, 1983, 12 young people on the highway to the new Miskito settlement, a village by the name of Tronquera, were also killed. On July 14, 1984, 12 employees of TELCOR, the government telecommunications system that our revolution recently inaugurated, were ambushed. On August 16, 1983, the harbor was bombarded, damaging the freight ship *Stevedor* and killing one child. This makes a total of about five ambushes against 2,500 inhabitants. If the counterrevolutionaries had destroyed this area, a community of poor people who are struggling for life, this whole community, would have been destroyed and we would have been living in mourning for a long time.

On May 14, 1983, Puerto Cabezas was bombed. Imagine the contribution that this dock, where the food comes in, makes to the lives of the people and to the stevedors. The poor people who are unemployed go to the wharf to catch a fish or two, which is their only source of livelihood. Once the wharf was destroyed, all of these possibilities were also destroyed.

You can imagine, you can think as a human being. It is reasonable and it is time to cast judgment on this kind of thing. All of the legal actions, and all of the quotations of the laws, cannot substitute for any of these things. [In this passage, the speaker is addressing Prof. Francis Boyle, who presented the U.S. case. — Ed.] My dear sir, I want you to pardon me and excuse me, you are very eloquent in your exposition of the law, because you are a professor. But this does not justify the fact that your words are not facts and this aggression is destructive to a nation that is struggling, a nation that is trying to survive in this particular universe.

EVIDENCE OF THE AGGRESSION

Mother and children murdered by contras at Palo de Arco, Río San Juan, May 1984.

Following a November 1984 contra attack near Nueva Guinea, the brain (in lower left) and blood of one worker were found splattered across the inside of this Nicaraguan Energy Institute jeep.

Unarmed civilian worker who was murdered and his
throat slit by contras in Nicaragua, November 1984.

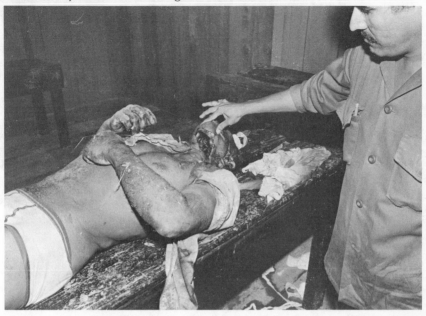

Andrew Ritchie

Funeral of Nicaraguan journalist Juan Matus, killed by contras near
Matagalpa, November 1984.

Andrew Ritchie

Mourning the dead in San Rafael del Norte,
following an August 1983 contra attack.

May 1984 contra attack on San Juan Río Coco.
Destruction of the economic infrastructure is key
to the Reagan administration's efforts to overthrow
the Nicaraguan government.

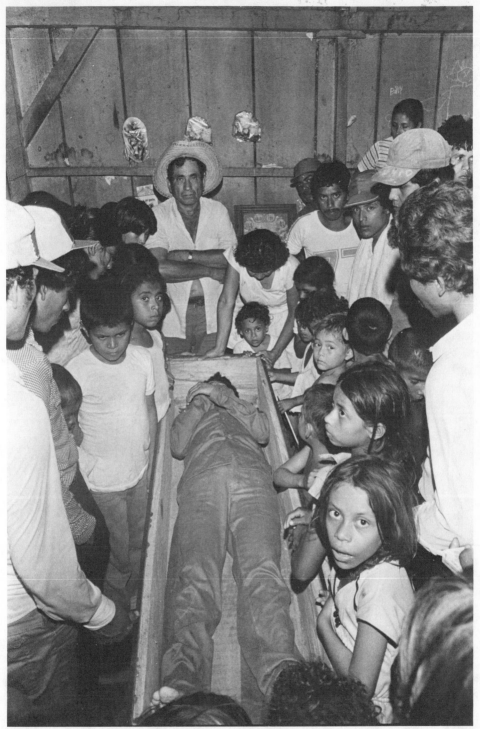

Family and friends receive the body of a 16-year-old soldier
killed by contras near El Serrano, November 1984.

Andrew Ritchie

Other victims of the CIA's contra mercenaries.
San Rafael del Norte.

Facing page: Sandinista
soldiers discover the
body of a Nicaraguan
Energy Institute worker,
Francisco Borge, killed
by contras outside
Nueva Guinea.

Andrew Ritchie

June 1984, Ocotal,
following attack by
contras.

III

FROM THE
UNITED STATES

Reagan's Central America Policy: A New Somoza for Nicaragua

Marlene Dixon

Director, Institute for the Study of Militarism and Economic Crisis

This presentation was prepared with my colleagues at the Institute for the Study of Militarism and Economic Crisis, ISMEC, in San Francisco, California. The Institute has done extensive research and publications on Nicaragua and Central America generally, with a view to educating and informing the American public. As the Institute's Director, I am making the presentation on behalf of the Institute.

INTRODUCTION

On July 19, 1983, the House of Representatives held an unusual secret session prior to voting on covert aid to the contras. After hearing the administration make its case, Rep. Bill Alexander (D-Ark.) expressed his concern that the Reagan administration "has a hidden agenda, undisclosed to Congress and the American people, and while talking about peace in the region, it is seeking a military victory" (*New York Times* [NYT], July 20, 1983; see also *Washington Post* [WP], July 20, 1983).

In November, 1983, in the wake of the U.S. invasion of Grenada, the Reagan administration openly warned Nicaragua: according to one U.S. State Department official, "If [Nicaragua] had any doubts about our willingness to use force under certain circumstances, those doubts should be erased" (*San Francisco Examiner* [SFE], Nov. 14, 1983; see also *NYT*, Nov. 7, 1983; *Newsweek*, Nov. 4, 1983).

I begin with the preceding quotations to emphasize that the conclusions and interpretations offered in this presentation are based upon the words and actions of officials of the Reagan administration. It is difficult to comprehend that such inhumane, callous, and brutal mentalities govern the greatest collection of lethal weaponry the world has ever known.

There are times when humanity cries out for eloquence; there are other times when the magnitude of the injustice, the extent of the crimes against humanity, the barbarity of the actions of the powerful are such that the weight of evidence speaks for itself, where comment is by necessity trivializing or an offense to the dignity of a whole people.

Such a time confronts us now, at this moment when we, the collective "We" of civilized humanity, are gathered together to judge a great power determined to reduce a sovereign nation to the status of colonial servant, and a free and independent people to the terror and brutality of yet another bestial military dictatorship. It might be said that we exaggerate, for the "great power" has proclaimed that:

> The United States has also sought to promote a set of political and economic values in Central America. . . . (1) to oblige governments to respect the human rights of their citizens. . . . (2) to promote the development of pluralist, democratic societies. . . . To bring about economic progress and social justice within a Western framework ("U.S. Policy for Central America," Rand Corporation, 1983, quoted in the Appendix to the Report of the National Bipartisan Commission on Central America, March 1984, p. 723).

But the great power that articulated these high-sounding humanitarian principles of justice and democracy is also the power that created human conditions of such barbarity that children below the age of consent died in the streets of Somoza's Nicaragua to liberate their people from the tyranny imposed by force by the United States of America.

In order to understand what the consequences would be for the Nicaraguan people of a successful U.S. policy of counterrevolution against the popular government of Nicaragua, to comprehend what a contra (Somocista) victory would mean, we shall briefly review the nature of "Somocismo" in power for more than 40 years — what it was that the Nicaraguan people fought for decades, what they finally defeated by force of the people in arms against the dictator Somoza.

The Somoza dictatorship was born as an instrument of U.S. imperialism. In 1927, in the midst of a civil war in Nicaragua, the U.S. sent 4,600 Marines to "protect American lives and property"; the Marines remained in Nicaragua to put down a popular nationalist uprising led by Augusto César Sandino. In the face of the resistance of the Nicaraguan people, the U.S. retreated to training and building a native Nicaraguan occupation force — the National Guard — to substitute for the Marines. By creating and maintaining control over the National Guard, the U.S. would be able to rule indirectly, through a puppet chosen by the U.S., Anastasio Somoza. Thus the Somoza dictatorship was a direct creation of U.S. imperialist intervention in the internal affairs of a sovereign nation. It was Somoza who arranged the assassination of Sandino in 1934; it was his National Guard that "pacified" the popular movement; and it was the U.S. government which kept both in power for the next 45 years. The political role of the Somozas and the National Guard as the jailers of the Nicaraguan people is contained in a statement made by the first Somoza, back in 1933: "I'll give this country peace, if I have to shoot every other man in Nicaragua to get it" (quoted in *Time*, Oct. 8, 1956, 43).

What did this form of rule mean for the Nicaraguan people? A few statistics tell the story most graphically (unless otherwise indicated, figures are from the U.S. Agency for International Development, the 1971 Nicaraguan Census, and the U.N. Economic Commission for Latin America):

— literacy was less than 50% among the general population, less than 30% in the countryside — and a mere 7% among women;

— 60% of the population lived in extreme poverty, and 95% of the urban population lived a marginal existence (Bendaña, 2);

— half of the rural population earned less than $39 a year (Bendaña, 2);

— 50% of all children over the age of five suffered from malnutrition, and 46% died before the age of four (Bendaña, 2);

— 50% of all deaths were among children under the age of 14;

— Nicaragua had the lowest rate of spending on public health and education in Central America, and the highest on per capita military expenditures (Bendaña, 3);

— 47% of the homes had no sanitary facilities (81% in the countryside); in Managua, 80% had no running water (in the countryside, 99%).

The brutality of the repression of Somoza and the National Guard was an internationally known and denounced phenomenon. Particularly in the countryside, in the operating zones of the Frente Sandinista, the repression was ferocious. Entire villages were devastated or evacuated — with, in one case, only a single child remaining to describe the slaughter. The government relied not only on the Guard but also on paramilitary death squads. Both in the city and in the countryside, hundreds of the known political prisoners (not counting those who were simply "disappeared") were held in jail in subhuman conditions, deprived of all rights. International human rights observers from the U.N. and the Red Cross were systematically denied permission to visit the prisoners. Not only the official political prisoners but the entire Nicaraguan people directly and daily experienced the country as a concentration camp, under a permanent state of siege. Before the victory of the popular revolution in 1979, Nicaragua was a country that never enjoyed even the most minimal democratic guarantees.

These are the atrocities which pushed the Nicaraguan people to the point of open insurrection and victory in 1979. The massive insurrection of the people of Nicaragua succeeded in driving out Somoza and the Somocista National Guard. In the aftermath of that revolution, out of the poverty, destruction and bestial repression of the Somoza dictatorship, the Nicaraguan people undertook to combat illiteracy, eliminate

many dread diseases, guarantee health care for their children, build new
housing and sanitation facilities — in short, to build a vibrant new society based on social equality and justice. Yet the new Sandinista government was faced with Somoza's legacy of barely $3.5 million in interna-
tional reserves (*NYT*, Dec. 15, 1979, and *Financial Times* [FT], Sept. 16,
1980) and a massive $1.6 billion foreign debt (in reality a personal debt
of Somoza, which he had amassed in voraciously building his own personal fortune) (*NYT*, Sept. 29, 1979; *Miami Herald* [MH], Sept. 5, 1979.

Reagan's stance toward this popular, democratic revolution was
unmistakably expressed by Jeane Kirkpatrick, Reagan's Ambassador to
the United Nations, when she called for the "ouster" of the Sandinista
government in Nicaragua (*SFE/San Francisco Chronicle* [SFC], July 24,
1983). The present claims of the imperial government of the United States
to special "democratic" virtue allow it, in the full cynical arrogance of
its imperial power, to spew forth the absurd cant of the Rand Corporation in the same breath that it states the real and actual position of the
U.S. and its actual and real attitude toward the nations and peoples of
Central America and the Western Hemisphere:

> From a strategic viewpoint, Central America is part of our strategic rear area,
> the Caribbean Basin, because "the Soviet Union seeks to exploit new targets
> of opportunity" there, and because "adverse regional trends will erode the
> strategic position of the United States." U.S. security depends heavily on
> preventing "the consolidation of any hostile regime in Central America. . .";
> maintaining "secure lines of communication" throughout the Basin; and
> ensuring "continued access to strategic raw materials, primarily oil and natural
> gas in nearby Venezuela and Mexico" (Rand Corporation, op. cit., 720-21).

The present government of the United States does not concern itself
for an instant with "human rights" or "pluralist, democratic societies"
or "economic progress and social justice"; its officials, as we will demonstrate, have said this repeatedly in many contexts. It cares only that
capitalist ("free") governments be subservient to the Reagan perception
of "national interest," that they recognize the right of the Right (in the
form of the government of the United States) to resume an uncontested
hegemonic domination of the entire globe. As we will show, the Reagan
administration has made its attitudes and intentions quite clear: (1) it
means to destroy the Sandinista government in order to secure a "strategic rear area"; (2) it means to establish a puppet government of
Somocistas in order to guarantee another subservient client state such
as those comprising the "iron triangle" of El Salvador, Guatemala, and
Honduras in Central America; (3) it means to establish a military presence
in Honduras, which will enable it to intimidate other small states in the
region; (4) finally, there is every reason to believe, given the number of

belligerent statements from members of the Reagan team, that they dream of planning an eventual assault on Cuba. This would be an attempt to secure the entire hemisphere for U.S. exploitation and for use as a secure base for a "rollback" foreign policy of nuclear intimidation against the Soviet Union. Once again we turn to the Rand Corporation:

> A relatively secure Southern perimeter has facilitated our role as a world power, enabling us to deal with problems in Europe and Asia . . . it is strategically imperative that the United States prevent extra-hemispheric threats from developing in the region [Central America and the Caribbean] so as to avoid the diversion of U.S. military and other resources that will diminish U.S. global strength and flexibility (Rand Corporation, op. cit., 722).

THE CASE AGAINST U.S. POLICY TOWARD NICARAGUA

It is our thesis that U.S. policy toward Nicaragua today has as its fundamental goal the overthrow of the Sandinista government by one means or another. We base this conclusion on both public statements and actions by U.S. government leaders. Among the public statements by U.S. leaders that express — directly or indirectly — their intent to overthrow the Nicaraguan government, we find the following:

— On July 18, 1983, the administration's Ambassador to the United Nations, Jeane Kirkpatrick, called for the "ouster" of the Sandinista government in Nicaragua (see above) and told anti-Sandinistas that "there was no truth to the [Brezhnev Doctrine] that Marxist revolutions are irreversible" (*NYT*, July 20, 1983).

— In his July 21, 1983, press conference, President Reagan stated that it would be extremely difficult to bring about stability in Central America so long as the current Nicaraguan government remains in power (*NYT*, July 22, 1983; *SFE/SFC*, July 24, 1983; *MH*, July 22, 1983).

— At various points during the summer of 1983, the administration no longer claimed to rest its case for aid to the Nicaraguan contras on the grounds that Nicaragua exported arms to El Salvador, but rather began to argue openly and through deliberately "leaked" reports that the Nicaraguan government itself was the source of the problems in Central America (see Halperin in *NYT*, July 19, 1983; *NYT*, July 22, 1983 and July 25, 1983; *WP*, July 27, 1983).

— Under Secretary of Defense Fred Ikle, one of the administration's main Central America policymakers, stated in a September 12, 1983, speech, "We do not seek a military stalemate. We seek victory for the forces of democracy" [i.e. the counterrevolutionaries, popularly known as contras, who are attempting to overthrow the Nicaraguan government] (Ikle speech, reprinted in Rosset and Vandermeer, 21-26; see also *WP*, Sept. 13, 1984; Wicker in *NYT*, Sept. 19, 1983; Szulc in *Los Angeles Times*

[LAT,] Sept. 18, 1983).

— Following the invasion of Grenada, the Reagan administration openly warned that if Nicaragua "had any doubts about our willingness to use force, . . . these doubts should be erased" (*SFE*, Nov. 14, 1983; see also *NYT*, Nov. 7, 1983).

— The Kissinger Commission Report on Central America, commissioned by the Reagan administration, stated in January 1984 that "the consolidation of a Marxist-Leninist regime in Managua" would be seen by its neighbors as constituting a permanent security threat (Kissinger Commission Report, 114).

— The 1984 Republican platform upon which President Reagan is running for a second term calls for support of the "democratic freedom fighters in Nicaragua" (referring to the contras who are attempting to overthrow the Nicaraguan government) and states that "Nicaragua cannot be allowed to remain a Communist sanctuary" (*NYT*, Aug. 22, 1984).

Our thesis that the basic goal of U.S. policy toward Nicaragua must be described as seeking to overthrow the present government does not, however, rest primarily on public statements; it is substantiated by the historical role of the U.S. in Nicaragua and by the actions of the Reagan administration. In the following sections of this testimony we will document:

A. the CIA war on Nicaragua;

B. the U.S. military build-up throughout Central America, which has set the stage for possible full-scale U.S. military aggression;

C. the economic war designed to undermine the Nicaraguan economy and thus its government;

D. the propaganda war that falsely portrays Nicaragua as a military aggressor and exporter of terrorism;

E. the destabilization of Nicaragua's neighbors;

F. the stifling of dissent against Reagan's policies within the United States Congress;

G. international pressure on other nations to support U.S. policy;

H. Reagan's sabotage of the peace negotiations process; and finally

I. the likely escalation of military intervention.

A. THE CIA (CENTRAL INTELLIGENCE AGENCY) WAR ON NICARAGUA

We refer here to both the covert and overt support for the contras that has been provided by the CIA in a number of forms, including economic-military sabotage.

The involvement of the CIA began under former U.S. President Carter;

it consisted of providing financial assistance to opposition elements within Nicaragua and to expanding U.S. intelligence operations (LeoGrande, 1983, 1). Shortly after President Reagan took office, on March 9, 1981, he authorized covert military actions against the government of Nicaragua that were supposedly designed to interdict Nicaraguan supplies to El Salvador (*WP*, Feb. 14, 1982; *NYT*, Feb. 15, 1982, and April 8, 1983). At the same time, the Reagan administration cut off all aid to Nicaragua, including food shipments, and launched an economic and diplomatic war against Nicaragua, which we shall describe below. During the spring of 1981, the contras began to receive training at camps run by Cuban exiles outside Miami and in Tampa and Okeechobee, Florida, as well as in Honduras and other countries; contra leaders refused comment when asked if they were receiving CIA and/or Pentagon support (*NYT*, Mar. 17, 1981, Apr. 2, 1981; *LAT*, Apr. 6, 1981). On December 1, Reagan approved and signed a 10-point covert action plan drawn up by the U.S. National Security Council (NSC), which called for the creation of a 500-man commando force and the expenditure of $19 million to conduct paramilitary operations against Nicaragua. Again, the supposed primary function of these operations was to interdict the flow of arms from Nicaragua to the opposition movement in El Salvador (*WP*, Mar. 16, 1982, and Mar. 10, 1982; *NYT*, Mar. 14, 1982, and Apr. 20, 1983).

More open forms of sabotage by the contras became evident during the spring of 1982. Between April and June, there were 106 contra attacks, including sabotage of economic and other targets. By the summer of 1982, the U.S. Congress learned that the CIA-led contra forces had grown to 1,500, well beyond the 500-man operation initially authorized. In December 1982, the CIA informed Congress that the contra forces had grown to 4,000 (see *MH*, Dec. 19, 1982, and *WP*, May 8, 1983).

The CIA was attempting to transform the contras from diverse bands of counterrevolutionaries into a single terrorist force (Riding in *NYT*, March 24, 1983; *MH*, July 15, 1983). In December 1982, the contras began daily raids into Nicaraguan territory from their camps in Honduras, and on December 17, they penetrated Nicaragua with a force of about 1,000 troops (*Uno Más Uno*, Dec. 18, 1982). It became apparent that the Honduran government was closely cooperating with the CIA in the covert operation against Nicaragua, and it was known that U.S. Ambassador to Honduras John Negroponte, a counterinsurgency expert who served in Vietnam and Cambodia, was in immediate charge of the contra activities (*NYT*, Apr. 3, 1983, and Apr. 4, 1983; *Time*, April 4, 1983). By that time, investigations by the establishment U.S. media, in particular *Newsweek*, had established that the goal of the contras was to overthrow the Nicaraguan government and not simply to stop the flow of arms to El Salvador (*Newsweek*, Nov. 8, 1982). The role of the CIA in supporting this effort was also clear. A public furor developed in the United States, resulting in the passage by Congress of the Boland-Zablocki bill of December 8, adopted 411-0 in the House and later incorporated by the Joint Conference Committee, which prohibited the U.S. from giving aid to paramilitary groups for the purpose of overthrowing the Nicaraguan government or promoting a war between Nicaragua and Honduras (*MH*, Dec. 9, 1982; *NYT*, Dec. 23, 1982).

Nevertheless, covert U.S. aid continued. Throughout the first part of 1983, the operations intensified, and in March a contra force of over 2,000 invaded Nicaragua from Honduras (*NYT*, Mar. 23, 1983; *WP*, Mar. 24, 1983). In May, the southern front of contras in Costa Rica opened up operations against Nicaragua. They were supplied with some 500 v. `pons and a few hundred thousand dollars from the CIA (White, 64; see also *WP*, May 15, 1983). On May 4, President Reagan acknowledged publicly that the United States was providing direct assistance to the contras (*WP*, May 5, 1983; see also *WP* Editorial, May 7, 1983; *NYT*, Apr. 12, 1984).

With this assistance, the contra armies had grown to 10,000 combatants by July 1983 (*NYT*, June 29, 1983) and, in the first six months of that year, they killed over 600 Nicaraguans and caused $70 million in damage (Ortega speech, *NYT*, July 22, 1983). On September 8, two contra airplanes, which were proven to be (and later admitted to be by U.S. government officials) supplied by the CIA (*NYT*, Oct. 6, 1983; CBS Nightly News, Oct. 6, 1983), bombed the airport at Managua. Frequent contra raids occurred in the north with the aim of disrupting Nicaragua's coffee harvest. However, the fact that the contras had won no significant support among the Nicaraguan population was confirmed in September 1983, when the CIA admitted to the U.S. Congress that the contras were failing in their mission to defeat the Nicaraguan government (*SFC*, Nov. 25, 1983, reprinted from *WP*; for previous reports, see *NYT*, July 24, 1983; *WP*, July 31, 1983).

At that time, a new CIA strategy was put into operation: attacks against industrial and transportation targets and Nicaragua's infrastructure. The CIA also began moving toward a direct role in these operations (*WP*, Sept. 29, 1983; *LAT*, Oct. 30, 1983; *NYT*, Oct. 16, 1983, and Oct. 23, 1983). This process had already begun earlier in 1983. In July, attacks on the port of Corinto and the oil pipelines at Puerto Sandino were planned. Also in July, according to one report, U.S. officials acknowledged to the press that the CIA had been asking (since February-March 1983) for detailed maps of three Nicaraguan ports, including Corinto; this was part of a covert plan to mine the harbors to prevent Soviet ships from docking there, to develop contingency plans for landing troops, or for other purposes, such as bombing the ports (*SFE/SFC*, July 17, 1983).

On October 10, 1983, an air and sea attack destroyed five oil storage tanks in Corinto, causing a fire that required the evacuation of the city's 25,000 people. Oil pipelines at Puerto Sandino were also attacked. These actions, designed to cripple Nicaragua economically by paralyzing industry and transport, were attributed to the contras at the time, with CIA planning and support (*NYT*, Oct. 16, 1983). The Nicaraguans maintained that the attacks had directly involved the CIA. Only months later was it publicly acknowledged that in fact the CIA had played a direct role in carrying out the whole operation at Corinto and Puerto Sandino, aboard a "mother ship," in a fashion similar to its role in the mining, using specially trained commando units (*NYT*, Apr. 18, 1984; *WP*, Apr. 18, 1984).

All of these activities culminated in the mining of Nicaraguan harbors in the spring of 1984 — although there were plans for such mining as early as the spring of 1983 (*SFE/SFC*, July 17, 1983). The mining was directly supervised by CIA operatives aboard a "mother ship" lying just outside Nicaraguan territorial waters. This operation resulted in damage to ships from Nicaragua, the Netherlands, Panama, Liberia, Japan, and the Soviet Union (thus risking the possibility of a confrontation with the Soviet Union). The Reagan administration defended the mining as a form of "self-defense by El Salvador and its allies under international law" (*NYT*, Apr. 9, 1984; Kirkpatrick speech in *WP*, Apr. 15, 1984). In regard to the public furor raised over the mining, Senator Patrick Leahy, an opponent of the contra operation, had this to say:

> Any senator who thinks the mining operation is somehow unique and different in kind from all the other military activity undertaken as part of the covert action program hasn't learned what is going on down there. Mining the harbors of Nicaragua is a logical consequence of a program aimed at conducting an undeclared secret war by proxy against a sovereign nation with whom we maintain full diplomatic relations (*WP National Weekly*, Apr. 30, 1984).

Although the mining caused enough of a scandal within the U.S. to jeopardize CIA funding for the contras on an ongoing basis, it is evident that CIA-backed contra activity continues. At the same time, opposition in the U.S. Congress does appear to have led the Reagan administration to introduce a new means of channeling support to the contras: the use of private, right-wing organizations that mobilize mercenaries (supposedly not connected with the government).

On September 1, 1984, Nicaraguan government forces shot down a helicopter used in a contra attack near the Honduran border. The wreckage of the helicopter contained two Americans, identified by contra spokesmen as members of a group called "Civilian Military Assistance" (CMA), which has been sending military advisers and equipment to the contras for over a year (*NYT*, Sept. 5, 1984). The CIA admitted that it "knew" about the existence of a paramilitary organization of U.S. veterans aid ing the contras (*NYT*, Sept. 12, 1984). In fact, five different branches of the U.S. government — the State Department, the Defense Department, the Treasury Department, the CIA, and the FBI — admitted to knowing about CMA (*NYT*, Sept. 10, 1984). At least one State Department official even admitted implicitly what a number of congressmen charged directly: that the State Department permitted these activities in order to side-step congressional orders limiting U.S. support to the contras (*NYT*, Sept. 12, 1984; see also *NYT*, Sept. 10, 1984).

Despite possible violations of the Neutrality Act, the U.S. Justice Department has done nothing to stop CMA activities (*NYT*, Sept. 10, 1984). Despite the fact that the group had no export license for the military equipment it was sending the contras, the U.S. State Department has done nothing (*NYT*, Sept. 10, 1984). What is more, administration officials have actively aided the mercenaries. As reported extensively in September by the *New York Times*:

— CMA spokesmen report that U.S. embassies in El Salvador and Honduras put them in contact with local military authorities, who escorted them to the contras. (The State Department says it has "no knowledge of this" but admits "we do our best to be helpful.")(*NYT*, Sept. 6, 1984)

— A U.S. army officer arranged the CMA's initial contact with Central American army officials. The mercenaries then carried combat weapons and 4,000 rounds of ammunition through Honduran customs without inspection, using a letter from General Gustavo Alvarez Martínez, then commander of the Honduran military (*NYT*, Sept. 6, 1984).

— The chief U.S. logistics officer in El Salvador, Major C.A. McArney, did most of the liaison work for CMA, which sent a dozen boxes of military equipment to McArney. He presumably distributed this equipment to Salvadoran (and possibly contra) forces (*NYT*, Sept. 7, 1984).

Finally, we can also note these recent examples of CIA support for the contras:

— The contra raid that occurred on September 1 was carried out by three rocket-equipped Cessnas supplied by the CIA (*SFC*, Sept. 15, 1984, based on *WP* coverage). The planes had been juggled from the U.S. Air Force to a Secret Joint Chiefs of Staff group, then to the CIA (free of charge), and from the CIA to a Delaware defense contractor, who armed the planes with rockets (*SFC*, Sept. 15, 1984). These planes had "disappeared" from government records in December of 1983, and represent spending in excess of congressional aid limits (*SFC*, Sept. 15, 1984).

— The CIA has helped "advise" the contras in fundraising (*NYT*, Sept. 9, 1984), with apparent success since, over the past six months, the contras have received up to $10 million (some estimates run as high as $15-20 million) in private contributions from sources that include a front group for Rev. Moon's Unification Church and other right-wing groups in the

U.S., as well as close U.S. allies, such as Guatemala, Israel, and Taiwan (*NYT,* Sept. 9, 1984; *MH,* Sept. 9, 1984; Anderson in *SFC,* Sept. 14, 1984).

— In June 1984, it was revealed that the CIA had produced a manual on sabotage, bombing and disruption of all kinds as part of the "final battle" to overthrow the Sandinista government (*Baltimore Sun,* June 30, 1984). This was particularly important as the contras were moving at the time from bases and camps in Honduras into Nicaragua.(*NYT,* July 30, 1984).

These hard, cold facts, which translate into the deaths of thousands of Nicaraguans and a tremendous sacrifice and hardship for the entire country, leave no doubt that the U.S. Central Intelligence Agency has been training, equipping, financing, and directing an army of mercenaries and Guardsmen of the former Somoza dictatorship in an effort to overthrow the legitimate government of Nicaragua.

B. U.S. MILITARY BUILD-UP IN THE REGION

The most frequently heard justification for the funding of the contras is that they provide an alternative to direct U.S. military involvement in the region, which would lead ultimately to a land war involving U.S. combat troops. The reality, however, is that the covert war has gone hand in hand with an increasing military build-up of U.S. forces and military infrastructure in Central America — both an increase in U.S. military "assistance" to the contras and the armies of El Salvador and Honduras, and a growth of direct U.S. presence. The Reagan administration initially assessed that the U.S. did not have the operational capacity to overthrow the Nicaraguan government (see Rand testimony, 710, 718-19). Various efforts have since been undertaken to prepare the U.S. for the possibility of effective military action in the region.

There has been a constant expansion of U.S. military presence in Central America throughout the period of the Reagan administration, taking many different forms. The blueprint for the U.S. military build-up was laid out in considerable detail in the National Bipartisan Commission on Central America (Kissinger Commission) Report of January 1984, causing relatively scarce opposition at the time. In the aftermath of the mining scandal, however, the escalation of U.S. military activities in Central America became a major public issue. On April 8, a *New York Times* article carried reports that administration officials had been drawing up plans for the use of U.S. combat troops in Central America, should this be necessary. The existence of these plans was denied by Defense Secretary Caspar Weinberger on April 8; but, on April 9, top officials affirmed the existence of the contingency plans for direct U.S. combat involvement — a shift from previous policies of the Defense Department

(*NYT*, Apr. 8-10, 1984). Later that month, the *New York Times* (Apr. 23, 1984) reported, "The Pentagon is now in a position to assume a combat role in Central America," and cited such indicators as the following:

— In the last year alone the number of U.S. military advisers in El Salvador and Honduras has multiplied more than tenfold, from 150 to over 1,800 (plus 800 on a temporary basis).

— The role of the Pentagon in policymaking has increased.

— Instances of U.S. troops being fired upon in combat situations have increased.

— Personnel attached to the bases being built in Honduras are being used to get around the U.S. congressional limits on U.S. advisers in El Salvador (e.g., such personnel are used for flying regular reconnaissance missions in tactical support of the Salvadorans).

Generally, the policies of the Reagan administration have led to a militarization and destabilization of the entire region. We will highlight the most important aspects of the U.S. military build-up, focusing particularly on the militarization of Honduras.

1. The U.S. Military Build-Up in Honduras

The transformation of Honduras into a virtual U.S. military base in the last five years began as a direct response to the Nicaraguan Revolution of 1979. With Somoza's defeat, the U.S. lost its Central American policeman; in addition, the Sandinista victory raised the specter of revolution throughout the Central American region. Thus the U.S. needed a new nerve center for its military operations in Central America. In the words of General E.C. Meyer, the U.S. should "anchor the defense of the Central American region initially in Honduras"(*WP*, June 20, 1983).

The particular formula for Honduras was to combine a nominally civilian government with militarization, turning Honduras into a base for U.S. military operations (including a staging area for attacks against Nicaragua). Hence, the U.S. pushed for the elections of 1981 (*WP*, Dec. 25, 1981), which brought into office the first elected government with a civilian President in 18 years. The logic was that an elected civilian government performing the role of "stabilizer of Central America" for the U.S. would avoid some of the contradictions that the U.S. had encountered with the discredited Somoza regime. (This combination of civilian facade with U.S. military occupation is reminiscent of the era of the Méndez Montenegro regime in Guatemala [1966-1970], under which the first great counterinsurgency offensive against the Guatemalan guerrillas was carried out by the U.S. in collaboration with a nominally civilian government — a government clearly subordinate to the military, and whose subordination in this regard was a condition for its taking office.)

According to one interpretation, Honduras became the linchpin in a Washington-conceived "Iron Triangle" (Honduras-El Salvador-Guatemala), with the three countries bound together by coordinated activity of their respective military and paramilitary forces (Wheaton, 1983, 250ff; see also Gregorio Selser in *El Día Internacional* [Mexico], Feb. 11, 1981). The key was to prevent "another Nicaragua" in El Salvador and to use Honduras in the U.S. war against Nicaragua. The latter purpose soon became clear as Nicaraguan contra bases were established in Honduras, and contra attacks against Nicaragua from Honduras were encouraged (Riding in *NYT*, Apr. 5, 1981; see also *NYT*, Apr. 2, 1981).

At the same time (1979-80), the U.S. began a program of increasing military aid and advisers, initiating the process of converting Honduras into a center of the Central American regional war zone. In 1980, officials of the Carter administration State Department asserted that the location of Honduras made it central, and proposed to Congress a military "reprogramming" (which meant in practice militarization), beginning with a seven-fold increase in U.S. military assistance (Rosenberg testimony, 47-48).

Since that time, the militarization of Honduras has continued unabated. The principal elements in this military build-up have included the following:

— U.S. military assistance grew from $4 million in 1980 to $78.5 million in 1984 — with the Reagan administration requesting $137 million for Fiscal Year 1985 (Barbieri, 1984a, 1; Central American Historical Institute Briefing Packet, based on Defense Department figures and administration requests).

— U.S. military personnel stationed in Honduras increased from 26 in 1980 to 2,000 as of the spring of 1984, in addition to a fluctuating number of U.S. troops participating in military exercises (up to 5,500 in the second part of 1983) (*WP*, Mar. 24, 1984; Central American Historical Institute). According to statistics compiled by the Central American Historical Institute, one report estimated that at the height of the 1984 military maneuvers, 33,000 U.S. military personnel would participate (including those involved in construction, communications, etc.).

— As of the second part of 1983, U.S. personnel in Honduras included 125 Green Berets training Salvadoran troops, plus 75 military advisers for training Honduran troops, and 60 Air Force electronic surveillance specialists. Since there are no congressional limits on the number of U.S. advisers in Honduras, this circumvents the limits established on the number of advisers in El Salvador (*NYT*, July 21, 1983 and July 23, 1983; see also Center for Defense Information, 5-7).

— The CIA has also played a crucial role in Honduras. As the contras' operation geared up in 1982, the size of the CIA station greatly increased — according to various sources — to about 200 people (*Time*,

Dec. 6, 1982; *NYT*, Dec. 4, 1982; *LAT*, Dec. 20, 1982). The official stated objective was again:

> ...to help interdict the arms supplies [to the opposition forces in El Salvador by training the Honduran intelligence and security forces in intelligence gathering and interrogation, providing logistical support for raids into Nicaragua, aiding the Honduran coast guard, and helping the Argentines and other non-Nicaraguans in sabotage operations using small arms supplied by the Americans (*Newsweek*, Nov. 8, 1982, 46; see also *NYT*, Dec. 4, 1982).

— Further, the U.S. military operations in Honduras have involved Honduran troops crossing the border into Nicaragua in support of the contras, as well as flying reconnaissance missions for them (*Oakland Tribune*, Oct. 2, 1983). Even for American advisers in Honduras, there has always been a thin line between advising the contras and actually planning their missions. That line was ultimately crossed in the case of the mining of Nicaragua's harbors.

The command structure for the contras included the U.S. Ambassador to Honduras, John Negroponte. He headed a team of CIA and U.S. military experts who developed the day-to-day strategy for the contras. These general orders were then passed to the second-level command center, which included General Alvarez and the Honduran high command, and also the CIA station chief in Tegucigalpa, Colonel Bermúdez, plus a representative (at least initially) from Argentina. Then orders would flow to the operational level of the contras, most of whose leaders were former Somoza National Guardsmen (White, 60, citing *NYT*, Apr. 3, 1983; *Time*, Apr. 4, 1983; see also *Newsweek*, Nov. 8, 1982, 47-48; *NYT*, Dec. 4, 1982).

In addition, veteran CIA officer Nestor Sanchez, now in Reagan's Defense Department and one of Reagan's principal Central American advisers, was seen in Honduras frequently during 1983, when intense contra operations were taking place. CIA Director William Casey personally inspected the operation in a secret trip to Honduras (Ray and Schaap, 8).

2. Military Exercises and Military Construction in Honduras

Simultaneous with the conventional build-up through U.S. military assistance and increased U.S. military personnel, the period since 1980 has also seen an unprecedented build-up through military exercises (maneuvers) held in Honduras and, related to this, military construction.

Military Maneuvers

— The first in the current series of maneuvers were those called Halcón Vista, held in October 1981; they were primarily naval.

— The "Combined Movement" maneuvers in 1982, held near the Honduran border with Nicaragua, were designed to train the Honduran army in rapid deployment techniques, use of weapons, and logistical support.

During the course of this exercise, a permanent base was constructed at Durzuna, 25 miles from Nicaragua (Quixote Center, 6).

— The Big Pine I maneuvers in February 1983, near the Honduran-Nicaraguan border, involved 4,000 Honduran and 1,600 U.S. troops (Central American Historical Institute, Appendix). They left behind equipment and facilities for the use of the contras (Nairn, 40). According to another study, "The location and nature of U.S.-Honduran joint military exercises in 1982 and 1983 have raised questions as to the intent of these maneuvers. . . . Both maneuvers took place within a few miles of Nicaraguan rebel bases, on the Honduran side of the border. The Nicaraguan government alleged that U.S. communications and military equipment transferred to the Mosquitia as part of both Combined Movement and Big Pine I were ultimately destined for the U.S.-backed counterrevolutionary forces" (Central American Historical Institute, 1).

— By far the largest and most multi-faceted of the exercises was Big Pine II, held from July 1983 through February 1984, and involving 6,000 Honduran and 5,000 U.S. troops. The Big Pine II maneuvers took place in several different locations in Honduras. The purpose was largely to intimidate the Nicaraguan government — and, some charged, to prepare for an invasion of Nicaragua (INSEH, 86). They provided the context for "extensive construction of airstrips, housing, and other facilities for U.S. personnel, a radar site, and tank traps" (Central American Historical Institute, 2, based on Defense Department figures). In addition, subsequent to these maneuvers, 1,500 U.S. troops were left permanently based in Honduras.

— In April-June 1984, the Grenadero maneuvers provided the occasion for the construction and expansion of two airfields near the Honduran borders with El Salvador and Nicaragua.

Military Construction

Military construction has proceeded both under the cover of the military maneuvers described above and independently. To summarize, the U.S. has vastly expanded airstrips in both the northern and southern parts of Honduras, has built roads and radar and communications centers for military use, and has spent $150 million for air and naval bases on the Atlantic Coast (*NYT*, July 23, 1983). U.S. officials have admitted privately that the U.S.-built airfields serve as supply depots for the contras (*NYT*, Apr. 23, 1984). Radar and telecommunications centers were established near Tegucigalpa, with equipment on Tiger Island. Of particular note is the Regional Military Training Center, constructed in June 1983. Its function was principally to train Salvadorans, 3,400 of whom had been trained there as of April 1984 (*Wall Street Journal*, Apr. 10, 1984). In February 1984, the Reagan administration sought $45 million from Congress in order to make this Center permanent (Center for Defense Information, 7; and Central American Historical Institute, Appendix, based on Department of Defense figures).

3. The Broader Import of U.S. Operations in Honduras

Is the U.S. Heading for Permanent Involvement in Honduras?

Particularly after the Big Pine II maneuvers and the attendant military construction and stationing of permanent U.S. troops in Honduras, questions began to be raised about the permanence of U.S. involvement in Honduras. On the one hand, Reagan administration officials have on occasion made statements to the effect that U.S. troops will be sent to Honduras for training exercises every year for possibly the next 20 years (*NYT*, Feb. 24, 1984). The Pentagon has actually drawn up a proposal for a $150-$200 million permanent naval and air base at Puerta Castilla, as well as the conversion of the Regional Military Training Center into a permanent base (*WP*, Jan. 11, 1984, Feb. 17, 1984; Sasser in *NYT*, Feb. 29, 1984; Center for Defense Information, 7).

On the other hand, the general stance of Reagan administration officials has been to deny allegations by critics such as Senator James Sasser and Representative William Alexander as to the permanence of the facilities, or of U.S. involvement. On other occasions the Reagan administration has refused to give information at all. Senator Sasser has charged that real evidence exists of a semi-permanent and permanent presence being constructed, without congressional authorization, and that this permanent military infrastructure has been established under the guise and under the cover of the various military maneuvers (*NYT*, Feb. 2, 1984, Feb. 9, 1984, Feb. 29, 1984; *Congressional Record*, Feb. 8, 1984. Similar conclusions about the "virtual permanency" of the installations were reached by the Military Construction Subcommittee of the House Armed Services Committee, and a June 1984 report by the General Accounting Office agreed that the facilities are not in any real sense temporary (*WP*, Feb. 1, 1984; *WP National Weekly*, Feb. 13, 1984; *NYT*, June 25, 1984; see also Washington Office on Latin America, 1984).

Are the Military Operations in Honduras Getting the U.S. More Deeply Involved in the Regional War in Central America? Is this Involvement Bringing U.S. Forces in Violation of the War Powers Act?

The official justification for the build-up in Honduras has been the need to bolster Honduran "defenses" against the Sandinista government in Nicaragua. This justification is refuted in a subsequent section of this testimony (D. The Propaganda War). In fact, the Honduran military build-up must be seen in the context of U.S. plans for offensive action

in Central America. In addition to the use of Honduras as a base of operations against Nicaragua, it also serves U.S. policy vis-a-vis El Salvador
in particular and Central America more generally:

El Salvador: The U.S. operation in Honduras is part of the U.S. war
against the Salvadoran Farabundo Martí National Liberation Front
(FMLN). We have already seen that the Regional Military Training Center
was built largely for the purpose of training Salvadorans. Further, the
operation in Honduras directly serves the U.S. military effort in El Salvador by getting around congressional restrictions on the number of U.S.
advisers in El Salvador (*NYT,* Apr. 23, 1984).

But there are also indications that the operations in Honduras are
part of the active combat in El Salvador. As long ago as May 1980, joint
actions by Salvadoran and Honduran troops prevented Salvadoran refugees from crossing into Honduras at the Río Sumpul and ended in a massacre of 600 refugees (Wheaton, 1983, 17, citing Church documents of
June 1980 on the massacre). More recently, during the Big Pine II maneuvers, U.S. helicopters regularly flew from Honduras into El Salvador on
reconnaissance missions (this was alleged by the FMLN and confirmed
by the Salvadoran military). Further, "It was suspected that U.S. personnel in Honduras — CIA employees, helicopter pilots, and others — have
entered El Salvador to assist government troops." That this is a regular
practice of American pilots based in Honduras was acknowledged as well
by the Pentagon (Center for Defense Information, 10; Robert Manning
in *NYT,* July 26, 1984; *NYT,* Apr. 23, 1984).

In the region generally: Reflecting the Defense Department's policy
of preparing for the possible use of combat troops in Central America
if leftist forces cannot be defeated any other way (*NYT,* Apr. 23, 1984),
U.S. officials and ex-officials describe what has been established in the
region as "a forward base structure." This makes rapid U.S. military action
possible, if it is determined that U.S. forces should intervene. The bases
in Honduras, already used to fly reconnaissance missions for the Salvadorans and to provide support for the contras in Nicaragua, are clearly part
of this "forward base structure," in fact essential to it (*NYT,* Apr. 23, 1984,
and Manning in *NYT,* July 26, 1984). Further, as pointed out in one study,
"In requesting money to build weapons storage bunkers [in Honduras]
in FY [fiscal year] 1985, the Pentagon noted, 'Forward storage of muni-
tions . . . will significantly enhance the [U.S.] Air Force's tactical air contingency capabilities throughout Central America'" (cited in Center for
Defense Information, 4; see *MH,* Feb. 3, 1984).

In short, there is little doubt that the build-up in Honduras has been
and remains part of an overall contingency plan for direct U.S. combat
involvement in Central America, a contingency that has not been authorized by the U.S. Congress. Already U.S. involvement has raised serious

issues of illegality and violation of congressional authority, particularly
the War Powers Act — which requires the President of the United States
to notify Congress within 48 hours of the introduction of U.S. personnel
into potentially hostile situations. In fact, a number of the U.S. operations from Honduras have placed American troops in hostile combat situations, or in situations of being fired upon. As early as November 1983,
four Democratic congressmen charged Reagan with violating the War
Powers Act by failing to notify Congress officially when U.S. troops were
sent to Honduras in August for the Big Pine II maneuvers, which were
to last over six months (*SFC*, Nov. 25, 1983). In January 1984, American
advisers with a Honduran platoon were involved in a fight with Salvadoran guerrillas (*NYT*, Apr. 23, 1984). In perhaps the most notorious incident of all, an American Marine at the Tiger Island radar station in Honduras was shot, and American Special Forces operating nearby in
Honduras were fired upon; the Marines have told Defense Department
officials that they consider Tiger Island a potential combat area. They
were removed at the time but are currently being returned to the area
(*NYT*, Apr. 23, 1984, July 26, 1984, Aug. 14, 1984; see also *Newsweek*,
Sept. 3, 1984).

C. ECONOMIC WARFARE

As part of its program of destabilization of the Sandinista government,
the United States has been engaged in policies of economic aggression
since the first days of the Reagan administration. Under the Carter
administration, despite intense opposition from some quarters, the policy
was to extend minimal aid to the new revolutionary government in
Nicaragua — in hopes of keeping Nicaragua in line, retaining a certain
degree of leverage over the policies of the Sandinistas, preventing them
from turning to the socialist bloc for assistance, and assuring that they
would comply with the repayment of the $1.6 billion debt left by Somoza.

In the last days of the Carter administration, and beginning immediately under Reagan, that strategy changed entirely. Instead, a policy of
economic aggression was adopted in which the U.S. had particularly strong
weapons, given the traditional economic dependence of Nicaragua upon
this country, for example, in matters of trade and aid. To quote one close
observer of the Reagan policies (Conroy, 3), "The Nicaraguan experiences
provide, in fact, a frightening example of the power of international capital
over the development potential of the Third World nations and a lucid
demonstration of the damages that can be wrought when those who control that power choose to exercise it."

To trace briefly some of the specifics:

a) In April 1981, the Reagan administration formally cut off U.S. aid and food shipments to Nicaragua and began pressuring international agencies not to lend to Nicaragua — even as Nicaragua was complying with its agreement to repay the huge Somoza debt, a tremendous sacrifice given the needs of the Nicaraguan economy and the necessity of using all resources for reconstruction. At this very time, according to the *New York Times*, "Some State Department officials are known to favor a policy of 'strangling' the Sandinista government economically, and then. . 'financing dissent groups'" (*NYT,* Apr. 2, 1981). The justification was to pressure Nicaragua on the issue of its aid to the Salvadoran guerrillas — but in fact the U.S. had already begun financing the contras, whose goal was the overthrow of the Nicaraguan government.

b) From the beginning, the Reagan administration pressured the international banks as well as U.S. private banks not to extend any credit to Nicaragua. Because of U.S. vetos, the World Bank has not provided any assistance to Nicaragua since January 1982, and a similar pattern has occurred at the Inter-American Development Bank. The State Department also interfered with private U.S. banks, for example, the Bank of America, making loans to Nicaragua (Conroy, 19; see also Cavanagh and Hackel, 14-16). As Conroy concluded (p. 22), "There is virtually no explanation for depriving Nicaragua of its access to credit from the U.S., whether suppliers' credits or bank credit, other than a conscious policy of economic aggression." This is especially the case given Nicaragua's good faith in the negotiations to repay Somoza's foreign debt.

c) In 1982, the U.S. took a further measure, slashing the Nicaraguan sugar quota for fiscal year 1983 by 90%. Nicaragua was thus forced to find new sugar markets overnight (*NYT,* May 11, 1983, in Cavanagh and Hackel, 13), since traditionally the U.S. had been the principal market for nearly all of Nicaragua's exports. Thus, the measure created a serious shortage of foreign exchange earnings. Combined with the restricted access to loans, the hard currency shortage has cut devastatingly into Nicaraguan reconstruction programs.

d) As a further measure against Nicaragua, the United States has refused to permit the selling of replacement and spare parts to Nicaragua, rendering inoperative a large percentage of Nicaragua's machinery. This has had untold repercussions in every sector of the economy, including humanitarian sectors like health.

e) The U.S. has sponsored direct attacks on the economic infrastructure. The clearest examples of this are the October 1983 attacks on the oil storage tanks at Corinto; attacks on the oil pipelines at Puerto Sandino; and the contra attack on the town of Pantasma, a major coffee growing center. The Pantasma action was designed to destroy economic targets related to the coffee harvest, in an attempt to reduce Nicaragua's export of coffee, which is essential to obtaining foreign exchange. (See Cerna, Stein, and Bush and Schauffler in Dixon, 1984a.)

These and a number of other open attacks were followed by the mining of Nicaragua's harbors, an attempt to cut the country off from trade with the rest of the world. If successful, the mining operation would have prevented ships from bringing Nicaragua needed imports, such as oil, and would have stopped Nicaragua's export crops from reaching foreign markets. Although the Reagan administration has yet to impose a formal trade embargo of the type imposed against Cuba in the 1960s (because they know none of the European allies would be likely to go along with it), the mining of the harbors was to be a functional equivalent.

To summarize the economic damage to Nicaragua: From May 1982 to May 1983, the U.S. war against Nicaragua caused losses of at least $61.2 million (destruction, damage, and idle capacity in production) (*Barricada*, "Lunes Socio-Económico," June 27, 1983, in Dixon, 1984a, 35). Since 1980, Nicaragua lost $112.5 million in loans and in 1983 alone it lost $354 million in trade and loans, as a result of U.S. economic sanctions and U.S. international pressures (*Christian Science Monitor* [CSM,] Dec. 6, 1983, in Cavanagh and Hackel, 12).

D. THE PROPAGANDA WAR

A major part of the Reagan administration's policy toward Nicaragua has been a persistent war of propaganda against the Nicaraguan government. The same falsehoods have been stated over and over again, so as to subject the American people to a veritable wall of misinformation. The propaganda war attempts to label the Nicaraguan government as an aggressive, totalitarian regime, which threatens the security of the United States. Such Cold War falsehoods are projected in order to justify the covert and overt military actions against Nicaragua and to prepare the American people to accept outright U.S. aggression, if and when it is carried out. The propaganda war has two major themes of disinformation: the alleged arms flow to El Salvador and the image of Nicaragua as an aggressive totalitarian nation.

1. The "Arms Flow" to El Salvador

As the evidence presented above demonstrates, the Reagan administration's objective in Nicaragua is to overthrow the current Nicaraguan government, in violation of both U.S. and international law. The Boland-Zablocki bill of December 1982, for example, prohibits the U.S. from providing military equipment, military training or advice, or other support for military activities, "for the purpose of overthrowing the Government of Nicaragua..." (*MH*, Dec. 9, 1982; *NYT*, Dec. 23, 1982).

In order to circumvent this restrictive legislation, therefore, the Reagan administration has generally claimed that its goal is not to overthrow but merely to pressure the Sandinistas to stop Nicaraguan support, particularly the shipment of arms, to the opposition movement in El Salvador. However, as numerous U.S. officials, journalists, and scholars as well as numerous articles in the established U.S. media have pointed out, the Reagan administration has been unable in four years to prove its case or to produce the evidence that such arms shipments are taking place (for example, *Washington Post,* June 13, 1984, and July 8, 1984; *CSM,* May 2, 1984; *Boston Globe,* June 10-12, 1984; AP wire story, June 11, 1984).

In March 1984, Under Secretary of Defense Fred Ikle acknowledged that 50% of the arms reaching the Salvadoran resistance come from the United States itself, captured from the Salvadoran army (*NYT,* Mar. 28, 1984, Apr. 11, 1984). Other U.S. officials and intelligence reports have acknowledged that the aid coming from Nicaragua and Cuba is minimal and in no way critical to the opposition movement in El Salvador (C. Dickey in *WP,* Feb. 21, 1983; *NYT,* June 30, 1984; Bonner, 268-69; Nairn, 33). Various investigative reporters and ex-U.S. military officers have confirmed statements by the Salvadoran resistance to the effect that most of their arms are obtained from the international black market centered in the U.S. or, even more to the point, are captured or bought outright from the U.S.-supplied Salvadoran military (Bonner, 267-68; based on direct interviews; statements by ex-Ambassador White to Congress; *Washington Post,* July 8, 1984; ex-Lt. Col. Edw. King in *NYT,* Sept. 12, 1984).

Furthermore, administration claims about funding the contras to "pressure" Nicaragua to stop the arms flow are contradicted by the fact that the contras themselves have always stated clearly that they had no goals related to El Salvador, and have never once intercepted an arms shipment to El Salvador (*NYT,* Apr. 13, 1984; Kenworthy, 188; interview with contra leader in Rosset and Vandermeer, 236-42).

All this was confirmed on June 11, 1984, by David MacMichael, until 1983 a high-level CIA analyst specializing in political and military developments in Central America, "There has not been a successful interdiction or a verified report of arms moving from Nicaragua to El Salvador since April 1981" (AP wire story, June 11, 1984; *NYT,* June 11, 1984; *WP,* June 13, 1984). Furthermore, MacMichael confirmed what had become clear since 1983 at least, that the arms flow argument is a deliberate deception by the Reagan administration. He stated that arms interdiction was never the goal in Nicaragua, that "the U.S. systematically misrepresented Nicaraguan involvement in the supply of arms to Salvadoran guerrillas to justify its efforts to overthrow the Nicaraguan government" (*NYT,* June 11, 1984; *NYT,* Editorial, June 18, 1984).

Combining MacMichaels's revelations with evidence presented above, we can conclude that the Reagan administration has deliberately promulgated disinformation about the supposed arms flow to El Salvador in order to circumvent the legal and political constraints on a policy aimed directly at overthrowing the Nicaraguan government.

2. The Myth of Nicaragua as an Aggressive Nation

The Reagan administration has repeatedly projected an image of Nicaragua as a powerful threat to the United States of America, rather than what it is: a small, poor nation attempting to reconstruct itself from 40 years of dictatorship. To cite some examples:

— Reagan stated on May 9, 1984 that Central America has "become the stage for a bold attempt by the Soviet Union, Cuba and Nicaragua to install Communism by force throughout the hemisphere" (*NYT,* May 10, 1984).

— In the same speech, Reagan charged "Cuban and Nicaraguan aggression, aided and abetted by the Soviet Union" (*NYT,* May 10, 1984). The Reagan-appointed Kissinger Commission on Central America called Nicaragua "a crucial steppingstone for Cuban and Soviet efforts to promote armed insurgency in Central America" (Kissinger Commission Report, 91).

— Reagan has said that the Nicaraguan people are "trapped in a totalitarian dungeon" (*NYT,* July 24, 1984), under a "Communist regime of terror" (*NYT,* May 10, 1984).

— Reagan has stated, "The Sandinistas are not content to brutalize their own land. They seek to export their terror to every other country in the region" (*NYT,* May 10, 1984).

What is the evidence against this view?

Initially Nicaragua sought both economic and military aid from the U.S., and only subsequently turned to the socialist bloc and elsewhere to get assistance when turned down by the United States (Sims and Schwab, 24).

Of the medium to long-term loans from 1979 through March 1982, Nicaragua received 67% from the West (Europe and Latin America), 17% from the Eastern bloc (6% from the Soviet Union), less than 1% from Cuba, and the rest from the Third World (Kenworthy, 189). A number of scholars show approximately the same figures (Malley, 25, citing Xavier Gorostiaga, "The Dilemmas Confronting the Sandinista Revolution Three Years After the Victory"; Sims and Schwab, 22, based on direct information and interviews published in *Envío,* July 1982 and *Baltimore Sun,* July 28, 1983).

In fact the Soviet Union has been called "niggardly" in its aid to Nicaragua (Gliejeses, 129, 133) and, according to a number of scholars, does not want to take on economic responsibilities in Nicaragua (Kenworthy, 183; "The Policy Paper," in Atlantic Council Report, 13, 52; LeoGrande, 1984b, 269). Anti-Sandinista writer Arturo Cruz Sequeira acknowledges that Nicaragua has received little Soviet aid (Cruz Sequeira, 96).

In testimony before the U.S. Congress, U.S. Marine Corps Lt. Col. John Buchanan (Ret.) has demonstrated that the Nicaraguan military capacity is purely defensive in nature (Buchanan, 1982, 52ff).

No military bases of foreign powers exist in Nicaragua, and Nicaragua has given assurances to the U.S. that no foreign bases will be allowed (Barnet interview with Sergio Ramírez, 672; see also Ramírez in *NYT*, July 26, 1983; LeoGrande, 1984b, 209).

It is Nicaragua that has consistently made proposals to the U.S. regarding the removal of all foreign advisers and bases from Central America.

Nicaragua bears no resemblance to a totalitarian regime. Its government has the support of the great majority of the people. It is currently engaged in a process of elections involving seven political parties. There is broad representation of the people in the Council of State (Nicaragua's legislative body, or congress), elected neighborhood bodies, labor unions, peasant associations and other popular organizations in many levels of society, and there is complete freedom of religion. Reports from such respected human rights organizations as Amnesty International and Americas Watch have given Nicaragua an excellent human rights record (*NYT*, Sept. 14, 1984; *WP*, Sept. 8, 1984).

Thus the campaign of disinformation by the Reagan administration that portrays Nicaragua as an aggressive, totalitarian, Soviet-aligned threat to the United States is entirely false, and is used simply as a justification for U.S. intervention in Nicaragua.

E. DESTABILIZING NICARAGUA'S NEIGHBORS

1. Internal Developments in Honduras

The transformation of Honduras into a virtual military base for the United States has had broad effects throughout Honduran society. The most obvious and dramatic effects have been on the political process. Numerous experts on Central America have concluded that the effect of the supposed incipient "democratization" of Honduras (the election of a civilian government) has been extremely negative (Booth testimony, 75; LeoGrande, 1983, 7-8; Rosenberg, op. cit.; Barbieri, 1984a). Similarly, in terms of human rights and repression, U.S. militarization of the country has been accompanied by the operation of right-wing death squads

(Barbieri, 1984a, 7-8; *Newsweek,* Nov. 8, 1982, 50). Generally, the U.S. military build-up of Honduras has exacerbated social and political contradictions, contributing to the destabilization of Honduras.

An alliance of U.S. power and the most reactionary elements in Honduras was consolidated, with U.S. Ambassador Negroponte running the country through General Gustavo Alvarez Martínez (and the two of them controlling nominal President Suazo Córdova). This alliance resulted in a virtual purge of the Honduran armed forces, particularly of those who resisted training the Salvadoran military (historically the enemy of the Honduran military) on Honduran territory, and of those who were rebellious (i.e., not subordinate to U.S. wishes) (*Newsweek,* Nov. 8, 1982; INSEH, 79).

According to some inside sources, the March 31 coup overthrowing the U.S.'s closest ally, General Alvarez, came as a surprise not only to President Suazo Córdova but also to the U.S. Embassy (Barbieri, 1984b, 4; Quixote Center, 7). Although the full dynamics leading up to the coup are complex, there is little question that it was a result in part of pressures both within and outside of the Honduran military against the repression and warmongering for which Alvarez was held responsible. In part the coup was also an expression of widespread misgivings about what the U.S. military operations were doing to Honduras (Barbieri, 1984b; *NYT,* Feb. 9, 1984, May 27, 1984, June 7, 1984, July 3, 1984, July 8, 1984).

Walter López, who succeeded the exiled General Alvarez as Chief of the Armed Forces, announced the military's decision to temporarily discontinue training Salvadoran soldiers in Honduras. There was also discussion about curtailing the activities of the contras. The interpretation of these moves was that they do not represent a fundamental change in Honduras's posture toward the U.S., but rather are a warning for Washington to come up with more aid for Honduras to pay for the privileges the U.S. enjoys in Honduras (*Central America Update,* July 1984).

According to Edward L. King (a retired Army Lieutenant Colonel, who often travels in Central America), in a report released by the Unitarian Church, both El Salvador and Honduras would prefer to end the training of Salvadoran troops in the regional training base in Honduras. King said that "there is increasing resentment in Honduras over the prolonged presence of substantial numbers of U.S. troops," and that this opinion had been given to him in interviews with the new leaders of the Honduran military. King further maintains that it is possible that Honduras will try to get the contras out of Honduras (*NYT,* Sept. 12, 1984).

There is considerable debate both within Honduras and abroad as to the full implications of the March coup. It remains to be seen whether some democratic space has been created, whether Honduran dependence on, and subordination to, the U.S. has been reduced, and whether the

U.S. has really lost ground as a result of the coup. Most observers tend to see the change as a renegotiation of the relationship between the U.S. and Honduras, on terms somewhat more favorable to Honduras. For example: fewer Salvadorans and more Hondurans are to be trained at the U.S.-run center at Puerto Castilla; Honduras is seeking more economic aid from the U.S.; and the military maneuvers conducted by the U.S. in Honduras are being scaled down. On the other hand, the U.S. has apparently made sure that it, and the Alvarez faction of the army, retain control over the intelligence apparatus, which is crucial for continuing U.S. operations in Honduras. (For the above, see *NYT*, June 7, 1984, June 10, 1984, July 3, 1984, July 22, 1984).

Whatever the ultimate outcome of the March coup, it is clear that the overall effect of the U.S. operations in Honduras has been to destabilize rather than stabilize the country. In this regard, the effects of U.S. policy in Honduras are entirely consistent with the more general effects of U.S. policy in the Central American region as a whole. The U.S. militarization of Honduras is indeed extending the war in Central America to Honduras.

2. The Attempted Militarization of Costa Rica

Costa Rica has the second highest per capita foreign debt in the world (*NYT*, Nov. 21, 1982). In 1981, Costa Rica's President Carazo declared a moratorium on interest payments (this was after Costa Rica had refused to implement International Monetary Fund (IMF) austerity policies) (Shirley Christian in *New Republic*, Dec. 1982, cited by White, 215). The financial community blacklisted Costa Rica; it could get no loans, there was a crisis, devaluation, and 90% inflation. Finally, the current President, Luis Alberto Monge, agreed to an IMF austerity program in 1982 (*Central America Report*, May 13, May 20, June 10, 1983).

The Reagan administration helped arrange the bailout of Costa Rica on the condition that Costa Rica start cooperating in Reagan's actions against Nicaragua. In 1982 the Costa Rican government issued a "white paper" accusing Managua of exporting revolution to Costa Rica, with virtually no evidence (White, 219). President Monge welcomed Edén Pastora into Costa Rica at about that time, though Pastora had previously been banned because his contra activities violated the Costa Rican traditional pacifist stance (*Excelsior*, Sept. 15, 1982; Christian, cited in White).

Monge also built up Costa Rica's security forces. Costa Rica does not have an army, but has a 7,000 member police force. Monge initiated the 10,000-man Organization for National Emergencies, which is a kind of paramilitary organization (*Uno Más Uno*, Dec. 19, 1982; *The Nation*, May 21, 1983; *Central America Report*, June 1983). The Reagan administration dramatically increased security aid to Costa Rica from $100,000 in 1981 to $128 million in 1983 (White, 219, 234-36, based on official Department of Defense figures). U.S. counterinsurgency training has been provided to 14,000 members of the regular security forces and the Organization for National Emergencies (White, 220, based on reports in Mexican press, *El Día*, Nov. 30, 1982, and *Uno Más Uno*, Dec. 19, 1982).

However, by mid-1983, Pastora's presence was destabilizing Costa Rica, especially the northern areas where he operated. Fighting between Costa Rican supporters and opponents of the contras erupted, and there was considerable political ferment against Pastora's operations (*NYT*, Sept. 20, 1983.). On some occasions Costa Rica would harass contras or their sympathizers; on other occasions the government would support them. When the contras attacked the Nicaraguan border station at Peñas Blancas, Costa Rica first accused the Nicaraguans of attacking Costa Rica, but then had to admit that it was in fact the contras who had attacked Nicaragua (*Uno Más Uno*, Nov. 6, 1983). In general, Costa Rica's vacillating stance toward the contras was very different from the all-out Honduran support for the contras in its borders. (For the above account, see White, 220ff, based on accounts in the U.S. and Mexican press.)

Reagan continued to pressure Monge. In 1983 the IMF was on the verge of refusing to pay the next installment of its loan because Costa Rica was not imposing all the austerity measures required by the loan agreement. Suddenly, about the time of a trip by Monge to the United States, the IMF gave special dispensation and paid the loan installment without the conditions having been met (*El Día*, Dec. 4, 1983, and Dec. 5, 1983; *Central America Report*, May 18, 1983). Clearly, the financial crisis gives the Reagan administration enormous leverage over Costa Rica.

However, more recently Costa Rica has increasingly refused to go along with Reagan. Costa Rica voted to condemn the U.S. invasion of Grenada in the U.N. Costa Rica declined to participate in CONDECA (Central American Defense Council), has refused to allow exercises near the Nicaraguan border, and stopped the sending of 1,000 U.S. Army engineers to build roads, bridges, and airstrips near the Nicaraguan border. Also, on May 15, 1984, Costa Rica signed an agreement with Nicaragua to monitor their common border. There will be a Supervision and Prevention Commission made up of members from the two countries and from the Contadora nations, to inspect the border and prevent border incidents. On May 14, 50,000 people had marched in Costa Rica's capital, San José, in a neutrality demonstration.

Clearly, there is a very strong neutralist tendency within Costa Rica. At the same time, Costa Rica is economically vulnerable to U.S. pressures. The effect of U.S. military policies in the region threaten to undermine Costa Rica's traditionally democratic and independent traditions.

F. THE STIFLING OF DOMESTIC DISSENT AND ATTACKS ON THE U.S. CONGRESS

Opinion polls since 1979 have consistently shown strong public opposition to U.S. intervention in Central America. As a reflection of this sentiment, the Reagan administration has faced consistent opposition in Congress. We should note that public opposition may fade if Reagan succeeds in winning a strong 1984 election victory, and public opinion may become more militarist; it is not realistic to be overly hopeful about the role of U.S. public opinion. Up to now, however, and especially since the main concern of the administration in 1984 is re-election, Reagan has found it essential to avoid a major public debate over Central America. The administration's actions to stifle dissent include attacks on Congress and on the authority of Congress. The following examples of its actions can be cited:

a) The Kissinger Commission Report. According to *Washington Post* polling director Barry Sussman (*WP National Weekly,* Jan. 30, 1984), the Reagan administration has successfully used other "bipartisan commissions" (on Social Security and the MX missile) to neutralize public opposition in preparation for a battle with Congress. Similarly, the objective of pushing Reagan's increased aid requests for Central America through a reluctant Congress, and of removing Central America as an issue in the 1984 election, required a "bipartisan" report by the Kissinger Commission. Despite some opposition to the Commission's report, Reagan has managed to push many of its recommendations through Congress — through methods described below.

b) When necessary, the administration has lied to Congress — the most notorious recent example being the case of the mining of Nicaragua's harbors (see press accounts throughout April 1984). On other occasions, the administration has refused to provide information, particularly about operations in Honduras, including information as to whether American advisers had been fired upon in Central America (see for example, *NYT,* July 26, 1984). In February 1984, top Pentagon officials ordered that all communications with Congress about U.S. military activities in Central America be cleared in advance; this muzzle regulation came in response to congressional inquiries, particularly in regard to whether the Pentagon was establishing a permanent military presence in Honduras without congressional authorization. Congressional inquiries, for example from Senator Sasser and Representatives Alexander and Studds, have run into Pentagon stonewalling; Rep. Alexander charged that the administration was engaged in a "systematic effort" to withhold information from Congress — as in the days of the U.S. build-up in Vietnam. (For the above, see *NYT,* Feb. 24, 1984, Feb. 25, 1984, July 26, 1984; *Congressional Record,* Feb. 8, 1984, 5122ff; Studds, 443ff).

c) At the same time, the Reagan administration has maintained that it should not be bound by Congress. One example involves violation of the War Powers Act, which requires the President to notify Congress when U.S. troops are in a combat zone or face imminent hostilities. The President must withdraw those troops within 60 days unless Congress grants authority to remain there longer. The administration acted in violation of the War Powers Act by flying reconnaissance missions in direct tactical support of Salvadoran combat units. When this was challenged, and Congress threatened to investigate, both Reagan and Schultz responded by questioning the constitutionality of the entire War Powers Act (*NYT,* April 3, 1984; see also examples of violations of the War Powers Act in Section B.3 above).

d) The administration has openly attacked congressmen who raised questions and, more generally, the authority of Congress. For example:

— Reagan's U.N. Ambassador Jeane Kirkpatrick stated that some members of Congress "want to see Marxist victories in Central America" (LeoGrande, 1984a, 74).

— Speaker of the House Tip O'Neill was almost charged with treason for his questions about U.S. policy in Lebanon, clearly a warning about his opposition to the Central American intervention (*NYT,* April 8, 1984).

— Reagan's speech of April 6, 1984 (*NYT,* Apr. 7, April 8, 1984) criticized Congress for not supporting the use of force in Lebanon and Central America. Reagan charged that it was "undermining" U.S. interests and influence, and encouraged the "enemies of democracy."

— National Security Adviser MacFarlane has made statements to the effect that debate is permissible only before a policy decision is made; subsequently, the policy must be supported (*NYT,* April 7, 1984).

This, then, is what Reagan means in speaking of the need to "restore bipartisan consensus in support of U.S. foreign policy."

e) The administration has also bypassed Congress to get funds; to cite only a few examples:

> The Reagan administration is using a variety of methods to finance military and intelligence activities in Central America that bypass normal congressional consideration and exceed spending limits set by Congress, according to administration officials, members of Congress, and classified documents. The methods involve accounting procedures and circuitous arms transfers that disguise both the value and quantity of military aid the U.S. has sent to Central America to support friendly governments and Nicaraguan rebels....It runs into millions of dollars more than Congress has approved...(*New York Times,* May 18, 1984).

The recent revelations by CIA operative Ron Rewald show that the CIA has a vast network of deeply clandestine operations throughout the world which allow U.S. administrations to circumvent controls established by Congress (Kelly).

On November 30, 1983, while Congress was not in session, Reagan attempted to pocket veto the legislation to extend certification requirements (linking aid to El Salvador to improvements in human rights) — attempts which, nine months later, were judged in the courts to be illegal and to exceed his constitutional authority (*NYT,* Aug. 30, 1984).

f) The Reagan administration has also attempted to circumvent Congress in the military build-up in Honduras. We have already discussed how it has withheld from Congress information about operations in Honduras. In addition:

— The Honduras operation has enabled the Reagan administration to violate the intent of the restrictions on U.S. advisers in El Salvador. Further, as charged by Senator James Sasser, the Pentagon "may be trying to subvert Congress" by building in Honduras "a military infrastructure that is far beyond anything necessary for the military exercises being undertaken there," and far beyond what has been authorized by Congress (*NYT,* Feb. 2, 1984; *Congressional Record,* Feb. 8, 1984, 51122ff).

— In June 1984, a General Accounting Office (GAO) Report provided to Senator Sasser and other congressional critics found that the Department of Defense had used "improper" funding sources for military construction, the training of Honduran troops, and providing medical facilities to Honduras; the expenditures of funds for a number of projects exceeded the legal limits. On June 26, in a letter to congressional colleagues, Representative William Alexander charged that the irregularities were "intentional" on the part of the Pentagon (*Washington in Focus,* July 24, 1984; see also *NYT,* June 25, 1984). Earlier in the year, on April 13, House Democratic leaders had used stronger language, charging the Reagan administration with illegal use of federal funds for military installations in Honduras (including one airfield that was likely used to support Nicaraguan contras) (*NYT,* Apr. 19, 1984).

— The Pentagon attempted to get around congressional resistance to funding assault airstrips in Honduras by building these airstrips under the cover of military maneuvers (*WP National Weekly,* Apr. 30, 1984).

These violations of Congress and its authority are related to the growing role of the CIA in making policy. The attacks on Congress, coupled with the increasing influence of certain elements of the military (for example, such ideological right-wing officers as Paul Gorman), indicate that the making of U.S. foreign policy is increasingly removed from the public realm. This phenomenon has been described as a national security state emerging to replace the nation-state. It is clear that the tendencies emerging in the formulation of U.S. policy toward Central America under Reagan threaten not only Central America, but also the norms of democracy within the American polity.

G. DIPLOMATIC PRESSURE TO ISOLATE NICARAGUA

The primary U.S. goal at the level of international diplomacy has been to isolate Nicaragua from the countries of Western Europe and the Socialist International (SI) — and then to claim that Nicaragua has become dependent upon the Soviet Union and the socialist bloc. It has been a continuing contradiction for the Reagan administration that the Socialist International (while having its own internal debates about Nicaragua, especially since there are Pastora sympathizers within this grouping) has more or less consistently remained in support of the Nicaraguan revolutionary government. The Western European countries, while not providing as much aid as the Nicaraguans needed after the U.S. aid cutoff, and while in some cases having criticisms of Nicaragua, nevertheless have given no indications that they would under any circumstances support an open aggression by the Reagan administration against Nicaragua.

Since 1981, the U.S. has attempted to correct this situation, beginning with the February 1981 mission by Under Secretary of State Lawrence Eagleburger to gain support for the U.S. view of Nicaragua as a communist springboard for Central America and as the source of arms for El Salvador's FMLN. In 1982, the U.S. put pressure on the French government, which was not falling in line with the U.S. on the issue of Nicaragua. The Reagan administration has attempted to divide the Socialist International on the question of Central America, working through Latin American members susceptible to U.S. pressure, and even created a special staff whose function was to serve as a means of pressure on the SI (they called it "communication"). There is no evidence that these policies have succeeded, but neither is there evidence that the U.S. has any plans of abandoning its efforts (for the above, see Malley, especially pp. 27ff, based largely on interviews).

H. REAGAN'S REFUSAL TO NEGOTIATE

The Reagan administration has actively undermined any efforts at a negotiated peace by stepping up aggression while ignoring or attacking peace initiatives by others, such as the Contadora Group and Nicaragua itself. At the same time, Reagan publicly claims the U.S. has been trying to negotiate with Nicaragua.

1. The U.S. under Reagan has not even given formal, written demands to Nicaragua (Gutman, 4). "Nothing in writing" is the motto. For example, according to the detailed study by Roy Gutman of the Washington bureau of *Newsday*, in August 1981 U.S. Ambassador Quainton delivered a set of what amounted to demands regarding changes in Nicaragua's internal functioning:

Quainton read from his cabled instruction but did not leave any documents behind. Only when the Nicaraguans asked for a copy did he furnish one. He sent no aide-memoire or formal document, rather what diplomats called a "nonpaper." This two-page copy of his talking points lacked a heading or signature or anything to identify its origin. In addition, the nonpaper said fulfillment of these conditions [related to Nicaragua's internal politics] was "essential" for future relations. A version issued by the U.S. embassy in Managua uses the word "important." Neither Quainton nor Johnstone could explain the discrepancy (Gutman, 12).

2. The U.S. has framed negotiations with extreme and impossible conditions. For example, in October 1981, the U.S. presented through Arturo Cruz a set of U.S. positions that almost amounted to Nicaragua disarming in the face of growing U.S. military aggression. Nicaragua was supposed to return to the country of origin all armed or unarmed helicopters and planes, armored personnel carriers, howitzers, and armed vehicles. Even Cruz, who is close to the U.S. government, was flabbergasted at the demands and the proposal was shelved (Gutman, 3, 7).

Further, the U.S. under Reagan has demanded that Nicaragua change its internal politics as a precondition to negotiations. One instance of this occurred in April 1982. Craig Johnstone, a Deputy Assistant Secretary of State and a major designer of U.S. policy towards Nicaragua, has stated: "At that point we elevated democratic pluralism in Nicaragua to be the sine qua non of restoring relations." As a Sandinista official said: "A state that agrees to negotiate on internal matters wounds its substantive reason for being a state" (Gutman, 11).

On what basis does the Reagan administration think it can place such demands? In the words of former Reagan administration official Thomas Enders, as recalled by Saul Arana of the Nicaraguan foreign ministry: "You can never forget that the United States is exactly 100 times bigger than you" (Gutman, 5, based on interviews). Enders, who was eventually (May 1983) forced to leave the Reagan administration because he was not extreme enough on Central America, although he favored aid to the contras (Gutman, 11; Enders), was quoted by *Newsweek* (Nov. 8, 1982) as talking about the need to "get rid of the Sandinistas," and was known as "Attila the diplomat" to other U.S. officials. His replacements were even more hard-line (Gutman, 5).

3. The strongest evidence of the charade of U.S. negotiations is that the Reagan administration has either ignored peace initiatives or actively undermined them by upping military aggression to disrupt any possible peace discussions.

When the Nicaraguans expressed time and again their willingness to enter into serious negotiations, and when in August and December 1982 they offered to negotiate unconditionally with the U.S., the U.S. responded by rejecting the initiatives and lying about the Nicaraguan position (W. Smith, 21, 23).

Focusing on the process during 1983-1984: since the summer of 1983, Nicaragua has sent numerous signals for peace to the United States (Gutman, 17-18, and numerous press reports).

— On July 19, 1983, Daniel Ortega announced that Nicaragua was willing to negotiate in multilateral talks ("Nicaragua's Proposal for Peace" in Dixon, 1984a, 101-03).

— On September 9 of the same year, Nicaragua signed, along with Costa Rica, El Salvador, Guatemala, and Honduras, the Contadora countries' 21-point peace plan.

— In October 1983, Nicaragua announced draft treaties that would prohibit Nicaragua from providing aid to El Salvador guerrillas in return for no CIA aid to the contras.

— On November 29, 1983, Nicaraguan Minister of the Interior Tomás Borge announced Nicaragua's willingness to ask Cuba to withdraw military advisers as part of a regional agreement.

— On December 1, Nicaragua offered, through the Contadora Group, to discuss a freeze on arms imports, limitations on the size of standing armies, and "measures which will lead to the establishment and, where applicable, the improvement of democratic, representative and pluralist systems which guarantee the effective participation of people in the decision-making process. . ." (Gutman, 18).

— On September 22, 1984, Nicaragua announced it would accept a draft peace treaty proposed by the Contadora Group, including the holding of impartial elections, ending support for groups fighting to overthrow other governments, and an end to foreign military bases in the region (*NYT*, Sept. 23, 1984).

What has been Washington's response to the clear Nicaraguan signals for peace? First, it either has deliberately ignored them or attacked the proposals as "wholly inadequate" or not to be taken seriously (Gutman, 18-20). But the second and major response to Nicaragua's peace initiatives has been an escalation of military aggression. Contadora countries began to see that the U.S. was actually working against negotiation and was rejecting Contadora as well as Nicaraguan peace proposals. In the spring of 1984, Mexican Foreign Minister Bernardo Sepulveda said that the "shelling of the City of Managua, the attack on Puerto Corinto, the attack on Puerto Sandino, or border incidents" had led the Contadora countries "to believe that there is a connection between our meetings and the desire to disrupt them with actions of this sort" (Gutman, 22). In January 1984, after receiving new U.S. reservations about Contadora proposals, Colombian Foreign Minister Rodrigo Lloreda Caicedo had pointed out, "What is happening is that the United States has not discarded a possible military solution, and the [Contadora] Group insists that a military solution must be discarded . . ." (Gutman, 20).

Given all of the above, it is stretching credibility to believe that the U.S. is undertaking negotiations with Nicaragua in good faith, in any sense. Given, too, that the only attempt to appear serious about negotiations is occurring this year, we must view Reagan administration "negotiating" as primarily a manipulation for the sake of winning the 1984 elections. Thus, for example, Secretary of State George Shultz's visit to Managua in the summer of 1984 was designed purely as a campaign maneuver for Reagan.

In fact, even the much-touted pro-negotiations people in the administration (such as Secretary of State Shultz) do not believe that negotiations should be an alternative to the policies of aggression against Nicaragua; they merely want to use negotiations as a more political instrument of pressure on Nicaragua. And the hard-liners within the administration acknowledge openly that they have no serious belief in negotiations — the Department of Defense's Nestor Sanchez warns against falling for "the lure of negotiations" (in El Salvador *or* Nicaragua) (Sanchez, 46). In essence, the extreme right in the United States has made it clear that it is ideologically committed to the obliteration of "communism," and "communism" is defined as any government not subservient to the United States.

As is reflected in the Kissinger Commission Report, the Reagan administration is opposed to any kind of negotiations that would leave the Sandinista government intact (Kissinger Commission Report, 114-15; LeoGrande, 1984b, 275). In other words, the Reagan administration will not negotiate anything but the defeat of the Nicaraguan government and all the popular and democratic forces of Central America. When the U.S., through its candidate for the 1984 Nicaraguan elections, Arturo Cruz, tries to force the Nicaraguans to negotiate with the contras, it is merely another demonstration that the U.S. is not willing to negotiate anything but a basic change in the Nicaraguan government. This, then, is not a serious position of good faith in regard to negotiations.

I. THE PROSPECTS FOR FURTHER INTERVENTION

Since the Reagan administration does not want to negotiate, we can expect a heightened level of intervention. What might the nature of this intervention be?

Following the failure of the hostage rescue mission in Iran, the Reagan administration has put increasing emphasis on upgrading the special operating forces of the U.S. military. These are secret elite commando units like the Green Berets, with specialized capabilities in counterinsurgency warfare, which complement the covert CIA activities carried out in Central America (*NYT,* June 8, 1984).

Trained in destabilization and "counter-terror" activities, the special forces were formed to increase U.S. capability to defeat "low level" guerrilla activities in the Third World, where the use of conventional forces may be premature or not politically feasible (*SFC,* July 19, 1982; *WP National Weekly,* June 25, 1984; and Nairn, 1984). Special forces can "assist in the training of military and security forces of friendly nations and can also provide a rapid, surgical response capacity when U.S. citizens or facilities overseas are threatened by terrorists, dissidents or the irrational acts of foreign governments" (Joint Chiefs of Staff report, cited in Nairn, 43). If we look at the kinds of options open to the U.S. in Nicaragua, we can see why these units may play a crucial role in something short of an all-out U.S. invasion — just as they played a crucial role in the invasion of Grenada. Grenada was also, to some degree, a rehearsal for how the U.S. electorate might respond to a larger intervention in Central America.

Numerous analyses have discussed the options available to the U.S. — ranging from seeking accommodation with Nicaragua (on terms acceptable to the U.S.), opposing the Sandinistas through non-military means, and support for the contras at various levels, to an all-out intervention by U.S. forces (Rand testimony; Nairn; Moran in Leiken). What becomes clear from these scenarios is that the option of all-out military intervention is extremely costly; it cannot be carried out in Nicaragua with less than 60,000 to 100,000 U.S. troops, which has made the Joint Chiefs of Staff reluctant to get involved. The question becomes: given the cost, how likely is a direct U.S. intervention in Nicaragua, and what are the most likely alternative steps?

Some observers suggest that if the U.S. could make a "surgical and precise" intervention and, above all, a rapid one — blitzkrieg style, in and out in a matter of weeks — then there is good reason to believe the Reagan administration might risk it. One scenario has the U.S. military moving to bomb Nicaragua's airfields, destroying its oil facilities, and possibly occupying its ports, with the idea of bringing the economy and transportation to a halt. This would be followed with a major invasion by the contras, possibly with the help of Honduran troops. The concept is of a full-scale military intervention, but with Central Americans rather than U.S. troops getting killed.

The forces opposing an intervention are not strong. Within the administration itself, divisions over Nicaragua policy do not appear to be consequential, despite publicity to the contrary. At the time of the mining of Nicaraguan harbors, for example, press reports indicated that the State Department opposed the mining. Some State Department officials disapproved because they were concerned about the reaction from European allies, should one of their ships be damaged — an indication of the important role that Western European governments could play should they choose to actively oppose Reagan's Nicaragua policies. In the end, however, the differences inside the administration were clearly not serious enough to prevent the mining from being carried out. The one major obstacle inside the administration to increased intervention appears to be the opposition within the Joint Chiefs of Staff to U.S. troop involvement in a land war without broad, unequivocal public and congressional support (see, for example, *NYT*, June 21, 1983).

Finally, opposing Reagan's interventionist policy toward Nicaragua are the nations represented in the Contadora Group and public opinion in the U.S. Reagan cares little about the opinions of the Contadora or other Latin American nations, however. Nor does he care about U.S. public opinion — otherwise he would have heeded the consistent public opinion polls over the past several years which have registered majority opposition to U.S. intervention in Central America. If he wins the election with a healthy plurality he will claim a public mandate.

Ultimately, the only thing that can really stop the Reagan administration from moving against Nicaragua is the U.S. government's own estimation that it cannot win.

SUMMATION

We believe the record shows that the Reagan administration of the United States has adopted policies toward Nicaragua founded upon absolute intolerance for any government that is not subservient to U.S. interests. Such policies are hardly new. They have solid roots in U.S. society from the rape of the indigenous peoples through a series of imperialist wars; they have been expressed in numerous policy statements beginning with the Monroe Doctrine; they have been implemented by numerous administrations, from Theodore Roosevelt's cry to "Charge!" on the peoples of Latin America up to the present. Only 10 years ago, we saw the termination of a long and brutal war against the tiny country of Vietnam, also waged to deny independence and impose subservience so that U.S. interests could continue their untrammeled looting of the world.

But if it is not new, then it is also true that the manifestations of that intolerance for the sovereign rights of others have reached extraordinary dimensions under the Reagan regime. Last year we saw the swift annihilation of tiny Grenada. Today, we see a ferocious determination to destroy the new society being built in the small country of Nicaragua.

In its effort to destroy that society and restore a Somoza-type regime, the Reagan administration has committed crimes against humanity that are apparent from our evidence. It has also committed crimes against both U.S. and international law, crimes that make a mockery of the administration's condemnation of Nicaragua for supposed violations of civil and political rights, for supposedly failing to establish a rule of law.

It is not our intention here to make a full legal brief of the Reagan administration's violations of law; many of these are described in our supplemental document entitled "Above the Law: U.S. Violations of International Law From Truman to Reagan." But a few examples from international law alone will further confirm the determination of the U.S. government to deny Nicaragua's sovereign rights — even at the price of rampant illegality.

We accuse the Reagan administration of placing itself above international law by refusing to accept the jurisdiction of the International Court of Justice in the case brought by the government of Nicaragua (Article 36(2) of the Statute of the International Court of Justice and the August 2, 1946 resolution of the Senate of the United States of America).

We accuse the Reagan administration of violating the Convention Relative to the Laying of Automatic Submarine Contact Mines, signed by the United States at The Hague in 1907, by the mining of Nicaraguan harbors (*NYT,* Apr. 21, 1984).

We accuse the Reagan administration of violating Article 2(4) of the U.N. Charter, Articles 18 and 20 of the OAS Charter, Article 8 of the Convention of Rights and Duties of States, and Article I of the Convention Concerning the Duties and Rights of States in the Event of Civil Strife. By using military force against Nicaragua and intervening in its internal affairs, the United States violated Nicaragua's sovereignty, territorial integrity, and political independence. The U.S. has recruited, trained, armed, equipped, financed, supplied, and also directed military and paramilitary actions in and against Nicaragua. The U.S. has violated the sovereignty of Nicaragua with armed attacks by air, land, and sea; with incursions into Nicaraguan territorial waters; with aerial trespass into Nicaraguan airspace. It has violated Nicaragua's sovereignty by the use of direct and indirect means to coerce and intimidate the government of Nicaragua (International Court of Justice, Order, 1984: 6).

We accuse the Reagan administration of violating Articles 2(4) and 51 of the U.N. Charter and Articles 18, 20, and 21 of the OAS Charter by its military invasion of Grenada on October 25, 1983 and the overthrow of its sovereign government.

We accuse the Reagan administration of terrorism under the Organization of American States Convention on Terrorism: Commitment to Combat Terrorism, Articles 2 and 8. Acts of terrorism have been carried out by the Reagan-funded contras against individuals protected by the OAS

Convention.

To continue with Reagan's violations of U.S. law:

We accuse the Reagan administration of violating 22 U.S. Code, Section 2422, which states that the CIA may not engage in operations in foreign countries (except as necessary to gather intelligence) unless and until the President makes a finding that each such operation is important to the national security of the United States.

We accuse the Reagan administration, by its mining of Nicaragua's harbors, of violating the Intelligence Oversight Act, which provides that the President must fully inform the Committees on Intelligence of the U.S. Senate and House of Representatives of any such operations.

We accuse the Reagan administration of violating the Boland-Zablocki Amendment of December 1982, which stated that funds could not be used by the Defense Department or the CIA to "furnish military equipment, military training or advice, or other support for military activities, to any group or individual," for the purpose of overthrowing the government of Nicaragua (Continuing Resolution for Fiscal Year 1983, Section 793).

We accuse the Reagan administration of violating the Neutrality Act by planning, recruiting for, and assisting in attacks by Nicaraguan contras on Nicaragua.

We accuse the Reagan administration of violating U.S. firearms laws by employing unlicensed individuals and corporations to ship weapons and ammunition to Nicaraguan contra training camps within the United States.

We accuse the Reagan administration of violating the Defense Appropriations Act of 1984 by spending funds in excess of the $24 million authorized for the CIA in Fiscal Year 1984 for the covert operations against Nicaragua. The excess included funding for the "mother ship" used to mine Nicaraguan harbors.

We accuse the Reagan administration of violating 31 U.S. Code 1301 (a), which states that "appropriations shall be applied only to the objects for which the appropriations were made. . . ." In training Honduran military forces, the U.S. Department of Defense used monies for purposes other than those for which they were authorized.

We accuse the Reagan administration of violating the Military Construction Codification Act, which states that military construction over $200,000 should be funded only by military construction accounts; the Defense Department used unauthorized funds when it constructed airfields, access roads, camps, and other facilities at nine locations in Honduras in 1983-84.

We accuse the Reagan administration of violating the War Powers Resolution when it introduced U.S. military personnel into hostilities or imminent hostilities in Central America without reporting these introductions to Congress. U.S. military advisers have come under fire in at least nine incidents, including the shooting down of a U.S. Army helicopter over the Honduran-Nicaraguan border in January.

Such is the tyrannical imposition of one nation's will on another that U.S. policy toward Nicaragua represents. We condemn the Reagan administration for its covert and illegal war, for all its efforts to impose a new Somoza and establish a society in which the people will experience the same denial of freedom and lack of democracy that they fought for decades to overcome. We condemn the Reagan attempt to compel subservience from the Nicaraguan government and people, an attempt that flies in the face of civilized standards for relations between nations and peoples. We condemn the barbarous use of power by a giant nation against a small and weak country struggling to overcome a legacy of poverty.

Therefore, we call upon the Permanent Peoples' Tribunal to affirm that the people of Nicaragua have the same right to independence and self-determination as was demanded by the peoples of the 13 American colonies of Great Britain over 200 years ago. For us, as Americans, it is not tolerable that the U.S. government denies to others the very rights — the right to revolt against tyranny and establish a new rule — upon which the United States itself was founded. The people of the United States have never mandated the negation of our Declaration of Independence; ours was never a dream of tyranny and inhumanity but of freedom and equality.

We consider it of the greatest importance that this session of the Permanent Peoples' Tribunal on Nicaragua has been convoked here in Brussels at this particular moment in the history of the United States, Latin America, Western Europe, the whole world. Not since the 1930s has human survival been so threatened by the very danger that we have addressed here: a lust for power so willful and so arrogant that it negates to all others any right to independent existence, indeed to existence itself. Fifty years ago, this phenomenon took the name of fascism and led to a war in which millions of human beings died. Today, in a nuclear age, it again bears the earmarks of fascism but has the capacity to destroy our entire planet and all its civilizations.

It is for this reason that we call not only upon the Permanent Peoples' Tribunal but all the peace-loving peoples and nations to make every possible effort to constrain the exercise of unlawful U.S. policy toward Nicaragua. We make this call to Western Europe in particular, whose governments are traditional allies of the United States and powerful voices within the world community of nations, and whose peoples have mounted massive demonstrations for peace; at a time of decision-making, the European nations and peoples may be able to moderate Reagan's policy. We make this call now, for the continuation of such policy will mean not only the destruction of a struggling new society and a reborn people. Reagan's intervention in Nicaragua, as in all of Central America, promises to bear monstrous fruit: at the least, another Vietnam War, and at worst, the nuclear holocaust that all humanity dreads beyond words. Recognition of Nicaragua's right to independence and sovereignty is nothing less than the road to world peace.

References

(In addition to interviews and articles from the daily, weekly, and monthly press, as cited in the text.)

Atlantic Council Report, Working Group on the Caribbean Basin, James Greene and Brent Scowcroft, (eds.)
    1984   "Western Interests and U.S. Policy Options in the Caribbean Basin," Boston: Oelgeschlager, Gunn and Hain.

Barbieri, Leyda
    1984a   "The Militarization of Honduras and Its Impact on Honduran Society," Statement prepared for the Subcommittee on Military Construction of the Appropriations Committee, March 27.
    1984b   "Crisis and Continuity in Honduras," Washington Office on Latin America (WOLA), May 10.

Barnet, Richard
    1984   "Interview With Sergio Ramírez," *World Policy Journal*, Spring.

Bendaña, Alejandro
    1978   "Crisis in Nicaragua," in North American Congress on Latin America, *Report on the Americas*, Nov.-Dec.

Bolin, William
    1984   "Central America: Real Economic Help Is Workable Now," *Foreign Affairs*, Summer.

Bonner, Raymond
    1984   *Weakness and Deceit: U.S. Policy and El Salvador*, New York: Times Books.

Booth, John
    1983   Testimony in "U.S. Policy in Honduras and Nicaragua," hearing before the Subcommittee on Western Hemisphere Affairs of the U.S. House of Representatives Committee on Foreign Affairs, March 15.

Buchanan, Lt. Col. John (USMC, ret.)
    1982   "Honduras and U.S. Policy: An Emerging Dilemma," hearing before the Subcommittee on Inter-American Affairs of the U.S. House of Representatives Foreign Affairs Committee, Sept. 21.

Cavanagh, John and Joy Hackel
    1984   "U.S. Economic War Against Nicaragua," *Counterspy*, March-May.

Center for Defense Information
    1984   *The Defense Monitor*, Vol. 13, No. 3. Center for National Security Studies
    1984   Packet, July.

Central American Historical Institute
  1984   "United States-Honduran Relations: A Background Briefing Packet," May.
Christian, Shirley
  1982   "Careworn Costa Rica" *The New Republic,* Dec. 6, 1982
Conroy, Michael
  1984   "External Dependence, External Assistance, and 'Economic Aggression' Against
          Nicaragua," unpublished manuscript, June.
Cruz Sequeira, Arturo
  1984   "Nicaragua: A Revolution in Crisis," *SAIS Review,* Winter-Spring.
Dixon, Marlene
  1984a   *Nicaragua Under Siege,* San Francisco: Synthesis Publications.
  1984b   "The Suez Syndrome," *Contemporary Marxism,* No. 9, Fall.
  1983   *Revolution and Intervention in Central America,* San Francisco: Synthesis Publi-
          cations.
  1982   "Dual Power: The Rise of the Transnational Corporation and the Nation-State,"
          Contemporary Marxism, No. 5, Fall. Revised version available from the Institute
          for the Study of Militarism and Economic Crisis, San Francisco.
Enders, Thomas
  1983   "Revolution, Reform and Reconciliation in Central America," *SAIS Review,*
          Summer-Fall.
Falk, Richard
  1983   "Lifting the Curse of Bipartisanship," *World Policy Journal,* Vol. I, No. 1, Fall.
Gleijeses, Piero
  1984   "Resist Romanticism," *Foreign Policy,* Spring.
Gorman, Paul
  1984   Statement to House Foreign Affairs Committee Subcommittee on Western
          Hemisphere Affairs, August 1.
Gutman, Roy
  1984   "America's Diplomatic Charade," *Foreign Policy,* Fall.
Instituto de Investigaciones Socio-Económicas de Honduras (INSEH)
  1984   "A Permanent U.S. 'Maneuver,'" in Dixon, Marlene, *Nicaragua Under Siege,* San
          Francisco: Synthesis Publications.
Inter-American Dialogue, Linowitz Commission
  1984   "The Americas in 1984: A Year for Decisions," March.
  1983   "The Americas at a Crossroads," Woodrow Wilson Center, April.
Kelly, John
  1984   "Cover to Cover: Rewald's CIA Story," *Counterspy,* June-August.
Kenworthy, Eldon
  1983   "Central America: Beyond the Credibility Trap," *World Policy Journal,* Fall.
Leiken, Robert (ed.)
  1984   *Central America: Anatomy of a Conflict,* Carnegie Endowment for International
          Peace, and Pergamon Press.
LeoGrande, William
  1984a   "Washington's Wars, Slouching Toward the Quagmire," *The Nation,* January 28.
  1984b   "Through the Looking Glass: The Kissinger Report on Central America," *World
          Policy Journal,* Winter.
  1984c   "Central America and the Polls," special report for the Washington Office on Latin
          America (WOLA), May.
  1983   "The Not-So-Secret War in Central America," Report for the Democratic Policy
          Committee, April.
Lowenthal, Abraham
  1983   "Change the Agenda," *Foreign Policy,* Fall.

Malley, Nadia
  1984   "Nicaragua's Relations With Western Europe and the Socialist International,"
          manuscript prepared for the International Studies Association, March.
Moran, Theodore
  1984   "The Cost of Alternative U.S. Policies Toward El Salvador, 1984-1989" in Leiken,
          Robert (ed.), *Central America: Anatomy of a Conflict,* Carnegie Endowment for
          International Peace and Pergamon Press.
Nairn, Allan
  1984   "Endgame," *NACLA Report on the Americas,* May/June.
National Bipartisan Commission on Central America (Kissinger Commission)
  1984   Report of the National Bipartisan Commission on Central America, January.
O'Dell, J.H.
  1984   "Over the Rainbow: U.S. Foreign Policy and World Development," *Freedomways,*
          First Quarter.
Pastor, Robert
  1984   "Spheres of Influence: Seal Them or Peel Them?" *SAIS Review,* Winter-Spring.
Quixote Center
  1984   "Honduras: A Look at the Reality," July.
RAND Corporation
  1984   Testimony Before the Kissinger Commission, published in manuscript version,
          March.
Ray, Ellen and Bill Schaap
  1983   "CIA's 'Secret' War Escalates," *Covert Action,* 18, Winter.
Reagan, Ronald
  1984   Speech on Central America, May 9, published in U.S. State Department collection
          of speeches.
  1983   Speech on Central America, April 27, published in U.S. State Department collec-
          tion of speeches.
Rosenberg, Mark
  1983   "U.S. Policy in Honduras and Nicaragua," testimony before the Subcommittee on
          Western Hemisphere Affairs of the U.S. House of Representatives Committee on
          Foreign Affairs, March 15.
Rosset, Peter and John Vandermeer (eds.)
  1983   *The Nicaragua Reader,* New York: Grove Press
Sanchez, Nestor
  1983   "The Communist Threat," *Foreign Policy,* Fall.
Sanders, Jerry
  1983   "Empire at Bay: Containment Strategies and American Politics at the Crossroads,"
          World Policy Paper No. 25.
Sims, Harold and Theodore Schwab
  1984   "The Development of Post-Revolutionary Nicaragua's Relations with the Communist
          Bloc," paper prepared for the International Studies Association, March.
Singham, Archie
  1984   "Foreign Policy Held Hostage: The Jackson Rescue Mission," *Freedomways,* First
          Quarter.
Smith, Wayne
  1983   "U.S.-Central American Policy: The Worst Alternative Syndrome," *SAIS Review,*
          Summer-Fall.
Studds, G.
  1984   "Questions Submitted in Writing by Representative Studds, and Responses Thereto,"
          Appendix I of "Foreign Assistance Legislation for Fiscal Year 1985," Part 6 of Hear-
          ings and Markup before House Foreign Affairs Committee and its Subcommittee
          on Western Hemisphere Affairs, Feb. 8-March 1.

Trilateral Commission
   1984   *Trialogue,* excerpts from April 1984 Plenary Meeting on "Central America."
Walker, Thomas (ed.)
   1982   *Nicaragua in Revolution,* New York: Praeger.
Washington Office on Latin America (WOLA)
   1984   *Washington in Focus,* July 24.
Wheaton, Philip
   1983   "U.S. Strategies in Central America," in Dixon, Marlene, *Revolution and Interven-tion in Central America,* San Francisco: Synthesis Publications.
White, Richard Allen
   1984   *The Morass: United States Intervention in Central America,* New York: Harper and Row.

Statement on Behalf of
the United States of America

Francis A. Boyle

Professor of International Law at the University of Illinois in Champaign

This Statement does not contain the personal viewpoints of the author. It was presented at the express request of the organizers of the Tribunal in light of the refusal by the United States government to send a lawyer to defend itself before the Tribunal.

Mr. President, distinguished members of this Tribunal, ladies and gentlemen, may it please the Tribunal. My name is Francis A. Boyle, Professor of International Law at the University of Illinois in Champaign. And at the request of the organizers of these proceedings, I appear here today on behalf of the United States of America. Let me first say how honored I am to be here in the company of my distinguished colleague from Nicaragua, Rafael Chamorro, Dean of the Faculty of Law at the University of Nicaragua in Managua.

1. INTRODUCTION

For the past two days we have heard testimony raising the most grievous accusations against the United States government under fundamental principles of international law. The United States government must and does treat these accusations quite seriously because, as Professor Falk* said last night, historically the United States has taken the pioneer role for the entire international community in the development of the rule of international law, in the foundation of the United Nations Organization, in the establishment of the Organization of American States, in the creation of the International Court of Justice as well as its predecessors, and in the formation of the numerous international organizations and institutions that constitute the fiber of the contemporary international legal order. Without the vigorous support of the United States of America for the rule of international law, the world community today would be

*A reference to the presentation by Richard Falk in this volume.

an immeasurably far more violent, lawless, and dangerous place for all its member states. And it is because of the U.S. government's resolute commitment to the rule of international law, and to the maintenance of international peace and security, that I appear here today to explain to you why the U.S. government's policy toward Nicaragua is fully supported by those basic principles of international law, which to a great extent have been devised and historically supported by the United States of America.

2. UNITED NATIONS CHARTER, ARTICLE 51

The primary determinant of the United States' policy toward Nicaragua can be found in Article 51 of the United Nations Charter, which I shall quote here in relevant part because of its fundamental importance to these proceedings:

> Nothing in the present Charter shall impair the inherent right of individual or collective self-defense if an armed attack occurs against a Member of the United Nations, until the Security Council has taken measures necessary to maintain international peace and security.[1]

The United States government maintains that its foreign policy toward Nicaragua is fully warranted as a measure of collective self-defense on behalf of the democratically elected government of El Salvador against armed aggression mounted by the Sandinista junta with the assistance of Cuba, the Soviet Union, and other communist regimes and radical movements. Notice that in Article 51, a state's right of individual or collective self-defense is deemed to be "inherent." The text of the French version of the United Nations Charter is equally as authentic as the English.[2] It is even more descriptive in its denomination of this right of individual or collective self-defense. The French version refers to this right of self-defense as a *droit naturel,* that is, a "natural right."[3] The purposeful use of this particular terminology draws upon the rich heritage of Western legal philosophy articulated by such distinguished natural-right theorists as Thomas Hobbes, John Locke, and the illustrious Jean-Jacques Rousseau. These were and still remain the three leading proponents of natural-right theory in modern legal philosophy. Thus I think it would be instructive for us to spend at least one moment of our time examining the definition of the concept of "natural right" as expounded by the very founder of modern natural-right theory — Thomas Hobbes — in order to determine the true meaning of Article 51 of the United Nations Charter. Chapter 14 of Hobbes' classic work, *Leviathan,* defines the "right of nature" as follows:

> The right of nature, which writers commonly call *jus naturale,* is the liberty each man hath, to use his own power, as he will himself for the preservation of his own nature; that is to say, of his own life; and consequently, of doing

anything, which in his own judgment, and reason, he shall conceive to be the aptest means thereunto.[4]

According to modern natural-right theory, one of the essential characteristics of a "natural right" is that it is said to be "inalienable."[5] Later on in that same chapter 14 of *Leviathan*, Hobbes explained what it means to say that the right of self-defense is "inalienable":

> Whensoever a man transferreth his right, or renounceth it; it is either in consideration of some right reciprocally transferred to himself; or for some other good he hopeth for thereby. For it is a voluntary act: and of the voluntary acts of every man, the object is some good to himself. And therefore there be some rights, which no man can be understood by any words, or other signs, to have abandoned, or transferred. *As first a man cannot lay down the right of resisting them, that assault him by force, to take away his life; because he cannot be understood to aim thereby, at any good to himself.*[6]

Hence the "natural right" of individual or collective self-defense recognized in Article 51 is a right "inherent" to each state member of the international community that has not and indeed could never have been abridged by any terms found in the United Nations Charter. Thus, to reiterate the opening words of Article 51: "*Nothing* in the present Charter shall impair the inherent right of individual or collective self-defense . . . ," etc.

To be sure, President Franklin Roosevelt's sponsorship of the foundation of the United Nations Organization in 1945 put an end to the Hobbesist state of nature, which was tantamount to a state of warfare, characteristic of international relations from 1939 until then. Nevertheless, Article 51 of the Charter left the "natural right" of individual or collective self-defense untouched and completely intact, as it existed under the customary international law of that time. Yet, the United Nations Charter did create some procedural requirements that had to be complied with in order for a state's exercise of its natural right of individual or collective self-defense to be deemed fully valid and thus totally blameless.[7] Hereinafter, I will establish that the United States government has fulfilled all the procedural and substantive requirements prescribed by the United Nations Charter and customary international law necessary for its effort to defend El Salvador from Nicaragua's armed aggression to be completely justifiable.

3. "ARMED ATTACK"

First, let me dispose of a preliminary technical point. From a cursory reading of the text of Article 51, some have argued that one apparent procedural requirement for the legitimate exercise of the natural right of individual or collective self-defense is the occurrence of an "armed attack."[8] However, Professor Myres McDougal of the Yale Law School has already definitively established that the language used in Article 51 — "if an armed attack occurs" — is not intended to express an exclusive condition.[9] In other words, the language is not meant to limit the natural right of individual or collective self-defense only to cases of an actual "armed attack." Rather, the language simply indicates that one circumstance among many in which a state can exercise its natural right of individual or collective self-defense is an actual "armed attack." Otherwise, the English version of the U.N. Charter would have used the phraseology "if *but only if* an armed attack occurs." Yet that clearly is not the language of Article 51.

This interpretation of Article 51 can be confirmed by reference to the French version of the Charter, which, instead of using the terminology "armed attack," employs the broader concept of *"aggression armée,"* that is, armed aggression. So interpolating the true meaning of Article 51 in accordance with both the English and French versions of the Charter, it is clear that a state has a natural right of individual or collective self-defense which can be exercised whenever it or some other state is the victim of an armed aggression.

4. "AGGRESSION ARMÉE"

Accepting this interpretation of Article 51 as correct, it then becomes possible to make substantial progress in understanding the legal basis for the U.S. government's policy toward Nicaragua. For in 1974, the United Nations General Assembly formally adopted the "Definition of Aggression" to be used by the U.N. Security Council for the specific purpose of determining what is an "act of aggression" within the meaning of Article 39 of the United Nations Charter.[10] It is therefore perfectly appropriate for the United States of America, which is a permanent member of the U.N. Security Council,[11] likewise to use the General Assembly's Definition of Aggression in order to determine whether Nicaragua has perpetrated an "armed aggression" against El Salvador that would permit the United States government to take steps necessary and proportionate to defend El Salvador in accordance with Article 51.[12]

Hence it becomes instructive to review for this Tribunal the relevant provisions of the United Nations General Assembly's Definition of Aggression found in an Annex to Resolution 3314 (XXIX) of December 14, 1974.[13] First, Article 1 defines the term "aggression" to mean the use of armed force by a state against the sovereignty, territorial integrity, or political independence of another state, or in any other manner inconsistent with the Charter of the United Nations.[14] And Article 2 provides that the first use of armed force by a state in contravention of the Charter shall constitute *prima facie* evidence of an act of aggression.[15]

Article 3 then lists a series of acts which qualify as an "act of aggression" within the meaning of U.N. Charter Article 39.[16] For our purposes, the relevant "acts of aggression" by Nicaragua can be found in Article 3, paragraphs F and G. Thus, according to Article 3, paragraph G of the Definition, the sending by or on behalf of a state (here Nicaragua) of armed bands, groups, irregulars, or mercenaries, which carry out acts of armed force against another state (here El Salvador), qualifies as an "act of aggression" within the meaning of that term as used in U.N. Charter Article 39.[17] Furthermore, according to Article 3, paragraph F of the Definition, the act of a state in allowing its territory (here Nicaragua), which it has placed at the disposal of another state (here Cuba and the Soviet Union), to be used by that other state for perpetrating an act of aggression against a third state (here El Salvador) qualifies as an "act of aggression" under U.N. Charter Article 39.[18]

Finally, Article 5 of the Definition of Aggression proclaims most emphatically that no consideration of whatever nature, whether political, economic, military, or otherwise, may serve as a justification for aggression.[19]

It is therefore clear from the General Assembly's seminal Definition of Aggression that by means of their continuing political, military, and economic support for the rebels in El Salvador, the Sandinista junta, together with the Soviet Union and Cuba, among others, have committed repeated "acts of aggression" against El Salvador within the meaning of Article 39 of the U.N. Charter.[20] Therefore, Nicaragua's incessant and continued acts of armed aggression against El Salvador have triggered the natural right of collective self-defense for the United States government to come to the assistance of El Salvador in accordance with Article 51 of the United Nations Charter. And to the same effect are Articles 21 and 22 of the OAS Charter, which allow recourse to the use of force in cases of legitimate self-defense, despite the prohibitions found in Articles 18, 19, and 20 of the OAS Charter mentioned by Professor Chamorro last night.[21]

5. INTERVENTION

To be sure, there is today some debate in the United States as to the actual extent of the provision of weapons, equipment, and supplies by Nicaragua, Cuba, and the Soviet Union, among others, to the rebels in El Salvador. It is universally agreed upon, however, that prior to the Spring of 1981, the degree of political, military, and economic support given by Nicaragua, Cuba, and the Soviet Union to the rebels in El Salvador was enormous.[22] The debate today turns on whether or not there has been a falling-off in that more than substantial level of weapons, equipment, and supplies sent from Cuba and the Soviet Union to Nicaragua, and from there to the rebels in El Salvador.[23] However, I must point out that even those U.S. citizens most favorably disposed toward the position of the Sandinista junta are more than willing to concede that *some* quantity of weapons, equipment, and supplies is still being transshipped from Cuba and the Soviet Union, through Nicaragua, to the rebels in El Salvador.[24] In accordance with the U.N. General Assembly's "Definition of Aggression," that is a clear-cut act of aggression for which there is no valid excuse or justification.[25] Moreover, it is still the case that the political and military headquarters for the rebels in El Salvador are located in Nicaragua, that rebels from El Salvador receive military training in Nicaragua and Cuba, and that orders, instructions, and support for rebel military operations launched against the democratically elected government of El Salvador are originating from Nicaragua.[26] These measures of direct support by Nicaragua and Cuba for the rebellion in El Salvador likewise constitute blatant acts of armed aggression against that country within the meaning of the General Assembly's Definition of Aggression and Article 39 of the United Nations Charter.

Hence, the precise level of weapons, equipment, supplies, and trained rebels currently being transported from Cuba and the Soviet Union through Nicaragua to the rebels in El Salvador becomes totally immaterial and completely irrelevant to the natural right of the United States government to protect El Salvador from this armed aggression. It is a black-letter rule of customary international law that no state has any right to provide even one iota of military, political or economic assistance to rebels seeking to overthrow the government of another state.[27] For the Sandinista junta to provide even one iota of support to the rebels in El Salvador constitutes not only an "act of aggression" within the meaning of U.N. Charter Article 39, but also a flagrantly illegal intervention into the domestic affairs of El Salvador. On this point, Article 1 of the U.N. General Assembly's seminal Declaration on the Inadmissibility of Intervention in the Domestic Affairs of States and the Protection of Their Independence and Sovereignty of 1965 states unequivocally:

> No State has the right to intervene, directly or indirectly, for any reason whatever, in the internal or external affairs of any other State. Consequently, armed intervention and all other forms of interference or attempted threats against the personality of the State or against its political, economic and cultural elements, are condemned.[28]

And a preambular paragraph in this Declaration states quite clearly: "[A]rmed intervention is synonymous with aggression and, as such, is contrary to the basic principles on which peaceful international co-operation between States should be built. . . ."[29]

Finally, even one iota of Nicaraguan support for the rebels in El Salvador also constitutes a gross violation of U.N. Charter Article 2, paragraph 4, which is the cornerstone of the post-World War II international legal order:

> All Members shall refrain in their international relations from the threat or use of force against the territorial integrity *or political independence of any state,* or in any other manner inconsistent with the Purposes of the United Nations.[30]

In accordance with Article 51 of the U.N. Charter, the United States government has a natural right to resist these egregious violations of the most fundamental principles of international law perpetrated by Nicaragua, Cuba, and the Soviet Union for the express purpose of overthrowing the democratically elected government of El Salvador.

6. PROPORTIONALITY

To be sure, it is also a basic requirement of customary international law that, to be fully legitimate, any exercise of the natural right of individual or collective self-defense must be roughly proportionate to the threat presented to the victim state.[31] I submit that this is precisely the case in Central America today. The U.S. response to Nicaraguan armed aggression has been almost exactly proportionate to the threat presented to the government of El Salvador by Nicaragua, Cuba, and the Soviet Union, among others. It is clear beyond a doubt that since its ascent to power in 1979 the Sandinista junta has worked assiduously to establish a rebel force in El Salvador that now numbers in the range of between 10,000 and 12,000 guerrillas.[32] As a necessary and proportionate measure of collective self-defense on behalf of El Salvador, the United States government has assisted in the creation of an interdiction force along the border between Nicaragua and Honduras that now consists of approximately 8,000 to 10,000 Nicaraguan exile troops.[33] Hence, there exists an almost exact equivalence between the number of members in the rebel force created by the Sandinista junta in El Salvador, and the number of members in the interdiction force supported by the United States government along the border between Nicaragua and Honduras.

7. INTERDICTION VS. AGGRESSION

From the perspective of international law, however, this approximate numerical equality between the two military forces is not their only salient feature. For it was the formally announced policy of the United States government that the interdiction force along the border between Nicaragua and Honduras was created for, and only for, the express purpose of terminating the illegal flow of weapons, equipment, supplies, and trained rebels from Cuba and Nicaragua, through Honduras, into El Salvador.[34] The U.S. government's policy in supporting this interdiction force was in no way intended to overthrow the Sandinista junta in Nicaragua. This crucial issue of fact and law is proven by the 1982 Boland Amendment to the Continuing Appropriations Act For Fiscal Year 1983, which reads as follows:

> None of the funds provided in this Act may be used by the Central Intelligence Agency or the Department of Defense to furnish military equipment, military training or advice, or other support for military activities, to any group or individual, not part of a country's armed forces, *for the purpose of overthrowing the Government of Nicaragua or provoking a military exchange between Nicaragua and Honduras.*[35]

Moreover, both the United States government and the Sandinista junta, as well as all objective observers, were in complete agreement that there was absolutely no realistic possibility that this interdiction force could have ever overthrown the Sandinista junta.[36] To the contrary, the small size of the force, the insignificant level and unsophistication of its armaments, and the manner in which it conducted its hostilities, all indicated that its sole and exclusive purpose was to interdict the illegal flow of weapons, equipment, supplies, and trained rebels from Nicaragua, through Honduras, into El Salvador.

8. DEMOCRACY VS. AUTHORITARIANISM

There was, however, one major distinguishing characteristic between the rebel force in El Salvador and the interdiction force in Nicaragua that makes all the difference from the perspective of international law. Namely, in El Salvador, the rebel forces are fighting for the express purpose of overthrowing the legitimate government of President José Napoleón Duarte that was installed by a democratic vote of the citizens of El Salvador in May of 1984.[37] In other words, the Sandinista junta, together with Cuba and the Soviet Union, are providing weapons, equipment, supplies, and training, as well as political and economic assistance, to a rebel force seeking to overthrow a popularly-elected democracy.[38] By contrast, in Nicaragua it was always quite clear that the interdiction force previously supported by the United States government had neither the training, the equipment, the supplies, nor the intention to overthrow the Sandinista junta.

The height of tragic irony here is that the Sandinista junta has never been elected by anyone, but rather installed itself by means of the forceful deposition of the Somoza government in 1979.[39] In large part, the Sandinista victory was directly attributable to Resolution 25 of the 17th Meeting of Consultation of the Ministers of Foreign Affairs of member countries of the Organization of American States, which demanded that the Somoza government be "immediately and definitively" replaced.[40]

In consideration for this OAS Resolution of support, on July 12, 1979 the Sandinista junta made a binding and solemn international commitment to the OAS that they would "call Nicaraguans to the first free elections that our country will have in this century."[41] Over five years later, that promise has not yet been carried out. And it remains to be seen whether free, fair, and democratic elections will actually be conducted in Nicaragua on November 4, 1984, especially given the fact that the three main opposition parties, organized into the Democratic Coordinating Committee under the leadership of the respected Arturo José Cruz, have not been certified to participate.[42]

For example, on 7 July 1984, less than three months ago, Commander Carlos Núñez Tellez said on *Radio Sandino:*

> The electoral process is the result of a political decision made by the FSLN [Sandinista National Liberation Front], its revolutionary leaders, and the government to reinforce the historical popular plan. *There is nothing more alien to the electoral process than sectarianism, dogmatism, and other vices that are characteristic of certain so-called democracies.*[43]

Although the United States government would prefer to see the installation of genuinely democratic and fully representative government in Nicaragua, nevertheless, that is a matter for the Nicaraguan people to determine for themselves in accordance with the principle of international law dictating the self-determination of peoples, as recognized by Article 1, paragraph 2 of the United Nations Charter.[44] But the same principle must likewise apply to protect the fundamental legal right of self-determination for the people of El Salvador, who have democratically elected the current government of President José Napoleón Duarte. This non-elected junta in Nicaragua has absolutely no right to provide any type or amount of military, political, or economic assistance to the rebels in El Salvador for the purpose of overthrowing its democratically elected government. I submit that it is absurd and duplicitous for the non-elected and increasingly authoritarian Sandinista junta that has been perpetrating armed aggression against the democratically elected government in El Salvador, to file a complaint with this distinguished Tribunal against the United States for coming to the defense of its helpless victim in El Salvador under Article 51 of the U.N. Charter. The Sandinista junta has cynically turned the international legalities of the situation completely onto its head.

9. THE LAWS OF WAR

It is also a basic requirement of international law that any exercise of the natural right of individual or collective self-defense must be consistent with the laws of war and the international laws of humanitarian armed conflict.[45] The Sandinista junta has alleged that some innocent civilians have been killed as a result of military operations launched by the Nicaraguan interdiction force. To be sure, such allegations must be proven by the Sandinista junta beyond a reasonable doubt.[46] Even then, however, such allegations do not detract from the essential legality of the United States government's natural right of collective self-defense on behalf of El Salvador in accordance with Article 51 of the United Nations Charter.

This is because it is a fundamental axiom of public international law that there exists a material difference between what is called the *jus ad bellum,* that is, the right to go to war or use force, and the *jus in bello,* that is, the laws of war.[47] Today the traditional doctrine of *jus ad bellum* can be found, essentially, in U.N. Charter Article 51. Whereas the *jus in bello* can be found, basically, in the Four Geneva Conventions of 1949[48] and the 1907 Hague Regulations.[49] Thus Nicaraguan allegations of civilian casualties relate to the *jus in bello,* not to the *jus ad bellum* by the United States government on behalf of El Salvador in accordance with U.N. Charter Article 51.

The international laws of humanitarian armed conflict apply whether or not the right to use force is legitimate in the first place.[50] Conversely, however, the fact that the international laws of humanitarian armed conflict might be violated does not mean that the right to use force in collective self-defense is thereby negated. Thus, even if it is proven beyond a reasonable doubt that members of the Nicaraguan interdiction force have violated the international laws of humanitarian armed conflict, such violations would only render them personally responsible for the commission of war crimes.[51] These violations would not, however, negate the U.S. government's natural right of collective self-defense on behalf of El Salvador in accordance with Article 51 of the United Nations Charter.

Moreover, all the documentation that has so far come into the public record indicates that the United States government scrupulously observed the international laws of humanitarian armed conflict when it used to train members of the Nicaraguan interdiction force in Honduras. Despite extensive examination of allegations to the contrary by Amnesty International/USA, not one shred of evidence has so far indicated that the United States government had ever trained these exile fighters to violate the laws of humanitarian armed conflict during the course of their military operations in Nicaragua. Indeed, most observers in the United States and abroad have concluded that U.S. military advisers in Honduras did in fact train Nicaraguan exile fighters to obey the international laws of humanitarian armed conflict.[52] The allegation that some of these exile fighters might have, purely on their own accord, disobeyed the laws of war creates personal criminal responsibility for the commission of war crimes on their part, and perhaps on the part of their immediate commanders, but not on the part of the United States government.[53] The United States government did everything in its power to ensure that members of the Nicaraguan interdiction force obeyed the laws and customs of warfare.

Also, it seems very obvious from reading the factual accounts of military attacks by members of the Nicaraguan interdiction force that they directed their hostilities primarily against what international law deems to be legitimate military targets in Nicaragua — that is, soldiers and armed militia, airports, military bases and convoys, oil facilities, railroad terminals, etc.[54] So long as their hostilities are directed against such legitimate military targets, and not primarily against the civilian population, there is no violation of the international laws of humanitarian armed conflict if some incidental civilian casualties do occur.[55] Public international law recognizes full well that when it comes to the conduct of violent hostilities, there certainly will occur some incidental civilian casualties. It is not a violation of international law for a government or an organized military group otherwise authorized to use force under Article 51 to launch an attack upon a legitimate military target, even if it believes that there might occur some incidental loss of civilian lives.[56] Since the United States government had the natural right to take measures necessary and proportionate to protect El Salvador from armed aggression mounted by the Sandinista junta, and since the United States government trained the members of the Nicaraguan interdiction force to obey the laws and customs of war, and since the interdiction force essentially attacked only legitimate military targets in Nicaragua, the United States government bears absolutely no responsibility under international law for any incidental civilian casualties that might have occurred as a result of their activities.

Nevertheless, it recently came to the attention of the United States government that some members of the Nicaraguan interdiction force might have committed violations of the laws and customs of war, despite the best efforts of the United States government to prevent this.[57] Hence, as an extra measure of precaution, and as evidence of its sincere desire to fulfill and indeed exceed the basic requirements of international law, the United States government terminated the expenditure of any funds for the purpose of supporting the Nicaraguan interdiction force in June of 1984.[58] Thus, for the past four months the United States government has not been providing any support to the Nicaraguan interdiction force. And as for private efforts undertaken by U.S. citizens to assist the Nicaraguan interdiction force without the approval of the United States government,[59] the U.S. government is under no obligation under international law to terminate such assistance, so long as those individuals do not use U.S. territory for the express purpose of actually launching a military expedition against the Sandinista junta in Nicaragua.[60]

10. THE MINING OF NICARAGUAN HARBORS

A similar line of argument applies to defeat allegations that the United States government somehow violated international law by assisting in the mining of Nicaraguan harbors by members of the interdiction force. The legitimacy of the U.S. action is justified on the grounds that this was a measure of collective self-defense on behalf of El Salvador against Nicaraguan armed aggression.[61] The purpose of the mining was to interdict the substantial flow of weapons, equipment, and supplies sent by the Soviet Union, Cuba, Vietnam, Bulgaria, and other communist regimes and radical movements into Nicaragua through these ports for the express purpose of their transshipment by the Sandinista junta through Honduras and across the Gulf of Fonseca to the rebels in El Salvador.[62]

The fact that mines were used instead of other measures of interdiction only goes to the question of whether or not their use may have constituted a violation of the international laws of humanitarian armed conflict. However, the use of mines *per se* would not negate the right of the United States government to take this action as a necessary and proportionate measure of collective self-defense on behalf of El Salvador under United Nations Charter Article 51. The relevant law on the former point can be found in the 1907 Hague Convention on the Laying of Automatic Contact Mines, which expressly provides in Article 7 that the provisions of the Convention do not apply except between contracting parties, *and then only if all the belligerents are parties to the Convention.*[63] Although both the United States and Nicaragua are parties to this 1907 Convention, neither El Salvador nor Honduras are parties to it.[64] Hence, by its own terms, the Convention does not apply to this situation.

Furthermore, it was recognized by most informed observers both in the United States and Nicaragua that these mines never had the explosive power necessary to cause serious destructive damage to the ships involved.[65] But rather that the mines were merely intended to serve as a warning to the governments of the Soviet Union, Cuba, Bulgaria, Vietnam, and others to terminate their exportation of weapons, equipment, and supplies to Nicaragua for transshipment to the rebels in El Salvador.[66] Hence the use of these low-explosive mines by the United States government in Nicaraguan harbors was both necessary and proportionate to the threat presented to El Salvador. I should also point out that all these mines were placed within Nicaraguan territorial waters,[67] and therefore they did not interfere with international shipping on the high seas in violation of the 1958 Geneva Convention on the High Seas.[68]

11. GENERAL DEFENSE

Quite obviously, during the time allotted to me here today for oral argument, I will not have the opportunity to specifically address each and every allegation brought against the United States government by the Sandinista junta under international law, though I will be pleased to entertain any further questions you might have on these matters after my formal presentation. Nevertheless, in regard to these amorphous allegations that the United States government has somehow violated various other international conventions and principles of customary international law while exercising its natural right of collective self-defense on behalf of El Salvador, I believe the prestigious International Law Commission has correctly articulated the relevant principle of customary international law in Article 34 of its Draft Convention on State Responsibility: "The wrongfulness of an act of a State not in conformity with an international obligation of that State is precluded if the act constitutes a lawful measure of self-defense taken in conformity with the Charter of the United Nations."[69] Such is the case for the entirety of the U.S. government's policy toward Nicaragua.

12. THE PEACEFUL SETTLEMENT OF INTERNATIONAL DISPUTES

The final substantive point I would like to make today is that Nicaragua has violated its solemn obligation to seek a peaceful settlement of the conflicts it has created with its neighbors in Central America in the manner prescribed by the terms of both the United Nations Charter and the OAS Charter. Article 23 of the OAS Charter expressly provides that all inter-American disputes must be submitted to the peaceful procedures of the OAS Charter before being referred to the Security Council of the United Nations.[70] And Article 52, paragraph 2 of the United Nations Charter requires that all members of a regional organization such as the OAS must make every effort to achieve a pacific settlement of local disputes by such a regional agency before referring them to the Security Council.[71] Nevertheless, it has been Nicaragua, not the United States government, that has strenuously resisted having these self-induced conflicts with its Central American neighbors submitted to the OAS.[72] The Sandinista junta has made the completely spurious argument that for some unexplained reason, the OAS might be biased against it. In fact, as I previously explained, it was a resolution by the OAS General Assembly that played the determinative role in the delegitimization of the Somoza government and thus enabled the Sandinistas to come to power.[73]

Rather than engaging in futile arguments with the Sandinista junta over this point, however, the United States government went out of its way to settle the Central American conflicts with Nicaragua peacefully, even in the face of the Sandinista's refusal to discharge its elementary obligations under both the OAS and U.N. Charters. Once the Sandinista junta made clear that it had no intention to resort to the appropriate regional organization for settling these conflicts (i.e., the OAS), the United States government announced its support for the initiative undertaken by the Foreign Ministers of the so-called Contadora Group (i.e., Venezuela, Mexico, Colombia and Panama).[74] The United States government has fully supported the efforts by the Contadora Group to obtain a peaceful settlement of the numerous conflicts in Central America that have been created by Nicaraguan armed aggression against its immediate neighbors — El Salvador, Honduras, and Costa Rica. The foreign ministers of the Contadora Group have recently announced the completion of a draft treaty on the basis of their so-called 21 principles.[75] However, since the United States government was not a party to the negotiation of this Contadora Draft Treaty, it has reserved the right to insist upon the inclusion therein and effective implementation of provisions creating adequate security guarantees, as well as inspection and verification procedures, designed to protect El Salvador from continued and repeated acts of Nicaraguan armed aggression.[76] Under these latter circumstances, such demands for revision of the Contadora Draft Treaty by the United States, Honduras, El Salvador, and Costa Rica are completely justified and fully warranted by Article 51 of the United Nations Charter.[77]

Nevertheless, as a further demonstration of its good faith and of its sincere desire to achieve a peaceful settlement of the numerous disputes in Central America created by Nicaraguan armed aggression, the U.S. government has conducted bilateral negotiations with the Sandinista junta under the auspices of Ambassador Harry W. Schlaudeman and the Nicaraguan Deputy Foreign Minister Hugo Tinoco at the Mexican town of Manzanillo.[78] Six rounds of negotiations have already occurred, and both sides have indicated that substantial progress is being made. These vigorous efforts by the U.S. government to fully discharge its obligations under both the U.N. Charter and the OAS Charter to settle this dispute with Nicaragua in a peaceful manner bear a high probability of success in the immediate future. Nevertheless, so long as the Sandinista junta is continuing to provide weapons, equipment, and supplies to the rebels in El Salvador for the purpose of overthrowing its democratically elected government, the United States remains entitled to take measures necessary and proportionate to protect El Salvador from Nicaraguan armed aggression under Article 51 of the United Nations Charter.

13. RECAPITULATION

This concludes my oral presentation today, but I would like to take one moment to recapitulate the basic points of my explanation for the legal basis of the U.S. government's policy toward Nicaragua.

First

Under Article 51 of the United Nations Charter, the United States government has a natural right of collective self-defense to protect El Salvador from armed aggression mounted by the Sandinista junta in Nicaragua with the assistance of the Soviet Union and Cuba, among other communist regimes and radical movements.

Second

Support by the Sandinista junta for the rebels in El Salvador constitutes a blatant "act of aggression" within the meaning of the U.N. General Assembly's 1974 Definition of Aggression and Article 39 of the United Nations Charter, as well as a gross violation of the General Assembly's 1965 Declaration on the Inadmissibility of Intervention, and of Article 2, paragraph 4 of the United Nations Charter.

Third

The U.S. response to Nicaraguan armed aggression by the creation of an interdiction force along the border with Honduras was both necessary and proportionate to the threat created for El Salvador by the Sandinista junta.

Fourth

The U.S. government never established the Nicaraguan interdiction force for the purpose of overthrowing the Sandinista junta.

Fifth

Any violations of the laws and customs of war committed by members of the Nicaraguan interdiction force were not the responsibility of the U.S. government. Nevertheless, out of an excess of caution and respect for international law, the U.S. government has terminated all forms of support for the Nicaraguan interdiction force.

Sixth

The non-elected Sandinista junta is forbidden to supply even one iota of political, military or economic assistance to the rebels in El Salvador seeking to overthrow the democratically elected government of President José Napoleon Duarte. The Sandinista's armed aggression against the Duarte government violates the international legal right to self-determination for the people of El Salvador as recognized by U.N. Charter Article 1, paragraph 2.

Seventh

The Sandinista junta has violated the provisions of both the U.N. Charter and the OAS Charter by its refusal to work with the OAS for the purpose of settling its self-induced conflicts with the neighboring states in Central America — El Salvador, Honduras, and Costa Rica. Nevertheless, as a substitute for the OAS, the United States government has given its support to the multilateral efforts of the Contadora Group and has also pursued in good faith bilateral negotiations with the Sandinista junta. In the meantime, however, under Article 51 of the U.N. Charter, the U.S. government has the natural right to take measures necessary and proportionate to protect the democratically elected government of El Salvador from persistent armed aggression by the Sandinista junta with the assistance of the Soviet Union and Cuba, among other communist regimes and radical movements.

14. CONCLUSION

For all these reasons, then, I believe the U.S. government's policy toward Nicaragua is fully justified under fundamental principles of international law. If the United States were to fail to come to the defense of El Salvador, then no state in the Western hemisphere could feel safe and secure against threats of armed aggression directed by totalitarian regimes from outside the hemisphere, such as the Soviet Union, by means of like-minded regional surrogates such as Cuba and Nicaragua. It is in the spirit of inter-American unity and solidarity that the United States government has acted to protect the democratically elected government of El Salvador from armed aggression by the Marxist-Leninist junta in Nicaragua at the behest of its Cuban and Soviet masters. I submit that this Tribunal should heartily commend the United States government for its selfless defense of El Salvador, and likewise soundly condemn the Sandinista junta for its vicious attack upon a democratically elected government. The rules of international law and the requirements for maintaining international peace and security permit no other result.

Finally, I would like to personally thank the distinguished members of this Tribunal, as well as my distinguished colleague from Nicaragua, for your kind and patient attention to my explanation of the legal basis for the U.S. government's policy toward Nicaragua. It has been greatly appreciated. And now I will be happy to answer any questions you might have. Thank you.

Brussels, Belgium
October 6, 1984

The full title of this presentation was "Statement on Behalf of the United States of America in the Case of Nicaragua v. United States of America Before the Permanent Peoples' Tribunal." —Ed.

Notes

1. U.N. Charter Art. 51, reprinted in H. Briggs, The Law of Nations 1047 (2nd ed. 1952).
2. U.N. Charter Art. 3.
3. U.N. Charter Art. 51 (French version).
4. T. Hobbes, Leviathan 103 (M. Oakeshott ed. 1962).
5. See H. Rommen, The Natural Law n. 50 (1948).
6. Hobbes, supra note 4, at 105 (emphasis added).
7. U.N. Charter Art. 51.
8. See Kunz, "Individual and Collective Self-defense in Article 51 of the Charter of the United Nations," 41 Am. J. Int'l l. 872, 875 (1947). See also Tucker, "The Interpretation of War Under Present International Law," 4 Int'l L.Q. 11, 29-30 (1951).
9. See M. McDougal & F. Feliciano, Law and Minimum World Public Order 240-41 (1961).
10. G. A. Res. 3314, 29 U.N. GAOR Supp. (No. 31) at 143, U.N. Doc. A/9631 (1974). The draft version is reprinted in Text of Draft Definition of Aggression, U.N. Monthly Chron., May 1974, at 86, and is identical to the final version.
11. U.N. Charter Art. 23, para. 1.
12. Cf. A. Thomas & A. J. Thomas Jr., Legal Limits on the Use of Chemical and Biological Weapons 208 (1970); D. Bowett, Self-Defense in International Law 13 (1958); J. Murphy, The United Nations and the Control of International Violence 17 (1982).
13. G. A. Res. 3314, 29 U.N. GAOR Supp. (No. 31) at 143, U.N. Doc. A/9631 (1974).
14. Id.
15. Id.
16. Id.
17. Id.
18. Id.
19. Id.
20. See, e.g., Weintraub, "Cuba Directs Salvador Insurgency, Former Guerrilla Lieutenant Says," N.Y. Times, July 28, 1983, at A10, col. 1; Simons, "Nicaragua Offers to Join in Talks on Regional Peace," N.Y. Times, July 20, 1983, at 1, col. 6; Taubman, "U.S. Said to Plan Military Exercises in Latin America," N.Y. Times, July 19, 1983, at 1, col. 6; Reuters, "Nicaraguan Aid to Rebels," N.Y. Times, May 2, 1983, at A3, col. 3; Weisman, "President Appeals Before Congress for Aid to Latins," N.Y. Times, April 28, 1983, at 1, col. 6; U.S. Dep't. of State, "Communist Interference in El Salvador," (Bureau of Public Affairs Special Report No. 80) (Feb. 23, 1981).
21. OAS Charter, April 30, 1948, 119 U.N.T.S. 3, 2 U.S.T. 2394, T.I.A.S. No. 2361, revised by the Protocol of Buenos Aires, Feb. 27, 1967, 21 U.S.T. 607, T.I.A.S. No. 6847.
22. See, e.g., Miller, "Soviet Said to Ship Tanks to Nicaragua," N.Y. Times, June 3, 1981, at A15, col. 1; N.Y. Times, June 2, 1981, at A4, col. 3; G. Wertzman, "More Salvador Aid Backed in Congress," N.Y. Times, Feb. 18, 1981, at 1, col. 2; "Communist Interference in El Salvador," supra note 20.
23. See, e.g., Greenberger, "Congress Skeptics Balk at Nicaragua Evidence," Wall St. J., June 15, 1984, at 22, col. 1.
24. See Ullman, "At War With Nicaragua," Foreign Aff., Oct. 1983, at 39, 57.
25. G. A. Res. 3314, 29 U.N. GAOR Supp. (No. 31) at 143, U.N. Doc. A/9631 (1974).
26. See "The Cuban Connection," Newsweek, Nov. 8, 1982, at 49, col. 1. See also Weintraub, supra note 20.
27. See E. Shotwell, Intervention in International Law 345-55 (1921).
28. G.A. Res. 2131 (XX), 20 U.N. GAOR Supp. (No. 14) at 11, U.N. Doc. A/6014 (1966), reprinted in 5 I.L.M. 374 (1966).
29. Id.
30. U.N. Charter Art. 2, para. 4 (emphasis added).
31. See M. McDougal & F. Feliciano, Law and Minimum Public Order 241-44 (1961); I. Brownlie, International Law and the Use of Force by States 261-65 (1963).
32. U.S. Dep't. of State, El Salvador: Revolution or Reform (Current Policy No. 546) 6 (Feb. 1984).
33. "Honduras: U.S. Linchpin in Central America," U.S. News and World Rep., Nov. 28,

1983, at 13, 14.

34. Address by President Reagan to a Joint Session of Congress (Apr. 27, 1983), reprinted in U.S. Dep't. of State, Realism, Strength, Negotiation: Key Foreign Policy Statements of the Reagan Administration 128 (May 1984):

> We do not seek [Nicaragua's] overthrow. Our interest is to ensure that it does not infect its neighbors through the export of subversion and violence. Our purpose, in conformity with American and international law, is to prevent the flow of arms to El Salvador, Honduras, Guatemala, and Costa Rica. We have attempted to have a dialogue with the Government of Nicaragua, but it persists in its efforts to spread violence. Id. at 129.

35. Continuing Appropriations for Fiscal Year 1983 (Boland Amendment), Pub. L. No. 97-377, Sec. 793, 96 Stat. 1830, 1865 (1982) (emphasis added).

36. See, e.g., La Feber, "How We Make Revolution Inevitable," The Nation, Jan. 28, 1984, at 69, 71.

37. See N.Y. Times, May 7, 1984, at 1, col. 1; N.Y. Times, May 8, 1984, at 1, col. 1.

38. See supra notes 22-24.

39. See N.Y. Times, July 21, 1979, at 1, col. 1. See also U.S. Dep't. of State, Background Notes: Nicaragua 3 (Jan. 1983).

40. OAS Res. of June 23, 1979, OAS/Ser. F/II.17, Doc. 40/79, Rev. 2, reprinted in M. Nash, 1979 Digest of United States Practice in International Law 1674-75 (1983).

41. Paragraph 4 of the OAS Resolution of June 23, 1979 calls for "[t]he holding of free elections as soon as possible, that will lead to the establishment of a truly democratic government that guarantees peace, freedom and justice." Id. See Middendorf, "Review of Nicaragua's Commitments to the OAS," 84 Dep't. St. Bull. 69, 71 (Sept. 1984).

42. See Motley, "Democracy in Latin America and the Caribbean," 84 Dep't. St. Bull. 1, 12-13 (Oct. 1984).

43. See Middendorf, supra, note 41, at 71 (emphasis added).

44. U.N. Charter Art. 1, para. 2.

45. See generally I. Brownlie, International Law and the Use of Force by States 231-336 (1963).

46. Corfu Channel Case (U.K. v. Alb.), 1949 I.C.J. 4, 18 (Judgment of Apr. 9).

47. See generally Gorelick, "Wars of National Liberation: Jus Ad Bellum," 11 Case W. Res. J. Int'l L. 71 (1979); O'Brien, "The Jus In Bello in Revolutionary War and Counterinsurgency," 18 Va. J. Int'l L. 193 (1978).

48. Geneva Convention for the Amelioration of the Condition of the Wounded and Sick in Armed Forces in the Field, Aug. 12, 1949, 6 U.S.T. 3114, T.I.A.S. No. 3362, 75 U.N.T.S. 31; Geneva Convention for the Amelioration of the Condition of Wounded, Sick and Shipwrecked Members of Armed Forces at Sea, Aug. 12, 1949, 6 U.S.T. 3217, T.I.A.S. No. 3363, 75 U.N.T.S. 85; Geneva Convention Relative to the Treatment of Prisoners of War, Aug. 12, 1949, 6 U.S.T. 3316, T.I.A.S. No. 3364, 75 U.N.T.S. 135; Geneva Convention Relative to the Protection of Civilian Persons in Time of War, Aug. 12, 1949, 6 U.S.T. 3516, T.I.A.S. No. 3365, 75 U.N.T.S. 287.

49. Convention Respecting the Laws and Customs of War on Land (Hague IV), with Annex of Regulations, Oct. 18, 1907, 36 Stat. 2277, T.S. No. 539, 1 Bevans 631.

50. See, e.g., United States v. List (No. 7), XI Trials of War Criminals Before the Nuremberg Military Tribunals 757, 1247 (1950); M. McDougal & F. Feliciano, Law and Minimum World Public Order 531-34 (1961).

51. The International Military Tribunal at Nuremberg recognized that "[c]rimes against international law are committed by men, not by abstract entities, and only by punishing individuals who commit such crimes can the provisions of international law be enforced." XXII Trial of the Major War Criminals Before the International Military Tribunal 466 (1948).

52. Christian Science Monitor, Aug. 6, 1982, Sec. 2, at 5, col. 1 (U.S. advisors in Honduras to teach classes ranging from radio to counterinsurgency, most likely including instruction on the laws of humanitarian armed conflict as required by Article 144 of the Fourth Geneva Convention of 1949).

53. See supra note 51 and accompanying text.

54. N.Y. Times, Oct. 15, 1984, at A4, col. 1 (oil ports); N.Y. Times, Sept. 9, 1984, at A1, col. 4 (air base); N.Y. Times, Apr. 18, 1984, at A1, col. 2 (oil facilities); N.Y. Times, Jan. 10, 1984, at A13, col. 1 (air field); N.Y. Times, Sept. 28, 1983, at A11, col. 1 (bridge); N.Y. Times,

May 1, 1983, at A8, col. 5; N.Y. Times, May 17, 1983, at A3, col. 2; N.Y. Times, Apr. 11, 1984, at A10, col. 4.

55. See, e.g., Convention Respecting the Laws and Customs of War on Land (Hague IV), supra note 49; Department of the Army, Field Manual 27-10: The Law of Land Warfare 17-21 (1956).

56. Id.

57. N.Y. Times, June 4, 1984, at A3, col. 1 (food storage silo; 12 civilians killed); N.Y. Times, Mar. 31, 1983, at A13, col. 5 (attack on town killing 4 civilians); N.Y. Times, Jan. 26, 1983, at A2, col. 3 (economic targets).

58. N.Y. Times, June 26, 1984, at A1, col. 6.

59. N.Y. Times, Sept. 16, 1984, at E4, col. 3 (activities of U.S. mercenaries in Nicaragua); N.Y. Times, Sept. 3, 1984, at A1, col. 6 (helicopter operated by two U.S. mercenaries shot down near Santa Clara, Nicaragua).

60. See Definition of Aggression, supra note 10.

61. See U.N. Charter Art. 51.

62. N.Y. Times, Apr. 12, 1984, at A10, col. 1 (statements of rebel leaders).

63. Convention Relative to the Laying of Automatic Submarine Contact Mines (Hague VIII), Oct. 18, 1907, 36 Stat. 2232, T.S. No. 541, 1 Bevans 669, reprinted in The Laws of Armed Conflict: A Collection of Conventions, Resolutions and Other Documents 715, 717 (D. Schindler & J. Toman eds. 1981).

64. The Convention was signed by the United States on October 18, 1907, and ratified on November 27, 1909. The Convention was never signed by Nicaragua, but was ratified on December 16, 1909. Id. at 720.

65. N.Y. Times, Apr. 12, 1984, at A10, col. 1.

66. Id.

67. N.Y. Times, Apr. 15, 1984, at E1, col. 1 (map).

68. Geneva Convention on the high Seas, April 29, 1958, 13 U.S.T. 2312, T.I.A.S. No. 5200, 450 U.N.T.S. 82.

69. See International Law Commission, Draft Article 34 on State Responsibility, reprinted in Schwebel, "The Thirty-Second Session of the International Law Commission," 74 Am. J. Int'l L. 961, 963 (1980).

70. OAS Charter Art. 23: "All international disputes that may arise between American States shall be submitted to the peaceful procedures set forth in this Charter, before being referred to the Security Council of the United Nations."

71. U.N. Charter, Art. 52, para. 2: "The Members of the United Nations entering into such arrangements or constituting such agencies shall make every effort to achieve pacific settlement of local disputes through such regional arrangements or by such regional agencies before referring them to the Security Council."

72. N.Y. Times, May 7, 1983, at A5, col. 2.

73. See OAS Resolution of June 23, 1978, supra note 40.

74. N.Y. Times, June 17, 1984, at A4, col. 1; id., June 16, 1984, at A1, col. 5; id., May 15, 1984, at A1, col. 6; id., Mar. 3, 1984, at A3, col. 6.

75. N.Y. Times, Nov. 17, 1984, at A3, col. 1; id., Nov. 13, 1983, at A11, col. 1. The objectives of the 21 principles include democratization, arms control, an end to support for subversion, and gradual withdrawal of foreign military advisers. See Motley, "Is Peace Possible in Central America?" Dep't. St. Bull., March, 1984, at 67.

76. Motley, "Is Peace Possible in Central America?" Dep't. St. Bull., March, 1984, at 67. See also N.Y. Times, Dec. 15, 1983, at A5, col. 1 (Report of Bipartisan Commission headed by Henry Kissinger).

77. See U.N. Charter, Art. 51.

78. N.Y. Times, June 26, 1984, at A7, col. 1.

Presentation

Larry Birns

Director of the Council on Hemispheric Affairs, Washington, D.C.

Before I begin my remarks, I would just like to say that I was in Chile with the United Nations in 1973, and no man inspires me more than that man sitting over there, the Swedish Ambassador, Harald Edelstam [a member of the jury for this session of the Tribunal — Ed.]. During the aftermath of the bloody Chilean coup, he was a latter-day Scarlet Pimpernel, taking in hundreds of refugees, including leaders of the Allende government and other political refugees resident in the country, when the embassies of Canada, Great Britain, and many other countries shut their doors. This man indefatigably saved hundreds of people. He's a hero and deserves to be a Nobel Laureate, and in fact someday I'll make that proposal. Harald Edelstam. (Applause.)

I came here — even though I don't travel well and I've never been to Belgium — because I thought it was important to be here. Perhaps I should begin by spending a few minutes describing what our organization is and what it does. The Council on Hemispheric Affairs (COHA) is not a solidarity organization. COHA is looked upon by the Reagan administration as a lethal, strategy-formulating organization composed of some 30 researchers, with an extremely prestigious board of trustees, that cannot be dismissed by the Reaganites as a *fideliste* front, because it includes presidents of national professional groups and trade unions, major religious leaders, academic figures, members of Congress, businessmen, and so forth. Since our chairman is the president of the Newspaper Guild of the United States, representing some 40,000 journalists in our country and Canada, we're very related to the American media and are looked upon by them as the organization of record on U.S.-Latin American affairs. In the past, we have been frequently cited by *The New York Times, Washington Post,* and other national and provincial papers, and on an average of five or six times a week, our research memoranda are placed in the *Congressional Record.* One of the reasons why the media trust us is that, unlike the Reagan administration, we're also looked upon as an organization having a single standard. We constantly criticize Nicaragua as we constantly criticize Guatemala, El Salvador, Chile, Argentina during military rule, and other governments that lapse from democratic procedures. That is, we have a right to talk about press censorship in El Salvador because we talk about press censorship in Nicaragua.

In fact, our chairman, in his introduction to COHA's annual "Survey of Press Freedom in Latin America," compiled in conjunction with the Newspaper Guild and published a few months ago, said that there are cases of press censorship in Nicaragua but no journalist has ever been killed in Nicaragua. In El Salvador, there's no formal press censorship, but there's total self-censorship. There's no free press in El Salvador. Two families own most of the newspapers, and 40 journalists have been murdered in the past several years. Two newspapers, *La Crónica* and *El Independiente,* the Catholic newspaper, were forced to close because of bombings and threats against their editors. So, our chairman says, how can the Reagan administration say that the Salvadoran elections took place in an environment of press freedom, and how can you compare that situation to Nicaragua, which is immeasurably superior?

Yesterday we heard a presentation by my compatriot from the United States, Professor Boyle — now that was high theater! Professor Boyle was putting you on, as an academic exercise, when he told you in his address that U.S. covert operations against Nicaragua were justified. In fact, I read a previous research paper that he did in which he came forth with the opposite conclusion. He was just being a good lawyer in the Dickensian sense. He was a man presenting a case, but the case involved all sorts of lacunae, distortions, and departures from reality. In an adversary fashion, I thought that I would talk about a few points that he made.

First of all, he referred to revelations made to him in Cuba by several Cubans — not one, but several — about Cuban arms aid to the Salvadoran guerrillas [Mr. Birns is referring to a statement by Francis Boyle during the question-and-answer period, which is not included in this volume — Ed.]. There is no possibility that such an event took place. If it had, Professor Boyle would be looked upon as a national treasure by the Reagan administration, and he would be transported around the country, to prove what the CIA has never been able to establish — that there has been such Cuban aid. Here we have a situation where an American, whom the Cubans have no particular reason to trust and of an uncertain political paternity, goes to Cuba and several Cubans give him one of the most important state secrets available. Now it may very well be that some Cubans told the professor that weapons were sent to Nicaragua — there's no secret about some Cuban weapons going to Nicaragua — but these weapons going to El Salvador, that strains credulity and not even the State Department bothers to make such charges.

Secondly, a totally distorted account of the Nicaraguan issue in the OAS has been presented by Professor Boyle. Point one, if the United States was determined to make a case against Nicaragua concerning alleged arms shipments to El Salvador, the venue could obviously have been found in that body. He himself said that the OAS voted to oust Somoza; presumably Anastasio wouldn't have permitted that to be put on the agenda if he had had the power to prevent it, but he didn't have such a power. In other words, any state in the OAS can bring a charge. The truth is that the United States has skirted presenting the Nicaragua-Salvadoran issue to the OAS because it has feared a strong nationalism in that body on the issue of intervention and also felt it couldn't make its case.

Point two about the OAS, Professor Boyle spoke of the help that the Carter administration gave to the ouster of Somoza (yes, the last several weeks, right before the overthrow). But prior to that period (and the U.S. Ambassador who was in Managua at the time told me this), the U.S. Ambassador to Nicaragua was specifically instructed not to speak to any Sandinista. Until a few months before the overthrow of Somoza — I think it was up to six months before the overthrow — U.S. arms were going to Somoza.

Point three, the United States was looking for an alternative to Somoza and it proposed to the OAS that a peacekeeping force formed by that organization be sent to Nicaragua to preside over the transition from the Somocista regime to a successor government. This was unanimously defeated; even such unsavory countries as Argentina at that time and Chile voted against the U.S. proposal. They so voted because they saw it as an attempt by Washington to deprive the Sandinistas of their victory.

The truth is that the OAS was never provided with the opportunity to be an instrument for a resolution to the bilateral differences between the U.S. and Nicaragua. In fact, rumor has it that Professor Boyle's presentation yesterday was so galvanic, so impressive, that the Soviet Union is speaking of hiring him to explain its case in Afghanistan.

In looking at U.S. policy toward Nicaragua and Central America, you must understand that the Reagan administration is extremely sincere, down to its marrow, that Nicaragua must die and that the Salvadoran guerrillas must be defeated. This is its religious, its creedal belief. It's not open to moderation or modification. The tragedy is that this is a simplistic formulation. It represents the sum of President Reagan's sophistication on the question of pluralism: for him, it means a hemisphere without Marxism. It is a personal insult to the President of the United States that any semblance of Marxist regimes — or regimes which he describes as Marxist — exists in Latin America.

This worldview comes as no surprise; it represents the man's thinking for years. Before he became President, he campaigned against the Carter administration as he campaigned a number of years before against other political candidates, on the thesis that the incumbent was being soft on Marxism. Here's an administration that was not really interested in the interdiction of weapons going from Nicaragua to the Salvadoran guerrillas, and it's absurd to think that the Reagan administration really believed that former Nicaraguan National Guardsmen were prepared to give their lives to prevent weapons going from Nicaragua to the Salvadoran guerrillas. What do they care about that? They were not in business for that. In fact, the real lawlessness of the U.S. operation was present from the very beginning. Training camps opened up in Florida, Texas, California, New Jersey, and Louisiana, staffed by the CIA and Cuban exiles, to train Nicaraguan exiles and others in insurgency activities. This was a violation of the 1793 Neutrality Act passed at the beginning of our history. The United States knew that this activity was a violation. Certainly the Attorney General knew it, because he had prosecuted Haitians and people from the island of Dominica who had been plotting in the United States to overthrow a foreign government. This was a violation of the law. In fact, later on, Secretary of State Alexander Haig indicated that in any general negotiation with Nicaraguan officials, the United States would be prepared to crack down on the training camps in the United States in terms of a quid pro quo — something for something.

Were the contras an effective interdiction force? After $100 million was given to them over three years, Dean Hinton, U.S. Ambassador to El Salvador, testifying before a House of Representatives subcommittee, was asked how many weapons the contras had interdicted. "Not a *pistola*, sir; not one *pistola*; not one bullet, not one gun." Utilizing spy planes, having a task force in the Gulf of Fonseca, having major radar facilities on Tiger Island, and with thousands of Honduran troops, the United States has not been able to provide any evidence of an arms flow, not even a captured bullet. But let's look at that more closely.

The last arms shipment was interdicted in January 1981, when a truck coming from Costa Rica with a false top was discovered to be carrying arms. After that, the United States starts making its charges. Assistant Secretary of State Thomas Enders goes to Managua. The Nicaraguan authorities say to him, we are prepared to establish joint patrols with the Hondurans. We must borrow U.S. telemetrical equipment to look for illicit arms shipments. Mr. Enders responds by saying it's impractical.

Fifteen separate efforts were made by the Nicaraguan government to engage in bilateral negotiations with the United States. At the United Nations, Jeane Kirkpatrick [U.S. Ambassador] tells Miguel D'Escoto [Foreign Minister of Nicaragua], "If you want us to solve your problems, go to Contadora." The United States, of course, has always looked upon Contadora with contempt. The contempt for negotiations to bring about peace in Central America is not concealed. For example, October 1983, Baltimore, USA: Deputy Defense Secretary Fred Ikle, one of the three major policymakers in the United States on U.S.-Central American relations, makes a speech before that city's World Affairs Council. He says, U.S. policy finds that the survival of a Marxist regime in Nicaragua and the presence of guerrillas in El Salvador are totally counter to U.S. national interests and will not be tolerated. In the summer issue of *Foreign Policy* magazine, Deputy Assistant Secretary of Defense Nestor Sánchez writes that the United States cannot coexist with Marxist regimes in Central America. But Contadora would legitimate and guarantee the existence of Nicaragua and also recognize the Salvadoran guerrilla forces as a political factor (it would not eliminate either).

How could the United States live with Contadora? The United States couldn't live with Contadora; that is the answer. The whole policy was to stall, to buy time in order to forfend a negotiated settlement in the pursuit of a military victory. And the plans are very clear. The plans have hardly been concealed from the Congress and from other policymakers in Washington.

Our organization is uniquely tied in with the intelligence community in Washington. We are the recipients of countless leaks from intelligence agencies. We have received continuous communications from dissidents within the CIA about what is taking place in the agency. Some months ago, a number of professionals in the Latin American Section of the CIA went to CIA Director William Casey and told him that intelligence was being used for political and ideological purposes and that this was demoralizing the agency. The professionals told Casey that their intelligence findings were being perverted by their superiors and that ideologically transformed conclusions were being issued by the Latin American director, at the time Constantine Menges.

William Casey, perhaps the sleaziest man in the Reagan administration, was forced to oust Menges because of this. Menges was then transferred to the National Security Council, where his first action was to recommend to President Reagan that the United States should start getting tough on Mexico — of the four Contadora nations, Mexico is the most stalwart in support of the peace process — because Mexico's independent stand is an embarrassment to U.S. foreign policy in Central America.

Out of retirement John Horton, 20 years a CIA man, is called to replace Constantine Menges. He stays in the agency for several months and then quits. Not because he opposes the Reagan administration's Central America policy; he supports it. He resigns because he finds that the professional assessments that the agency is making are not being respected and listened to, and that the politicos in the CIA are coming out with statements that would be supportive of the Reagan administration, not objective intelligence.

The Reagan administration knows it has no evidence of any Nicaraguan arms shipments to El Salvador. Former CIA analyst David MacMichael revealed that there has been no arms intercept — nothing, no evidence — since April of 1981. In other words (and I've had many conversations with him since), he was privy to all pertinent U.S. intelligence coming from the Defense Intelligence Agency, from NASA, from all of the other instruments that deal in intelligence matters, and the evidence was in — nothing.

For the past three years, our organization has telephoned the State Department once a month asking for some information, some evidence that would justify the incessant administration charges that arms shipments — Nicaragua to El Salvador — were being made. Remember that such evidence would be extremely important: the centerpiece of U.S. policy in El Salvador is the claim that the uprising there is not a national revolution, not an indigenous revolution, but an imported one. It's being imported from Nicaragua via Cuba and the Soviet Union, and Managua is helping to arm the revolution. But there's no evidence of this.

The administration has suggested that it gave the Intelligence Committees of the House and Senate evidence to that effect. We had a contact with the House Intelligence Committee and asked "Has the administration given you any evidence of Nicaraguan arms shipments?" And we were told, "Information yes; evidence no." But during our routine monthly calls, we were informed by the State Department that, "To give you any information would jeopardize clandestine sources of information." We responded by saying, "Hey, you know, in Northern Ireland, whenever the British come across an arms cache, they reveal the house where it was taken, how much stuff was there. Can you not tell us about one bullet, one rifle that went from Nicaragua to El Salvador?" And it was repeated to us that "to do so would jeopardize clandestine sources of information."

Finally the Reagan administration presented its July 1984 revelation, the pay-off moment. What we saw was a spy-plane or satellite shot of a smudge which allegedly was a boat off-loading weapons to El Salvador. Now a paramount element of intelligence procedures is that you don't care so much about the off-loading phase; you must trace the boat back to where it came from. That's what you're concerned about, the source. There was no effort to give the source; we were told this was an arms boat off-loading weapons. It could easily have been a shrimp boat, since the Honduran military command routinely engages in shrimp smuggling. (Shrimp boats engaging in such operations off-load shrimp to other craft going to a refrigerator plant for eventual shipment to California.) But this was the administration's ultimate evidence. Then the July 1984 White Paper proceeded to give evidence quoted from the *Washington Post* and *Human Events,* a publication put out by an extreme right-wing group in our country called the John Birch Society. There was no effort at presenting classified documents, only references from the popular press and right-wing publications. But this came merely as the latest example of the Reagan

administration's strenuous efforts to justify its position, even if information had to be invented.

Earlier, in February 1981, the first of a series of White Papers was issued.
This White Paper set forth the revelations contained in a diary of a leader
of the Salvadoran Communist Party, Shaflik Handal, about a trip he made
to Moscow in search of arms. It was rather interesting that the State Department gave three different versions of how this diary fell into its hands.
It was found on a shelf in the supermarket; it was taken off a dead Salvadoran guerrilla; and it was seized in the office of Handal's architect
brother in San Salvador. Now, we read this diary rather closely. In it, the
total amount of weaponry that it cites would enable the Salvadoran guerrilla forces to fight for only one day. And that estimate was not made
by myself, but by the Pentagon. Now, it's interesting that for months the
White Paper analysis was not made public by the U.S. press. It stated
only that definitive information had been produced about Nicaraguan
arms shipments.

A reading of the Shaflik Handal diary obtained by the State Department indicates that he was extremely unhappy about his trip to Moscow.
He said, "I was greeted only by third-stringers. I was kept waiting. They
told me later that if I want weapons I should go off to Hanoi to see if
I can find them." The White Paper that contained Handal's disclosures
was compiled by John Glassman, a Soviet expert in the State Department,
who just happened to find himself in El Salvador at that particular time.
Although a number of experts on the Central American region felt at
the time that the diary was spurious, it was not until publication of a
June 1981 article in the *Wall Street Journal* that the document was definitively debunked. Glassman admits: number one, that the February 1981
White Paper was "full of embellishments"; secondly, "we made mistakes";
thirdly (these are almost the exact words), "we extrapolated things that
we perhaps had no reason to extrapolate." Conclusion in the *Wall Street
Journal* article: the White Paper was largely an invention.

A year or so ago, another White Paper came out. Thomas Enders,
Assistant Secretary of State at the time, a hardliner, an alumni of Cambodia, where he presided over the secret bombings, argued within the
administration against its release. He said that the White Paper would
bring derision upon the State Department, that the White Paper contained no new information, and that it was merely a rehash of old formulations. Here you have a series of White Papers presented before Congress to justify U.S. policy; none of them had any real substance or
information of integrity, even though they were supposed to provide the
ultimate justification of administration policy — to defend before the Congress and to the American people the controversial things that the United
States was doing in Central America.

What the United States is doing in the region is perfectly plain: it is attempting to win a military victory against the Sandinistas and to bring down the Salvadoran guerrillas. Most importantly, it is attempting to buy time. For Washington, Nicaragua is a dead star. It still shines, but it's dead. Washington works furiously to discredit the November Nicaraguan elections before the fact, because it doesn't want to be put in the untenable position of working to bring down a constitutionally elected government in that country. It repeatedly says that it supports Contadora, yet does everything it can to subvert that peace process. So, what are the dynamics?

The dynamics are these. Two Octobers ago, we came into possession of intelligence information from both the State Department and the CIA that a plan was being readied for a military action by the United States against Nicaragua; this was called plan "Pegasus." We sat on it for about four days, consulting with the "overt" people in the State Department, who dismissed it as being farfetched. But the sources that told us this had given us information a week prior to the Grenada invasion that the United States intended to invade the island. And so we felt impelled to move ahead on the "Pegasus" information.

This information appeared throughout Latin America and Western Europe, and in *Newsweek* magazine and a number of U.S. newspapers. Soon after, a Washington reporter from the Associated Press had lunch with one of his State Department sources, who told him that plan "Pegasus" had been delayed because of premature publicity that COHA had given it. About a month ago (and I wish that Daniel Ortega would read our press releases, he wouldn't get things all wrong), we came upon another burst of intelligence, that the United States was intending military action against Nicaragua in or around February 1985, after the elections. Why was this important? It was important for this reason: that the first plan — "Pegasus" — was based on the assumption that the United States would be able to lure Nicaragua into attacking Honduran forces after provocative forays by the latter. The next step would be for Honduras to convoke a meeting of CONDECA (the Central American Defense Community) and say "we are being attacked and we request your military assistance." At that point, following the scenario established by the Grenada intervention, U.S. aid would be solicited, and Washington would launch air and naval attacks on Nicaragua that would destroy military objectives broadly defined to include economic targets also.

But there were a number of other things happening, as well. One was the Beirut bombing, which killed over 200 Marines and produced negative public opinion in the United States about foreign involvement. Another was that the internal situation in Honduras was rapidly deteriorating, not only because — as we were told yesterday — of a great welling of Hon-

duran nationalism, but also because General [Gustavo] Alvarez, who had
pocketed all the corruption payments coming from Washington, had
generated a great amount of criticism from the 26 senior commanders
of the Honduran military forces. They wanted not only a share in the
decision-making, but a share in the bounty as well. Since General Alvarez was totally disinclined to develop a cooperative approach in these matters, he was overthrown.

Professor Boyle told us yesterday, as a justification for the Nicaraguan
contra interdiction forces, that not only was Salvadoran security threatened by Nicaragua, but that Honduras as well was being compromised.
The only problem with his argument is that the Hondurans to this very
day refuse to acknowledge that there is a single contra in their country.
Just two weeks ago General [Walter] López, who succeeded Alvarez, stated
"There are people saying that those people are in our country; those people are not in our country." That is the absurdity of the policy today.

Now let me quickly round out what I want to say. President Reagan
most likely is going to be re-elected. This means perilous times for the
Nicaraguan government. As was suggested in a statement yesterday, a Reagan White House unfettered by the need to follow caution in the face
of an upcoming election will act more boldly when the restraints and hin-
drances put on it by U.S. public opinion are removed. Earlier this year,
there was a discussion in the White House about whether to take military
action against Nicaragua immediately or wait until after the election.
There was a spirited debate, which was eventually reported upon in the
American media. It was decided that, particularly after Beirut, a delay
in offensive action against Nicaragua would occur.

Here you have a volatile situation in Washington, a confrontation of
forces. Arrayed against the President are a healthy segment of the Congress and the bulk of the American media. It may come as a surprise
to you that most of the U.S. media are against administration policy in
Central America. We have done a tally of editorials in the major
newspapers in the United States and have found that about 75% of them
are against U.S. involvement in Nicaragua. The news stories that appear
in the *Washington Post* and *The New York Times* are a constant source
of embarrassment to the administration. But the American public is worn
down by Presidential statements. The public can take only a certain
number of revelations at one time; after a while, even news of scandals
underlying current U.S. policy doesn't have much of an impact. The prevar-
ications, the manipulation of statistics, the inventions, have become so
routine that when you call up a newspaperman and say "Hey, I've got
a new scandal for you," they say "What's new? Come on, now. We all know
that the administration is lying — so what's new — it's not news any longer."
The Congress itself has become a scene of debilitation and weariness, as

administration deception after deception falls upon it.

Let's for a moment attempt to evaluate the quality of the opposition in the United States against a deepening U.S. intervention in Central America. The churches are very good; the Catholic Church and the National Council of Churches are very good. You'd be also interested to know that the charge made by a major Jewish organization in the United States, B'Nai Brith, about alleged anti-Semitism in Nicaragua was directly challenged by two major Jewish organizations, the Union of Hebrew Congregations and the American Jewish Congress. Both held press conferences denying that anti-Semitism existed in Nicaragua. The official who made the original charge about anti-Semitism, who happened to be one of our trustees, was immediately brought to the White House by the Reagan administration and briefly made into a hero.

The American people are very worried about Marxism. They have been schooled not in pluralism, but in a unitary political system of formalistic rather than substantive democracy. It doesn't matter if the political system is a bestial one, like that of Pinochet's Chile and the ones in Guatemala — as long as they're not Marxist, it's a sufficient credential to be acceptable in Washington. It's extremely difficult for a congressman who is well-informed, whose staff has provided him or her with good information, to take on the administration over the question of current U.S. actions in Central America, and we have seen in recent months a depressing wearing down of congressional opposition.

Right now the administration will be able to get what it wants for Salvadoran military funding. In the past, the administration routinely asked for twice as much as it needed, then permitted congressional liberals to cut it in half, and everyone was happy. The problem right now is that the administration is asking for double what it really wants and is getting most of what it is asking for. Presently, the Congress is still holding fast against funding the contras in Nicaragua. But it was rather curious that Professor Boyle yesterday (in perhaps the worst moment of his address) said that the administration — possibly in an excess of caution — had cut funding of the contras. It certainly would not have been because the White House had been offended by human rights violations by the contras, as we've heard in this forum. Rather, it would have been more honest for him to say that the House of Representatives voted against contra funding over the objections of the administration, and the administration ostensibly was forced to cut funding of the contras against its will.

In his address at the Republican National Convention in Dallas, where he put Reagan's name in nomination, Senator Paul Laxalt, one of Reagan's closest intimates, said that whatever action the Congress takes, the administration will not turn its back on the "freedom fighters" in Nicaragua. Take that remark seriously, because the cutoff of funding that allegedly is taking place under mandate of the Congress doesn't mean anything. The CIA has awarded funds to a host of organizations in Central America and in Western Europe to carry on surrogate funding of the contra activities in Nicaragua through a "laundering" process.

Such funds, once awarded, cannot be recaptured irrespective of congressional intent. Remember, the CIA has a long history of laundering funds. A couple of months ago, in Bonn, Germany, I made the charge that the CIA had laundered money through the Christian Democratic Adenauer Foundation in Germany to contra forces in Nicaragua. The president of the Adenauer Foundation, extremely indignant, wrote a letter to all of our trustees, saying, "You will not survive this foul accusation against this noble organization." Anyone who knows Chile during the 1960s and the activities of Adenauer-funded Roger Vekemans, the august Belgian priest, knows that the Adenauer Foundation's credentials are somewhat tarnished. After that threatening letter, as almost a *deus ex machina,* the *Washington Post* carried an article revealing that the Adenauer Foundation had been used by the CIA to launder illicit funds to the José Napoleón Duarte electoral campaign in El Salvador. Now we heard yesterday about the democratic election in El Salvador, but how can you have a democratic election when you have no free press and where one party was singled out to receive millions of dollars of illicit campaign funds to pull it over the top (and remember, the Duarte victory was not that large)? If such an occurrence took place in a country whose political system was opposed by Washington — such as Nicaragua — you can be sure that the Reagan administration would have powerful demurrers to make about it.

My last few words would go like this. A countervailing force is needed against Reagan administration policy. Congress today is an uncertain vehicle for opposition to the White House's goals for Central America. The suggestion was made yesterday that a strong voice from Western Europe is very important; it is indeed. The influence of the Socialist International has been very significant, and it has been a restraint on U.S. policy. I would also suggest that constant efforts on the part of Western European governments and the West European citizenry to attempt to redress the embarrassing immoderation, the hysteria and zealotry of U.S. policy, are very much in order to maintain some kind of equilibrium. Thank you.

IV

U.S. INTERVENTION AND INTERNATIONAL LAW

On the Legality of the Reagan Administration's Policies

Joe Verhoeven

Professor of International Law at the
Catholic University of Louvain, Belgium

I. INTRODUCTION

1. Having been formulated on numerous occasions and in various courtrooms, even prior to being submitted for international jurisdiction, Managua's accusations against the United States are well known.

In substance, the United States has been accused of illegal intervention in the internal affairs of Nicaragua, in contempt of Nicaragua's basic rights, and has been accused of "aggression" in violation of the United Nations Charter. This accusation is serious. The United States, however, scarcely seems to be concerned. To be sure, it denies the validity of such an accusation; but in order to justify its denial, it hardly shows the zealous concern about illegal conduct which it usually manifests in denouncing such conduct on the part of others.

This same attitude is widespread in international relations where, more than anywhere else, the bandit can put on the airs of an archangel. It is deplorable that a state can satisfy itself in this manner with such perfunctory denials, especially when this same state, as one of the "great" powers, claims to exercise a privileged role within "the family of nations." A state should not authorize itself, in the absence of enforceable judgments in the area of international relations, to completely disregard accusations made against it — especially when the accusations are serious. Rather, it should be incumbent upon the accused state, just as it is upon the state making the accusations, to bring forth all the elements of proof that would reasonably permit the reality of the contentious facts and the legitimacy of the policies underlying them to be established. To continue to follow the policies under discussion, without offering any means of assuring conformity with the law, is to neglect the basic rules of international society, particularly when these policies are met by major criticisms of

The full title of this presentation in the original French was "On the Legality of the Policies Followed by the Reagan Administration in Relation to the Sandinista Government of Nicaragua."

intervention and aggression. It is also neglecting the basic rules of cooperation among states to increase the obstacles to bringing about an impartial international justice, and under conditions that make one doubt the
presence of good faith; for example, in the case before the International
Court of Justice, as in the present case, it has been seized with a dispute
based on an issue of which the Court is the sole arbiter.

2. The accusations presented by Nicaragua mainly raise factual questions, and concern the reality of the deeds of intervention and aggression
for which the United States is being reproached.

It is not our role to make a ruling on these questions. That is the
province of any authority to which proper appeal has been made, taking
into account all the elements of proof which have been submitted to it.
Our intention is simply to establish the juridical framework within which
these questions must be addressed. This framework is defined by the laws
of intervention and aggression as indicated by the Nicaraguan accusations. Though this framework is indeed fundamental, it does not exhaust
all the juridical questions raised by the policies which the United States
has followed in relation to the Sandinista government; in addition to possible interventions or aggressions, these policies reveal even more circum-
stantial illegalities (See II). Although less basic, these must also be
denounced if the facts from which they are deduced are established.

The American practices — if we assume them to be established, which
we will not prejudge here — demonstrate a gradual increase in violations
of the law. First, conventional and customary rights and obligations are
in question, which, in terms of the importance of respect, are not basic
insofar as they do not directly affect the very essence of the state. Then
come the rules of non-intervention in internal affairs, which protect in
particular the sovereign rights of any state to decide freely its own political, economic, or social structures. And finally comes the ban on aggression, which is intended to guard each state from attacks on its integrity
and its independence that could be initiated by armed force, the most
detrimental instrument with regard to the peace and security of all states.
This gradation could be regarded as aesthetic or moral rather than juridical. It is true that, for a long time, international law refused to put the
violations of its rules in any order according to seriousness. However, following its special spokesman, Professor Ago, the International Law Commission has established a distinction between "offenses" and "crimes" of
a state in its draft articles on the responsibilities of states in international
law. It has clearly qualified as a "crime" the violation of the rule banning
aggression.[1] The exact scope of the distinction is certainly not free from
ambiguities, and it is possible that attempts will be made to deprive it
of all practical significance. But this does not negate the fact that the
distinction testifies clearly to the refusal to place all violations on the same

plane. Some of these violations must be the object of firmer condemnation because they call into question some of the more basic interests. Undoubtedly violations of the prohibition on intervention and aggression are among these.

It is in this spirit that we will make a distinction between "minor" (Section II) and "major" (Section III) illegalities in this case.

II. "MINOR" ILLEGALITIES

3. The question of aggression or intervention aside, the legality of U.S. policies in Central America, particularly with regard to Nicaragua, should be ascertained with reference to the ensemble of rights and obligations by which states are accountable to each other.

These rights and obligations are established by international custom and derive also from treaties currently in effect which establish law between concerned parties. It would serve little purpose to draw up a complete inventory of these rights and obligations or to enumerate all the hypotheses by which, given the available information, respect for their dispositions is subject to caution. We will limit ourselves to two examples here, remembering that violations of the law can be as much the result of ignoring obligations which have been clearly accepted as they can be the abusive exercise of a right whose principle is indisputable.

It is an incontestable fact that the United States has, unilaterally and in a drastic manner, reduced its import of sugar from Nicaragua, which dropped from 58,000 to 6,000 tons. This is a patent violation of the laws of the GATT (General Agreement on Tariffs and Trade) which accepts reductions of this sort when they are not discriminatory. To be sure, a spokesperson of the U.S. Department of Commerce stated that the question of sugar imports from Nicaragua "must be considered in a larger context."[2] This still provides no justification whatsoever for an action which the United States had no right to undertake without authorization from GATT. The Council of the GATT clearly stated this in its report, adopted "without opposition on the part of the United States," whose conclusion "was that the reduction. . .of the sugar quota attributed to Nicaragua was not compatible with the dispositions of the GATT in terms of being non-discriminatory."[3]

It is also an incontestable fact that the United States has, in recent months, greatly increased the number of large-scale naval maneuvers along the Nicaraguan coasts. Such maneuvers are in themselves perfectly lawful so long as they do not take place in sovereign Nicaraguan waters. The high seas are in fact free, which means that any state has the right to use those waters for ends compatible with international law. It is not incompatible with international law, at least given its current dispositions, for

military maneuvers to take place in those waters. It is not acceptable for
a state to undertake such maneuvers with the sole aim of intimidating
a coastal state, creating a climate of insecurity, and thereby give credibility to the threat of an eventual armed invasion. Such practices should
be condemned as an abuse of the freedom of the high seas; like any other
juridical system, the international order should not tolerate rights which
it grants, even if they are undisputed, being used by their holders for the
sole purpose of causing damage to others.

4. These two examples suffice to remind us that, even with the question of intervention and aggression set aside, American conduct toward
Nicaragua can in many respects be judged as contrary to the rules of the
law of nations.

It is possible that these violations are the sign of a more fundamental
failure to recognize the sovereignty, independence, and "integrity" of a
state, and at the same time the instrument of that failure. It is true that
the violations are, so to speak, "minor" compared to some of the infractions of international law which, assuming they are established, would
be far more serious. However, they should neither be put to rest nor ignored
under the fallacious pretext of "a larger context" within which they are
committed.

III. "MAJOR" ILLEGALITIES

5. The United States has been reproached for having illicitly intervened in the internal affairs of Nicaragua and for being guilty of "aggression" towards Nicaragua.

This accusation is particularly serious, as has been said, since it bears
on the violation of the most fundamental rights of a state. Intervention
should not be confused with aggression, and each should be treated dis-
tinctly.

a) The Rules of Non-Intervention

6. It is traditionally accepted within the law of nations that no state
has the right to intervene in the internal affairs of another. This ban is
the natural corollary of sovereign equality among states, which, rightly
or wrongly, remains one of the keystones of present-day international society. While it is not, to be sure, formulated *expressis verbis* in the United
Nations Charter, this ban has been affirmed in categorical terms on numerous occasions by the General Assembly. We can specifically cite the Declaration on the Inadmissibility of Intervention in the Domestic Affairs of
States and the Protection of Their Independence and Sovereignty (Resolution 2131 (XX);[4] the Declaration of Principles of International Law Concerning Friendly Relations and Cooperation Among States (Resolution

2625 (XXV);[5] or the Declaration on the Inadmissibility of Intervention and Interference in the Internal Affairs of States (Resolution 36/103 of the General Assembly).[6]

It is true that these resolutions by themselves do not possess any obligatory force since they are not the expression of any normative power held by the General Assembly. But it would be erroneous for this reason to deny them any authority, if only purely moral authority. It is not to be doubted that these resolutions express current customary and incontested rules, which are simply the inevitable consequence of the postulates of state sovereignty and independence. They are in this sense purely declarative; the fact that they were adopted by a quasi-unanimity can only serve to reinforce the authority of the explication of the right they convey. Moreover, the United States would have even less right to contest the rules of non-intervention, for it is, along with Nicaragua, a signatory to a Charter which confirms these very rules. It is specifically recalled in the Charter of the Organization of American States, signed in Bogotá on April 30, 1948 and modified in Buenos Aires on February 27, 1967. Article 15 states with precision that the rule of non-intervention excludes the use of "not only armed force but also any form of interference or attempted threat against the personality of the State or against its political, economic and cultural elements."

It is also true that non-intervention has been violated numerous times, and continues to be violated, as recent events attest. We should not conclude, however, that the rule is obsolete or outmoded. No more than the proliferation of robberies calls into question the existence of property laws, the multiplicity of interventions should not call into question the existence of the rules of non-intervention, nor be a justification for illicit interventions. It is in fact the essence of juridical logic that a rule or law can be violated, even though the sanction which should be applied to the offender may remain largely uncertain.

Consequently, it is not the absence of a rule prohibiting intervention that could justify the interventions in the internal affairs of Nicaragua for which the United States has been reproached. If they can be justified, it could only be on the basis of limits or exceptions which would then involve a denial of the principle.

7. The first difficulty lies in the very notion of "intervention." The rule prohibiting interdiction is formulated in reference to objectives, without taking into account the nature of the acts necessary to carry them out. Herein lies its originality, in the sense that a purpose — "to intervene" — makes certain acts unlawful that in themselves would be perfectly lawful; indeed such a purpose aggravates the illegality of illicit acts.

It is the purpose of the act rather than the nature of the act which causes the rule against non-intervention to be raised. All the same, the rule complicates the feasibility of the act. As rudimentary as it may be, "international society" rests in fact on the interdependence of its members, the very idea of a society based on interrelations more or less spread out among them. In this respect it is characteristic of our contemporary era that the dream of a law protecting the autarky of princes-peasants, according to the formula of Pierre Gothot, has definitely given way to constantly growing realities of intersecting and interdependence among "nations." It inevitably results that there are few policies which are without effects — and sometimes quite damaging ones — on other nations. Is this saying that we must condemn all policies as having the purpose of illicit intervention? Absolutely not.

It is difficult, however, to formulate the criteria with which one can easily separate national policies with international repercussions from condemnable interventionist policies. If the purpose characterizes the intervention, then probably condemnation should be reserved solely for those policies whose primary, if not exclusive objective is to put wrongful pressure on the decision-making of others, which should be free. It should be recognized that, insofar as this bears on a principally subjective element, the proof of this "interventionism" can be difficult. It is undoubtedly in accordance with the reserve with which the judge treats matters relating to sovereign states that he abstains, in his censure of particular policy options, from further probing into the motives of a state when plausible causes for these policies can be reasonably found elsewhere than in intervention.

It should be unnecessary to emphasize how delicate opinions can be in these cases. However, it seems useless to spend any more time on this point. In fact, it follows clearly from several statements or other pronouncements emanating from various authorities that, particularly since Reagan took office, the United States intends to put direct pressure on Nicaraguan politics in order to bring the Sandinista government back to creeds more compatible with the faith and mores of the American administration. In order to justify these dubious policies, national interests other than those dictated by the American conception of security have not been taken into account. In this respect the purpose of intervention is patently obvious; if the purpose is not necessarily to overthrow the Sandinista government, it is at the very least to force Nicaragua to comply with orders which it would have no right to challenge — notwithstanding Nicaragua's independence and freedom of choice, which are recognized by the law of nations. The ambiguity of the notion of intervention would never be a reason to allow the United States to escape condemnation, should the well-founded accusations on the part of Nicaragua be established.

8. The second difficulty lies with the notion of "internal" affairs. This term, which appears to imply the opposite of "external" affairs, seems to

draw a distinction comparable to the one usually established between national policy and "foreign" policy. Such a distinction must be isolated; the Charter of the OAS and the resolutions of the General Assembly state with precision that no state has the right to intervene "in the internal *or external* affairs" of another state.[7]

Thus, this ambiguous term "internal affairs" does not refer to the spatial domain of a jurisdiction or a certain sphere of competence, but its object. Within the sphere of "internal" affairs are those affairs which, according to international law, fall within the "national" sphere of each state.

Again, the distinction, even explained that way, is less clear than it seems. Insofar as the law of nations has advanced and is extending itself in sectors which it formerly ignored, the space reserved to the national sphere grows smaller, and therefore so does the notion of "internal" affairs. The most notable example of this is human rights: the law of nations is seen as exerting at least minimal control over conduct which, throughout the centuries, was exclusively reserved to the sovereign decision of the state. These developments only serve to complicate the application of the distinction between national affairs and international affairs. They obscure the uncertainties of a law whose formulation takes often very devious paths and whose meaning conflicts with cultural and ideological divisions among the members of the "family of nations." From this point of view, American policies toward Nicaragua scarcely raise a problem. Even if American policies marginally claim to be motivated by certain violations of human rights, they do not, as has been stated, hide their desire to bring about forms or modes of government more compatible with American wishes, if not to overthrow the Sandinista government.

Now, if there is indeed a national sphere which the law of nations respects to this day, it is the responsibility of each state to set up the government of its choice and to decide freely its political, economic, and social forms of organization, whatever the model or inspiration might be. The United States can certainly regret that some adopt formulas hardly compatible with the canons of so-called liberal democracy; the United States does not have the right to forbid them. The ambiguities of the notion of "internal" affairs cannot, any more than the ambiguities of the notion of intervention, serve as a legal justification for American policies toward Nicaragua.

9. The final difficulty concerns the exceptions which can be attached to the rule of non-intervention. Undoubtedly, the terms in which that rule is normally formulated do not foresee any. On the contrary, they insist on the fact that a state never has the right to intervene, "no matter what the reason," in the affairs of another state.

There are few prescriptions whose mandate is so categorical as to "absolutely" prohibit any departure from the law. Non-intervention does not escape from this; that one can depart from it under certain circumstances does not appear to have ever been seriously contested. However, there remains the difficulty of defining these exceptions in a precise manner, as the doctrine and the practice are in fact as abundant as they are contradictory in this case. Many so-called legitimate causes for intervention have been put forward and debated from various perspectives. It is not our intention to inventory all of these. It is sufficient to take a look at several, insofar as they seem to have been invoked to a greater or lesser degree in the Nicaraguan affair.

i) In a system where the United Nations has not succeeded in exercising the monopoly which the Charter seemed to bestow on it, states should probably be authorized to exercise some legal policing, at least to redress the violations of rights of which they are the victims. There are some reprisals, be they military or nonmilitary, whose specificity is the result of the legitimation that the sanction confers on acts which are illicit in themselves. The conditions remain as they were stated during the 1928 arbitration of the so-called Naulilaa Affair, based on an understanding that reprisal is the last resort for re-establishing legality, any demand for reparation having been in vain, and that the reprisal should be proportionate to the illicitness against which the party carrying out the reprisal intends to protect itself.

Reprisals which are understood as such must surely be considered lawful, in spite of their apparent condemnation by several international bodies.

However, we cannot see how this concept can seriously be applied to the Nicaraguan situation. The illegality against which the United States claims to protect itself — or protect its "friends" — would have to be unequivocally established. It must be said that this has not yet been done. The United States scarcely hides that it is the illegitimacy — in the eyes of the U.S. — of a policy rather than its proclaimed illegality that justifies U.S. intervention. Assuming that such an illegality were established, it nevertheless would remain difficult to accept the unilateral recourse to reprisals without having first exhausted the "collective" means (the United Nations or the OAS) which could have facilitated ending the illegality. And finally, the remedies used are not proportionate to the ills they are supposed to "cure."[8]

The American policies in this case are all the more debatable because the very prejudice endured by the United States is evanescent. It should not be excluded that a state intervene on another state's behalf when the latter's rights are threatened, indeed on behalf of all states when objective obligations of which no specific state has custody are violated. Certainly, in such a hypothesis, it is still important to assure oneself of the "sincerity" of a certain policy. For it does not normally pertain to a state, under the pretext of weaknesses in international society, to set itself up as the policeman of the law of nations. Any effort to police others can only be suspect, a priori, especially when it is made by a superpower as in the present case. The Nicaraguan affair would confirm without a doubt that there is some basis to this suspicion.

ii) Intervention for humanitarian reasons, by which a state intends to put an end to the inhuman treatment which certain people or certain groups suffer in other states, must in principle be forbidden under the current law of nations, whatever its use has been in the past.

This prohibition is easily understood. It is not certain that it can be as absolute as some wish, since certain rights of human beings are judged to be more basic than state prerogatives. However, whatever human rights violations the Sandinista authorities are criticized for, even assuming they were established, they would not in fact have the character nor the scope to justify an intervention on humanitarian grounds. It is not serious to maintain the contrary.

iii) The state of necessity is equally a monster that seemed to have been swallowed up and which seems to reappear in certain respects, as evidenced by its consecration — a limited one — in the draft articles on the responsibility of states adopted by the International Law Commission.[9]

This argument could not be seriously put forth in this case. The state of necessity, which cannot be invoked on behalf of others, requires that "vital" interests must be directly threatened; in that case, the Chief Executive of the state would move to protect these interests by an intervention that would normally be forbidden. We do not see what threat Nicaragua would pose to the "vital" interests of the United States. Undoubtedly empires manage to find threats to their security at distances farther from their own territory than is consequential. No more in the West than in the East is there a Brezhnev Doctrine that can be accepted.

iv) Civil war is the usual place for contradictory interventions, which have at times been legitimated.

This does not however provide any acceptable justification for American intervention in Nicaragua. This is principally for two reasons:

The first reason concerns the fact that the hypothesis of a civil war scarcely seems verified in the case of Nicaragua. Certainly there exists a serious situation, with problems and disorders, largely attributable to the acts of foreign elements in Nicaragua. This situation does not have the characteristics of civil war; civil war requires at least the minimal existence within the state of an organized (armed), conflict, which seems to be lacking in this case.

The second reason concerns the fact that under any hypothesis, a situation of civil war does not authorize foreign intervention. Without question, there was a time when it was apparently accepted that there could be intervention either solely for the benefit of the legal government, or for the benefit of one belligerent party or the other. This is no longer the case. Today the rule is that no intervention is acceptable, neither for the benefit of the legal authority, nor for the benefit of the rebel authority.[10] Thus the United States does not have the right to intervene for the benefit of the opponents of the Sandinista government. Perhaps they would claim some right to "counter-intervention," called legitimate defense by analogy, to counterbalance the support illegally given by a third state to the Sandinistas. It seems useless, however, to consider further the legality of this "counter-intervention." Suffice it to state that there are no reasons to carry it out; in this case the authorities in Managua have not in fact benefited, at least not before the intervention, from external aid "of a nature to exert substantial influence on the outcome"[11] of the conflict, which eventually would have justified an American "counter-intervention."

v) There remains finally the issue of legitimate defense. Some contest that legitimate defense can never justify an intervention.[12] This exclusion seems too radical; we cannot see why the victim of an illicit aggression should refrain from any intervention, which is justified by the right of legitimate defense. Legitimate defense necessarily presupposes an aggression; legitimate defense should be addressed only after having reviewed the rules governing it.

b) The Banning of Aggression

10. Aggression is undoubtedly one of the most serious infractions of the rules of the law of nations, in that it impinges on the very integrity of a state and that this violation is perpetrated by the use of armed force, which in principle belongs solely to the United Nations.

Aggression is clearly prohibited by the Charter. It is not, however, defined there, and agreement on a definition will require interminable discussions; these have already been undertaken by the Society of Nations. Today the definition of aggression is set forth in Resolution 3314 (XXIX), adopted on December 14, 1974 by the General Assembly of the United Nations.

No more than any other, this resolution is not in itself obligatory.[13] Nevertheless, we do not see what other definition to substitute for it since it does represent the most authorized interpretation of the Charter and, after lengthy negotiations, it received the unanimous consensus of all members of that body of the United Nations — the General Assembly — which is the most representative of the international community.

11. According to Article 1 of the Resolution, "Aggression is the use of armed force by a State against the sovereignty, territorial integrity or political independence of another State, or in any way inconsistent with the Charter of the United Nations. . ."

In its Article 3, the Resolution enumerates a series of acts which can be characterized as aggression, while stating, in its Article 4, that this enumeration is not restrictive and that the Security Council has the right to "determine that other acts constitute aggression under the provisions of the Charter."

Two points are worth underlining in this definition. On the one hand, aggression exists only when it relies on *armed force*, which excludes economic, ideological, or other types of aggression, no matter how reprehensible these may be in other respects. On the other hand, aggression exists only when armed force is *used*. This means that just the threat of using force cannot be constituted as aggression, even though such a threat would authorize the Security Council to undertake coercive action on the basis of Chapter VII of the Charter.

It is clear in other respects that the primary judge of aggression is the Security Council, since it was set up precisely to guarantee the peace and security which any aggression hypothetically endangers. The freedom of the Security Council to exercise its police function with a view to fulfilling that responsibility is definite; Article 4 of the Resolution expressly safeguards its autonomy with respect to the definition furnished in Article 1. Is this to say that the Security Council is the sole judge of an aggression? Absolutely not. It is the natural judge, insofar as aggression should normally provoke the setting into motion of the apparatus designed to stop it, which in principle comes back to the Security Council. It is not, however, the exclusive judge. Any authority can verify the reality of an act of aggression, from the moment that this verification is necessary to carry out the function with which it is duly invested. In this respect, it is immaterial that this authority should lack the competence to order certain peace-preserving measures which the United Nations Charter gives solely to the Security Council.

12. Two series of facts are called upon to support the accusations of aggression made against the United States: the mining of the ports of Nicaragua and the support given to the military and paramilitary activities of forces hostile to the Sandinista authorities.

The mining of the Nicaraguan ports — or at least the principal ones of Corinto, Puerto Sandino, and El Bluff — is an undisputed fact; no doubt exists that it was carried out under the orders of U.S. agents. Such an act unquestionably has the characteristics of aggression, given that Resolution 3314 (XXIX) includes among acts that qualify as aggression, "The blockade of the ports or coasts of a State by the armed forces of another State. . . ."[14] It could be claimed perhaps that the existence of a blockade has not been established in this case. Nevertheless, there is still an aggression since the actual mining constitutes at least "the use of armed force by one State against the. . .territorial integrity of another State," in the words of the same Resolution.[15]

The support given to the rebels operating out of Honduras, as the case may be, constitutes an aggression according to the terms of Resolution 3314 (XXIX), only if it represents a "substantial involvement." The resolution qualifies as aggression "The sending by or on behalf of a State armed bands, groups, irregulars or mercenaries, which carry out acts of armed force against another State of such gravity as to amount to the acts listed above [i.e., the acts qualified as aggression in the resolution — Ed.], or its substantial involvement therein."[16] American involvement on the side of the rebels must be presumed in light of the significant sums that the Reagan administration admits giving to them. To assess whether this involvement is "substantial," and the gravity of the acts, raises exclusively factual questions. Given this, there is no lack of arguments to affirm that all systematic support to subversive or terrorist movements on the territory of another state could constitute an act of aggression, since this is clearly condemned by Declaration 2625 (XXV) concerning the principles of international law with respect to friendly relations and cooperation among states. Article 4 of Resolution 3314 (XXIX) states in fact that the enumeration provided in its Article 3 is not restrictive; if necessary, it could be less demanding with regard to indirect aggressions.[17]

13. At least concerning the mining of the ports, the fact of aggression seems thus established.

Can it be justified by other means?

Article 2 of Resolution 3314 (XXIX) gives to the Security Council — and by extension to all other authorities normally appealed to — the power to spell out the criteria for aggression, notwithstanding the aspects of "taking into account other pertinent circumstances, including the fact that the acts either in cause or consequence are not of a sufficient gravity."

It would be injurious to the suffering of the Nicaraguan people to claim that the American actions are without sufficient gravity. What about "other pertinent circumstances?" The expression is strange in that it seems to cover both objective factors and factors of intent or motive.[18] We cannot understand what usefulness it could have in this case. The United States certainly claims the need to defend "American" freedom and security as the reason to undertake its disastrous crusades here and there. There are undoubtedly special circumstances; however, they could never take on the "pertinence" required to excuse an aggression.

Since all the "pertinent" circumstances are lacking, only legitimate defense could legalize an act that demonstrates a priori all the characteristics of aggression. The right to legitimate defense is in fact uncontested; the Charter emphasizes incorrectly that it reflects a "natural"[19] right, meaning that it is basic.

In the present case, it is principally on the basis of legitimate defense that the United States claims to justify its actions in Nicaragua. Again, the argument principally raises factual questions. And we must first be agreed upon the conditions within which this legitimate defense can be exercised.

14. Prevailing opinion deems that there is no right to legitimate defense outside of that which is recognized by Article 51 of the United Nations Charter.[20] The conditions as worded in this article must always be respected by whoever claims legitimate defense. It is possible that certain implicit demands can be added to those which are expressly stipulated; it is nevertheless certain that the right to legitimate defense cannot be exercised under conditions less onerous than those set by the Charter.

i) Legitimate defense authorizes the victim of aggression to utilize armed force to protect itself. It is an accepted fact that a third party can help the victim in such a case and participate in exercising its right to legitimate defense. This so-called collective legitimate defense, on behalf of another, has been criticized; some do not hesitate to see it as a fiction.[21] Nevertheless it is accepted; the Charter in fact expressly confirms it.

The victim in this case is El Salvador. In applying collective legitimate defense, the United States cannot in principle be reproached for intervening on behalf of El Salvador to put an end to the Nicaraguan aggression. Given that, one would have wished that the call for collective defense had been clearly made by the Salvadoran government from the moment of the aggression of which it claims to be a victim. To invoke legitimate defense a posteriori could cause one to doubt the credibility of the argument, especially when it is intended to legitimate the acts of a state which was not the direct victim of aggression.

ii) According to the terms of the Charter, there can be legitimate defense only when there is "armed aggression." This notion must be understood in the light of the definition given by the General Assembly in the previously cited Resolution 3314 (XXIX).[22]

To establish Nicaraguan aggression, it has been stated that the Sandinista authorities have provided assistance to the Salvadoran rebels, especially in the form of arms shipments. Therefore the aggression would be indirect in the sense of the Resolution. Unless the reality of this assistance is proven and shown to be "substantial," as required by Article 3, g, it cannot be considered decisive support which would justify by extension its being characterized as aggression.

Here there is a question of pure fact. And under any hypothesis, it is still necessary to establish the antecedence of an eventual Sandinista aggression. The measures taken cannot in fact be justified as legitimate defense unless they were subsequent to the aggression they claim to repress. It is not acceptable to say that legitimate defense can be exercised as a preventive measure. Again this is a question of pure fact, complex as it is.

iii) In the terms of Article 51 of the Charter, legitimate defense can-

not be exercised "until the Security Council has taken the measures necessary to maintain international peace and security"; and the state resorting to it must report "immediately" to the Security Council the measures
it is taking in the exercise of its right of self-defense.

These points make very clear the strictly exceptional character of the
right to legitimate defense. That right exists only because, provisionally,
the United Nations is unable to intervene effectively to protect the victim
of an aggression. Exercising that right remains, under any hypothesis,
subject to control by the United Nations so long as that body is not in
a position to substitute its collective action for the unilateral measures
which are normally forbidden.

In this regard, we can merely note that neither El Salvador nor the
United States appears to have duly notified the Security Council of the
measures taken in the alleged exercise of its right to legitimate defense.
There are, however, even more serious aspects. The obligation of the state
is not only to give notification of the measures that it is taking in the name
of legitimate defense after an aggression. Beyond all procedural duties,
before resorting to armed force or prolonging the use of it, a state must
exhaust all peaceful means at its disposal. In particular, it must activate
collective security mechanisms which should make pointless all use of
unilateral force. It is only under this condition, according to the spirit
and the letter of the Charter, that the individual right to legitimate defense
can be accepted.

In this respect, it must be stated that neither before nor after the so-
called Nicaraguan aggression did the United States (or El Salvador) seriously use the resources offered by the United Nations or the OAS. On
the contrary, it seems to have abused its "great power" status, which has
officially given it veto power in the Security Council, to prevent putting
these very resources to work. Under these conditions, any argument of
legitimate defense must be rejected. As basic as it is, the right to legitimate defense cannot be claimed when the necessity to resort unilaterally
to force is not the result of urgency or of the objective weaknesses of a
system for finding a solution to a problem, but is the result of the sole
desire on the part of a state to paralyze the functioning of the system in
order to intensively pursue partisan politics.

iv) While the Charter does not address the issue, it is traditionally
accepted that legitimate defense must be proportionate to the aggression.

We must add that this rule of "proportionality" is not easy to apply,
even if it is understood that, according to the terms of the arbitration
of the Carolines Affair (1841), legitimate defense must not lead to anything that is "unreasonable or excessive."[23] Out of concern with avoiding
any abuse of the use of armed force, the rule requires the state to abstain
from any measures which are not strictly necessary to put an end to aggres-

sion, while it awaits the decisions of the organs of the United Nations.

It is in the light of all these pertinent circumstances that we must consider what is concretely necessary and sufficient to put an end to aggression, and consequently to verify respect for the demand of proportionality. Given this reservation, it is nevertheless difficult not to find a priori some excessiveness in the American "counter-attack." It is difficult in fact to see how the aggression denounced by the United States is proportionate in an equitable manner to the enormity of the political, economic, diplomatic, and military means that it has employed to protect its Salvadoran protege.

IV. CONCLUSIONS

15. One summary study of the juridical framework in a case of contentious behavior cannot come to conclusions regarding facts which it has refused to prejudge, at least so long as their reality has not been clearly established.

Consequently, no condemnation whatsoever can be found there. Nevertheless, it would be difficult to contest that, on the three levels which have been identified here, the legality of the practices followed by the United States with regard to Nicaragua is at the very least dubious. It is dubious because these practices violate rights and obligations whose existence cannot be contested; it is also dubious because the conditions under which the U.S. practices could be exceptionally justified by particular causes, such as legitimate defense, scarcely appear to be fulfilled.

Notes

1. See Article 19. Text *in Ann. C.D.I.*, 1980, II, p. 31.
2. See Q.E. Number 378/84 of Mr. Vernimmen at the Council of the C.E.E., June 4, 1984, and their response, of July 30, 1984, J.O., Number C 232/26, September 3, 1984.
3. Ibid.
4. December 21, 1965.
5. October 24, 1970.
6. December 9, 1981.
7. See, for example, Article 18 of the OAS Charter or Section 1 of Resolution 2131 (XX).
8. See infra, number 14.
9. See Article 33. Text *in Ann. I.D.I.*, 1980, II, p. 32.
10. See the resolution on the principles of non-intervention in civil wars adopted in 1975, at Weisbaden, by the International Law Institute, *Ann.*, Vol. 56, p. 544.
11. Article 3 of the previously cited resolution.
12. See the provisional report by J. Zourek on the idea of legitimate defense in international law, *in Ann. I.D.I.*, Vol. 56 (1975), p. 59.
13. See supra, Number 6.
14. Article 3, c.
15. Article 3, b.
16. Article 3, g.
17. See H. Thierry, J. Combacau, S. Sur, and Ch. Vallée, Public International Law, 4th ed.,

1984, p. 512.

18. See B.B. Ferencz, Defining International Aggression, 1975, Vol. 2, pp. 30-32.

19. Article 51. The English text refers to "inherent" and the Spanish text "immanent."

20. See the report by J. Zourek, cited above, p. 52.

21. See D.W. Bowett, Self Defense in International Law, 1958, p. 216.

22. Supra, Number 12.

23. Cited in H. Thierry et al., op. cit., p. 498.

V

THE
TRIBUNAL'S
JUDGMENT

Judgment of the
Permanent Peoples' Tribunal

The Permanent Peoples' Tribunal Convened in Brussels on October 5 through October 7, 1984, having considered,

- the Charter of the United Nations of June 26, 1945;
- Law No. 10 of December 12, 1945, instituting the International Military Tribunal at Nuremberg, the Statute of the Tribunal, and the Judgment delivered by the same Tribunal;
- the Charter of the Organization of American States of April 30, 1948, amended by the Protocol of Buenos Aires of February 27, 1967;
- the Universal Declaration of Human Rights, adopted by the General Assembly of the United Nations on December 10, 1948, as well as the International Covenants;
- the American Convention on Human Rights, adopted at San José, Costa Rica, on December 22, 1969;
- the Havana Convention of February 20, 1928;
- the Río de Janeiro Pact of September 2, 1947;
- the Declaration on the Inadmissibility of Intervention in the Domestic Affairs of States and the Protection of Their Independence and Sovereignty, adopted with Resolution No. 2131 (XX), December 21, 1965, by the General Assembly of the United Nations;
- the Declaration of Principles of International Law Concerning Friendly Relations and Cooperation Among States in Accordance with the Charter of the United Nations, adopted with Resolution No. 2625 (XXV), October 24, 1970, by the General Assembly of the United Nations;
- Resolution No. 3314 (XXIX) on the Definition of Aggression, adopted by the General Assembly of the United Nations on December 14, 1974;

Having considered the Declaration of Independence of the United States of America, July 4, 1776;

Having considered the judgments handed down by the Second Russell Tribunal on Latin America in sessions held in 1974, 1975, and 1976;

In consultation with Professor Richard Falk, some stylistic changes have been introduced in this translation from the original French to bring out the meaning more clearly, but nothing of substance has been altered.

Having considered the sentences handed down by the Permanent Peoples' Tribunal, most especially in sessions on:

— Argentina (Geneva, May 3-4, 1980),
— El Salvador (Mexico, February 9-11, 1981),
— Guatemala (Madrid, January 27-31, 1983);

Having seen the encyclical Populorum Progressio (March 26, 1967); Having seen documents emanating from the conferences:

— Medellín (Colombia, August 26, 1968);
— Puebla de los Angeles (Mexico, January 27-February 13, 1979);

Having considered:

— the Universal Declaration of the Rights of the Peoples (Algiers, July 4, 1976);
— the Statute of the Permanent Peoples' Tribunal (Bologna, June 24, 1979);

Having studied the report of Francis Boyle, professor at the University of Illinois (United States), presenting, at the request of the Tribunal, the official position of the United States of America on Nicaragua;

Having had the benefit of the testimonies of the Nicaraguans, particularly the Miskitos, victims of the aggression:

— Digna Barrera,
— Brenda Rocha,
— Rev. Norman Bent,
— Rev. James Lloyd Miguel Mena,
— Orlando Wayland Waldimar,
— Tomás Alvarado,
— Ramón Sanábria
— Mario Barreda;

Having considered the reports of:

— Rafael Chamorro, Dean of the Faculty of Law at the University of Nicaragua, Managua,
— Richard Falk, professor at Princeton University (United States),
— Rosa Pasos, captain in the Army of Nicaragua (EPS),
— Freddy Balzán, Executive Secretary of the Antimperialist Tribunal of Our America,
— Marlene Dixon, Director of the Institute for the Study of Militarism and Economic Crisis (United States),
— His Excellency Ernesto Cardenal, priest, writer, and Minister of Culture of Nicaragua,

— Magda Henríquez of the Sandino Foundation, Managua,

— Lilly Soto, President of the Union of Nicaraguan Journalists (UPN),

— Larry Birns, Director of the Council on Hemispheric Affairs in Washington, D.C. (United States),

— His Excellency Alejandro Serrano Caldera, Ambassador of Nicaragua to France and Permanent Delegate to UNESCO,

— Joe Verhoeven, Professor of International Law at the Catholic University of Louvain (Belgium);

Having taken into account:

— audio-visual material,

— cartographical documentation,

put at the disposal of the Tribunal;

Having taken into account the special texts and other documents presented to the Tribunal,*

Considering that on the 4th of September, 1984, the matter was presented to the Tribunal by the following Nicaraguan organizations: Sandinista Workers Central (CST), Rural Workers Association (ATC), National Union of Farmers and Cattle Ranchers (UNAG), National Confederation of Professionals (CONAPRO), Union of Journalists of Nicaragua (UPN), July 19 Sandinista Youth (JS19), "Luisa Amanda Espinoza" Association of Nicaraguan Women (AMNLAE), Federation of Health Workers (FETSALUD), Sandinista Defense Committees (CDS), National Teachers Association of Nicaragua (ANDEN), Sandinista Cultural Workers Association (ASTC), Nicaraguan Committee in Solidarity With the Peoples (CNSP), Committee of Mothers of Heroes and Martyrs (CMHM), National Union of Nicaraguan Students (UNEN), Antimperialist Tribunal of Our America (TANA), all of whom charge the government of the United States of America with responsibility for the war imposed on Nicaragua and the peoples of Central America, and request the Tribunal:

a) to demand of the government of the United States of America to stop the war and all other types of aggression and intervention against Nicaragua;

b) to reach a verdict in favor of peace and support for the people of Nicaragua and its government so that they may, in an atmosphere of peace, reconstruct their country and achieve freedom, sovereignty, and independence.

Considering that this request was declared admissible by the Tribunal, in accordance with Articles 4 and 12 of the Statute of the Permanent Peoples' Tribunal, and that this decision was communicated to the govern-

---

*The complete list of documents and their authors, which was included here in the text of the Judgment, will be found in the List of Documents Submitted to the Jury, p.261.

ment of the United States of America on the 28th of August 1984, inviting it to participate in the proceedings, in accordance with Article 15 of the Statute;

Considering that the government of the United States has failed to respond to this invitation to participate in these proceedings;
Decrees the following judgment:

I. INTRODUCTION

The Permanent Peoples' Tribunal functions within a juridical framework established by the Universal Declaration of the Rights of the Peoples, adopted on July 4th, 1976 in Algiers.

This is the thirteenth session of the Tribunal.

The Tribunal holds proceedings primarily concerning the affirmation of the right of each people to choose freely the path of its political, economic, cultural and ideological development, without any outside interference.

The existence of the Tribunal is the result of efforts on the part of lawyers and moral authorities from all regions of the world, brought together to constitute a body capable of deciding whether the fundamental grievances of the people are justified. In the present case, the Tribunal has researched whether the grievances directed against the United States government by the government of Nicaragua are established according to international law.

Toward this end, the two parties were invited to the present proceedings.

Nicaragua provided testimony and reports by experts to the Tribunal.

The government of the United States failed to accept the invitation to take part in the debates.

However, at the initiative of the Tribunal, an expert in international law, Professor Francis Boyle, presented a complete report, orally and in writing, tending toward the justification of all the acts of which the government of the United States has been accused.

II. DESTABILIZATION AND GENERAL STATE OF WAR

1) Political Interventions and Military Actions

Military Actions

The victory of the Sandinista revolution over the Somoza dictatorship and the creation of a new State of Nicaragua was accompanied by the flight of a considerable number of former Somocista Guardsmen and other persons associated with the former regime. These people located themselves primarily in the United States, in Guatemala, and in Honduras, where they very quickly made efforts to organize themselves and find support for destabilizing, if not overthrowing, the Sandinista government.

In the beginning, this activity was directed toward the formation of bands lacking any political or military strategy and often any connections between them. They carried out a variety of subversive and criminal actions, particularly in the regions of Nicaragua bordering on Honduras, attacking among others those working in the literacy campaign.

These actions increased over the years and, since the end of 1981, have taken on the character of a counterrevolutionary effort which is more and more coordinated, well provided with funds and resources, and militarily equipped, with a well-defined strategy aimed at terrorizing the people, destroying the economic potential of the Nicaraguan state, and damaging the socioeconomic fabric of the country.

The extent of these attacks, which have continued to grow since 1981, has been documented in detail in reports presented to the Tribunal. This documentation establishes a series of aggressions, acts of sabotage, acts of terrorism, and acts of war, perpetrated by counterrevolutionary forces and their allies against the people and the State of Nicaragua.

From 1981 to September 12, 1984, documentation exists for 64 cases of kidnapping, 30 assassinations, 445 provocations, 289 infiltrations, 922 battles, 240 ambushes, 345 attacks, 98 acts of sabotage, making a total of 2,475 acts of aggression that bear witness to an incessant politics of aggression.

To this record can be added the numerous plans of aggression described in convincing detail before this Tribunal (the Red Christmas Plan, Plan C, the Marathon Plan, the Sierra Plan).

We shall recall here the most striking of the many imposing facts in this material. They are also well-known facts, since the international press has reported most of them:

— Bomb attack at the Mexican airport that damaged an Aeronica plane and injured three members of the crew (1981);

— Bomb attack at the Augusto C. Sandino International Airport in Managua that left four dead and three injured (February 22, 1982);

— Invasion attempt by the MISURA counterrevolutionary group directed by Steadman Fagoth in the Northern Zelaya region (Red Christmas Plan, December 1981);

— Attempt by the counterrevolutionary group, FDN, to take over the town of Jalapa in Nueva Segovia (Plan C, end of 1982 to April 1983);

— Bombings at the Augusto C. Sandino International Airport by a twin-engined plane of the counterrevolutionary group ARDE and bombings of the two ports, Puerto Corinto and Puerto Sandino, by T28 planes (September 1983);

— Naval attack by "Piranha" boats on the fuel depot at Puerto Corinto and at Puerto Cabezas, and bombing of the storage tanks at Puerto Sandino (October 1983);

— Attacks on Nicaraguan ships by Honduran marines, in the Gulf of Fonseca (November 1983);

— Attack by an NH-500 helicopter on the village of Opali in Nueva Segovia (September 1, 1984).

All the evidence shows that these massive aggressions could not have occurred without substantial outside aid to the counterrevolutionary forces. These forces not only failed to gain a foothold among the population at large, but on the contrary produced a reaction of rejection that increasingly cemented the cohesion between the people of Nicaragua and their legitimate government. This reality was even recognized by the U.S. Central Intelligence Agency, in U.S. congressional hearings held during 1983.

The complaint presented to the Tribunal, and the majority of the reports and testimonies which have been submitted, demonstrate that the government of the United States and the governments which it supports in the region (primarily Honduras and, to a lesser degree, Costa Rica) are responsible for this substantial foreign aid, and for the development of the strategy of aggression.

The Tribunal deems that these grievances are well founded.

American Policy in Latin America

As early as May 1980, the Santa Fe Committee drafted a report for the Republican Party entitled "A New Inter-American Policy for the Eighties." This report outlined the major directions of U.S. policy toward the Latin American continent.

The concepts central to this policy are derived from the national security doctrine: War is inherent to human experience and reflects ideological/political rivalries. The defense of the security of the continent against an alleged communist menace becomes the principal task. In this context, Nicaragua occupies a decisive place. The Sandinista triumph in Nicaragua is regarded in such circles as a manifestation of the communist menace because, in the words of the Santa Fe Report: "The Nicaraguan base on the American continent will now facilitate a repeat of the new Nicaraguan revolutionary model."

From this perspective, the defense of human rights is subordinated to ideological identity. What is alone valued is the capitalist model and its ideological attainment of formal political liberty. This view of human rights is tied to a conception of democracy as pure process, without regard to the actual situation of mankind.

The evolution of U.S. policy toward Central America reveals that the Reagan administration has acted in general accordance with the ideas set forth in the Santa Fe Document, whether as a matter of deliberate plan or by parallel determination of national policy.

In his July 21, 1983 press conference, President Reagan declared that it would be extremely difficult to ensure stability in Central America as long as the present government of Nicaragua remains in power (*New York Times*, July 22, 1983). The Tribunal has knowledge of similar statements that could be multiplied indefinitely. The same types of positions have been taken by the so-called bipartisan Commission on Central America named by the Reagan administration. The report of this Commission, headed by Henry Kissinger, contended that "the consolidation of a Marxist-Leninist regime in Managua" constitutes "a permanent security threat" (*New York Times*, Jan. 1, 1984). The same viewpoint is found in the analyses put forth by powerful brain trusts with close connections to the Reagan administration. For example, the 1983 report of the Rand Corporation, "U.S. Policy for Central America," affirms the view that the security of the United States of America depends essentially on having the capacity to prevent the consolidation of any hostile regime in the Caribbean Basin and in Central America.

Organization and Support for the Counterrevolution

These U.S. declarations have been accompanied by actions which involve actual support for the counterrevolution.

Since March 9, 1981, the Reagan government has authorized secret military actions against the government of Nicaragua while at the same time terminating all aid to that country. In fact, the U.S. government launched an economic and diplomatic war against Nicaragua. In the spring of 1981, counterrevolutionary elements that had taken refuge in Florida and Honduras began to receive military training from personnel associated with U.S. Special Forces (*New York Times*, Apr. 5, 1981). On December 1, 1981, Reagan signed a plan for secret actions against Nicaragua articulated in 10 points, as elaborated by the National Security Council of the United States, and aimed at creating a military force of 500 men, together with granting $19 million in financial aid to carry out paramilitary operations against Nicaragua.

These developments were confirmed by the former ambassador to El Salvador, Robert White, and have never been denied. During the summer of 1982, the U.S. Congress learned that counterrevolutionary forces directed by the CIA had increased to 1,000 persons. In December of the same year, the CIA communicated to the U.S. Congress that these same forces had grown to 4,000 men. The CIA sought to unite these rather distinct counterrevolutionary bands into a single opposition force dedicated to the overthrow of the government in Managua. It was during this same period that counterrevolutionary forces began to launch almost daily incursions into Nicaraguan territory from Honduras. Under the aegis of U.S. Ambassador John Negroponte, a notorious expert in counter-insurrection, Honduras had been transformed into a permanent base of secret operations. These developments were foreseen in the plan of December 1, 1981 (White, Richard Allen, *The Morass: United States Intervention in Central America*. New York: Harper and Row Publishers, 1984, p. 60). It appeared ever clearer, even to American public opinion, that the anti-Sandinista efforts of the United States were not aimed at interrupting an arms flow from Nicaragua to El Salvador, the existence of which had never even been demonstrated to any degree (*Newsweek*, Nov. 8, 1982).

The reaction of the American public to these interventionary policies finally influenced the U.S. Congress, especially in view of overwhelming evidence of the facts, to adopt the Boland-Zablocki Amendment in December 1982. This amendment forbids the U.S. government to give aid of any kind to paramilitary groups that seek the overthrow of the Nicaraguan government or that seek to provoke war between Nicaragua and Honduras.

These efforts on the part of the U.S. Congress represent to the Tribunal a considerable demonstration of the Reagan government's involvement on behalf of the counterrevolutionary forces. There is also evident a certain weakness on the part of the Congress (the House of Representatives being obligated, among other things, to make deals with the Senate, which has a Republican majority); the Congress has not acted effectively enough to end the involvement of the Reagan government in the counterrevolutionary enterprise. In May 1983, the counterrevolutionary forces opened another front of operations against Nicaragua, mounted from within Costa Rica. These forces were armed with 500 weapons and $100,000 furnished by the CIA (White, 64). And on May 4, 1983, President Reagan acknowledged publicly that the U.S. gave direct aid to the counterrevolution.

Furthermore, thanks to this aid, the counterrevolutionary forces expanded to 10,000 fighters during this same year. The CIA provided important military equipment to the counterrevolutionary effort: for instance, the two planes that bombed the international airport in Managua on September 8, 1983 had been directly furnished by the CIA (White, 65). One has reason to believe that other acts of aggression, such as the bombing and mining of Nicaraguan ports, were arranged and partly executed by the CIA. During the month of July 1983, representatives of the U.S. administration admitted to the press that the CIA was in the process of making detailed maps of the three ports of Nicaragua, including Corinto (*San Francisco Chronicle*, July 17, 1983). Several months after the attack on the fuel depot at Corinto, it was admitted publicly in the press that the CIA had directed the operation by using specially trained commandos (*New York Times*, Apr. 18, 1984).

The culmination of all these activities was the mining of the ports of Nicaragua at the beginning of 1984, an undertaking in preparation since 1983. The operation was directly supervised by CIA agents stationed on a boat at the edge of the territorial waters of Nicaragua. This operation caused severe damage to Nicaraguan, Dutch, Panamanian, Liberian, Japanese, and Soviet ships (and obviously risked a direct confrontation with the Soviet Union). The Reagan government did not hide its responsibility for the operation, which it defended by farfetched reasoning as an act of "self-defense" for El Salvador and its allies in accordance with international law (*New York Times*, Apr. 9, 1984).

The facts recounted above convince the Tribunal that the mining operation was the outcome of a wider policy of aggression conceived and implemented over a long period of time on both an ideological and an operational level. This opinion is also shared by some of the elected representatives of the American people: Senator Patrick Leahy declared, "Any senator who thinks that the mining operation is somehow unique and different in kind from all the other military activity undertaken as part of the covert action program hasn't learned what is going on down there. Mining the harbors of Nicaragua is a logical consequence of a program aimed at conducting an undeclared secret war by proxy against a sovereign nation with whom we maintain full diplomatic relations" (*Washington Post National Weekly*, Apr. 30, 1984).

In addition, financial aid to the counterrevolutionaries, which was $19 million in 1982, reached $54 million in 1983 and may have increased since. This sum, moreover, includes only official aid, for in reality the total aid at this point surpasses $100 million every year. It is also necessary to consider that, as a result of growing opposition in the U.S. Congress, the Reagan government has found a new means of getting aid to the counterrevolution: by utilizing private organizations that support the mercenary troops, as well as by encouraging third governments, such as Israel, to provide further military aid to the contras.

On September 1, 1984, the military forces of the Sandinista government shot down a helicopter used by the counterrevolutionaries for an attack originating from across the Honduran border. The remains of two U.S. citizens were identified among the crew; it was revealed that they were members of a group called "Civilian Military Assistance" (CMA). Five different U.S. governmental institutions (including the National Security Council, the Justice Department, and the CIA) acknowledged that they knew of the existence of this organization, which had been active for a year in aggressions against Nicaragua. Some official representatives of the government in Washington went even further in acknowledging that the mercenaries had been recruited so as to circumvent the decision of Congress (*New York Times*, Sept. 10, 1984). It is a fact that the Justice Department of the United States has never undertaken to investigate the CMA, despite the possible violations of U.S. neutrality legislation that forbids such activities within U.S. territory.

The Vassalization of Honduras and Costa Rica

The Sandinista revolution has radically modified power relationships in Central America. The United States lost its best ally in the region; confronted with this fact, the United States has looked for a new, primary ally.

Honduras has several characteristics which made it well suited to play this role: 1) its geographic location; 2) its relative political stability; 3) the weak economic power of the local bourgeoisie; 4) a military apparatus both docile and ready to collaborate on projects with the United States.

From 1979 to the present, the North American presence in Honduras has continued to grow; the militarization of the country is undoubtedly the most visible symptom. In four years, from 1980 to 1984, the increase in military aid multiplied by 10; it has now reached the level of over $40 million per year. The joint military maneuvers (United States/Honduras) go on and on and are ever-expanding; in the first six months of 1984, one can count only 41 days without joint military exercises. The presence of North American advisers and servicemen in Honduras is permanent; by the end of 1983 there were more than 5,000. The amount of military construction by the United States in Honduras increased in the fiscal years of 1982, 1983, and 1984, and several proposals already known to exist for 1985 come to more than $85 million.

Several of these construction projects were carried out without the knowledge of the Honduran Parliament or in violation of Honduran laws. The training center at Puerto Castilla, for example, is known to have been imposed by the United States. This shows, in an obvious manner, the subordination of Honduran sovereign rights and national interests to U.S. interventionary diplomacy in the region.

The situation with Costa Rica is different, its militarization being of a lesser degree and more recent. The growth in the militarization of this country has nevertheless been noted by numerous observers. This process began in January 1982, the period in which Israel and Costa Rica signed a military cooperation agreement. This agreement calls into question the traditional neutrality of Costa Rica and reinforces the alignment of this country with U.S. policy. Increasingly numerous aggressions by counterrevolutionary elements from Costa Rican territory suggest a growing involvement on Costa Rica's part. Greatly in debt, Costa Rica is at the mercy of the international entities that supply it with credit, the most important of these being controlled by the United States (IMF, IDB, IBRD).

Pressure on Allies

The government of the United States has likewise exercised constant pressures on its allies to terminate their military aid to Nicaragua (as in the case of France), their political support, and their economic cooperation. This interventionary effort is dramatically manifested in a letter from Secretary of State George Shultz to the Ministers of Foreign Affairs of the 10 countries of the European Economic Community, and of Spain and Portugal, on the occasion of their meeting in San José, Costa Rica, in September 1984.

Taken together, these facts show clearly that the Chief Executive of the United States intends to destabilize the Nicaraguan regime by the combined use of military, political, and economic coercion.

2) Economic Pressures

A sufficient number of factors indicate that the Reagan administration has currently undertaken the destabilization of Nicaragua's economy. These coercive efforts tend to:

— cause a substantial reduction in Nicaragua's access to international commerce in general and prevent the importing of goods to satisfy the fundamental needs of the country, most notably food products and materials essential to the reconstruction of the economy;

— cause international financial institutions, including the International Monetary Fund and the World Bank, to refuse to extend credit to Nicaragua;

— support and even instigate actions aimed at undermining the reconstruction of the Nicaraguan economy, such as the blockading of the maritime ports, giving aid to the armed invasion forces originating from Honduras and Costa Rica, and training these forces.

Comparable acts of hostility would not cause great damage to an economy as strong and resilient as that of the United States. They have catastrophic effects on a country as small as Nicaragua, already having an uphill battle to repair the damage done by the Somoza dictatorship, the long civil war, and a series of natural disasters, and to meet the fundamental needs of the Nicaraguan people, long poor and deprived.

Since the day — July 19, 1979 — when the present government of Nicaragua was brought to power, remarkable economic progress has been made. The former Somoza government left behind a foreign debt of over $1.6 billion, a very high figure for an economy of such restricted dimensions; the Nicaraguan Treasury did not have more than $3.5 million, about enough to last three days, when the Sandinistas took over. However, thanks to production being reorganized in fundamental ways, principally resulting from the agrarian reform, the country was able to revive its economy during the first three years of the Sandinista government.

Before July 1979, approximately 55% of the arable land of Nicaragua was owned or controlled by some 2,000 landowners holding vast or medium-sized properties, while more than 120,000 peasants had to survive on less than 3% of the arable land. At the end of 1983, the state of Nicaragua owned 23% of the land, small landowners and cooperatives owned 20%, and the medium-sized farmers owned 44%. In 1980, economic growth reached 10% per annum; in 1981 it was 8.7%, but in 1982 it fell by 1.4%. Fortunately, thanks to measures designed to thwart the disastrous effects of hostile U.S. policies, growth resumed in 1983 and reached 4.5%. It should be noted that a global recession and partial recovery had some influence on Nicaragua's growth performance during that year.

However, since the middle of 1984, the Nicaraguan economy has again experienced great difficulties, for the following reasons:

In the first place, the world economic recession has not spared the Nicaraguan economy. It is true that Nicaragua's agricultural production has increased, thanks to the agrarian reform, as has the production of manufactured goods, in certain cases by an average of 40%. But the world prices for the basic commodities exported by Nicaragua, such as cotton, coffee, sugar, and meat, as well as the prices of manufactured products, fell below the costs of production.

In the second place, the hostile economic policies of the Reagan government have virtually deprived Nicaragua of any access to the U.S. market; for example, the U.S. government reduced by some 90% the amount of sugar Nicaragua could export to the United States. Customs barriers to be imposed on Nicaragua are now being prepared.

In the third place, the urgent need for the Nicaraguan people to defend their country against military interventions, supported by the United States and originating from Honduras, Costa Rica, and El Salvador, has placed a heavy financial burden on the Nicaraguan economy. It has also caused a loss of manpower necessary for economic reconstruction. Twenty-five percent of the national budget has had to be transferred to national defense expenses (arms purchases, maintenance of the army, etc.).

In the fourth place, as a result of the gigantic debt inherited from Somoza, the present government was not in a position to prevent the Nicaraguan economy from being transformed into what is called "an international debt economy."

Like so many other Third World economies, the Nicaraguan economy will temporarily be looking for new foreign loans in order to meet obligations related to servicing its debt. Nicaragua's foreign debt had reached approximately $3.6 billion by the end of 1983. Since the boycott imposed by the Reagan government on foreign loans to Nicaragua, it has become extremely difficult for the government of this country to deal adequately with its foreign debt, either for purposes of financing imports or gaining access to world markets. Currently Nicaragua must devote 70% of its exports to servicing the foreign debt. The burden of this debt has catastrophic consequences for an economy as small as that of Nicaragua.

We must also note that the accusation that the Nicaraguan economy is tied to the economies of the socialist countries is entirely false. For example, regarding the foreign debt, Nicaragua received $600 million in foreign loans in 1983. Only 18% of this came from socialist countries; the rest was received from other Latin American countries, Western European countries, and transnational banks.

Between 1979 and the beginning of 1983, the present government of Nicaragua received a total of $1.88 billion in loans and gifts. Of this, only 21.4% came from socialist countries (of which one-quarter was provided by Cuba), 22.4% came from other Latin American countries, and 7.5% (the majority in the form of gifts) came from Western Europe. The rest of the cash flow came from international monetary institutions, including the IMF and the World Bank, transnational banks, and even financial institutions in the United States during the Carter administration. In 1982, only 5% of Nicaragua's overall international trade was with socialist countries.

Because of Washington's refusal to sell Nicaragua any arms, Nicaragua had no choice other than to buy small quantities of arms from Eastern European countries as well as from Italy and Libya. Before the Reagan government came to power, Nicaragua purchased small quantities of arms (worth approximately $40 million) in France. The Reagan government, however, succeeded in persuading the Mitterrand government to stop selling arms to Nicaragua. An appreciable number of Western European countries continued to provide aid to Nicaragua for its economic development despite Reagan attempts at intimidation.

Based on these elements of proof, the Tribunal has come to the conclusion that the economic policies of the Reagan administration toward Nicaragua have caused great damage to its economy. However, it is the military aggression, supported both financially and materially by the United States, that does Nicaragua the greatest economic and social damage. The ranching and agricultural sectors, so important to Nicaragua because they provide employment for almost 45% of the work force and represent 60% of the total foreign exchange generated by the export sector, were particularly damaged. The peasant population was hit very hard: 478 workers killed by counterrevolutionary attacks and 581 workers detained. 120,672 people had to be moved from combat zones and relocated elsewhere; it was also necessary to aid them in reconstructing their lives on a viable basis. The cost of this operation reached more than 550 million córdobas. Accumulated losses in these sectors (agriculture and ranching) reached 176 million córdobas in the form of damage to the infrastructure and mechanical equipment, as well as 196 million córdobas in losses from damaged crops. A minimum estimate of other damage to these sectors is 644 million córdobas.

The loss of earnings and the loss of production in the public sector for the rest of the economy has been estimated, for 1983, at 648 million córdobas. Damage was particularly significant in the forestry, fishing, energy, transportation, and construction industries. These figures are for the most part incomplete and they constitute the most conservative estimate of the damages. They do not take into consideration the tragic suffering of the people nor the loss of human lives, effects that it is impossible to express as statistics, nor the destruction of hospitals, schools, and therefore the services they perform.

3) The Ideological War

Far from considering that its intervention in Central America, and particularly in Nicaragua, is an exercise in violence, the American government insists that it is an act of solidarity with the people and a legitimate defense of collective interests. To justify its intervention, it disseminates worldwide an image of the Sandinista state as a military, political, and ideological threat, an image that calls into question the legitimacy of that state. Nicaragua is therefore not the victim of aggression but the aggressor.

The accusations used in creating this image are numerous. But the most fundamental is that of being "Marxist-Leninist."

Marxist-Leninist: By this reasoning, the Sandinista Front is charged with betraying the original democratic and pluralistic inspiration of the Nicaraguan revolution. It is charged with installing a totalitarian regime in Managua by taking over all the organs of the state and by excluding from power the other forces which had participated in the overthrow of the Somoza dictatorship. It is charged with having suppressed all liberties, and with the violation of human rights; it is also accused of persecuting, indeed exterminating, the indigenous minorities.

Marxist-Leninist: By this reasoning, the Sandinista Front is alleged, despite certain appearances, to be profoundly anti-Christian. The proof would be, for example, the conflict with the church hierarchy, the expulsion of foreign priests, and the lack of respect toward the Pope during his visit to the country. The Christians involved in the revolution are said to be manipulated by the Sandinista Front; the influence of its ideology has corrupted their faith and broken their loyalty to the real Church, it is said.

On the geopolitical plane, the Sandinista Front, being Marxist-Leninist, is alleged to have submitted to the hegemony of Moscow. Therefore it is said to represent a new frontier for international communism in the Central American region. Its tendency to export revolution is said to be flagrantly manifested by its constant military support to the El Salvadoran guerrillas.

The United States developed this campaign of accusations against Nicaragua thanks to the enormous means at its disposal, notably its diplomatic network and ideological apparatus. The United States exerts great control over the spread of information. The new Institute for Religion and Democracy, specializing in ideological warfare on the religious level, was accorded a special significance in this campaign. The accusations and arguments coincide, moreover, with positions taken by certain sectors of the Nicaraguan opposition, particularly the "Coordinadora Democrática," whose principal organ is the newspaper *La Prensa.*

Furthermore, broad sectors of the Catholic hierarchy, both Nicaraguan and international, contribute significantly to the campaign, as do the Evangelical churches and several Protestant sects active in Nicaragua. The accusations and arguments of these religious groupings coincide in a striking manner with those of the North American ideological apparatus.

On the various grounds we have mentioned, the Sandinista state has no legitimacy, according to the U.S. administration. The Sandinista power to govern is challenged. The armed opposition to the Sandinista government is therefore legitimated; on the other hand, the effort to provide an armed defense of the revolution is correspondingly de-legitimated. In this light, the intervention of the United States in Nicaragua appears as a crusade for the defense of democracy, the oppressed opposition, the indigenous minorities, the Church, and Western Christian civilization.

However, this image of the Nicaraguan revolution is based much more upon the ideology attributed to the Sandinista Front than its actual character. The disparity between the seriousness of the accusations and the inconsistency of the proof is notable. The ideological argument is not based on an appreciation of the facts, but substitutes itself for the facts.

Furthermore, the conception of Marxism-Leninism attributed to the Sandinista Front has nothing to do with the historical goals and theoretical perspectives that have inspired and continue to inspire the Sandinista Popular Revolution. These theoretical perspectives propose in essence to clarify the process of popular liberation by developing, in an original and anti-dogmatic manner, the contributions of the Sandinista, Marxist, and Christian traditions.

In addition, no convincing justification has been provided for placing in doubt the autonomy and Christian authenticity of the priests, religious, and lay people taking part in the revolution as a direct expression of their faith. The testimony of witnesses heard by the Tribunal, and of persons who have communicated with it, leads to this conclusion.

Even though it is a fabrication, the "Marxist-Leninist" image of the Sandinista Popular Revolution performs a precise function: to hide the economic and political contradictions by transforming them into ideological and religious contradictions; to overshadow, on the geopolitical level, the contradictions between North and South, between the forces of oppression and the oppressed, and to artificially place in a central position the contradiction between East and West; that is, between the Christian capitalist West and the communist world, labeled "Marxist-Leninist" and "atheist."

That is why Nicaragua is such a prime target for the United States. The national security doctrine as applied to Nicaragua coincides perfectly with U.S. policy as applied everywhere else on the continent and particularly in the Southern cone. To recognize the validity of this doctrine would mean for the oppressed peoples to renounce definitively their dreams of freedom.

For the United States, the ideological campaign against Nicaragua is part of its battle for worldwide hegemony. A hegemony which is called into question by the very attempt of the Nicaraguan people to break out of the logic of blocs, and to earn the right to control their own destiny; to break with the culture of domination and fatalism and to establish a culture of liberation.

In repressing the aspirations of the Nicaraguan people and other oppressed peoples, the United States contradicts the ideals of its own revolution, the revolution that for more than two centuries has inspired oppressed peoples to fight for their own right to life and liberty.

III. HISTORICAL SOURCES OF U.S. INTERVENTIONS

We must recall that U.S. interest in Central America and most particularly in Nicaragua has been continuous since the second quarter of the 19th century. The origin of that interest, like its various economic and political manifestations, is tied to the development of the capitalist system in the United States itself. U.S. leaders did not wait until either the Russian revolution of October 1917 or the Sandinista revolution of 1979 to consider this region as their zone of influence.

We can distinguish three periods in the history of U.S. interference in Nicaragua:

1. 1825-1860 (Approximately)

During the first period, U.S. interest was focused on obtaining a territorial concession that would permit the construction of a waterway for navigation between the Atlantic and Pacific Oceans. It was a matter of inflicting a partial loss of sovereignty upon Nicaragua so as to secure profits for private North American economic interests.

The U.S. government intervened on two levels. First, it intervened on the international level and in a direct manner, in response to the reaction of Great Britain, which sought to guard its supremacy on the seas (an accord was signed, the Clayton-Bulwer Treaty of 1850). Inside Nicaragua, it intervened in an indirect manner: by lending support to one or another faction of the bourgeoisie (the conservatives of Granada, the liberals of León), and then to an American national (William Walker) who came to set up a local dictatorship and was recognized officially by the United States in 1856.

2. The Second Period 1860-1932

The second period was one of the development in Nicaragua itself, especially in the Atlantic Coast regions, of American enterprises that exploited natural resources (rare woods, construction lumber, minerals) and monoculture enterprises that produced tropical products (sugar cane and bananas) in self-governing enclaves. They had their own currency and, except for the mines, they functioned principally through the creation of a totally dependent labor force and through the purchase by each enterprise of the products of small producers who received payment in currency that could be used only to buy consumer goods imported by the enterprise itself.

In addition, in the Pacific region, the development of the coffee economy led to a new system of agrarian production (the expulsion of peasants from any land suitable for coffee plantations, the formation of a rural proletariat deprived of its own land). This system was promulgated by the liberal bourgeoisie, which took political power (Zelaya); out of nationalism, it defended the interests of the Nicaraguan and Central American capitalists against the overseas interests of the United States. This nationalist policy was also a reaction against the American practice and rationale of imperial power, which justified not only the Spanish-American War but also military intervention in Nicaragua.

From the first decade of the 20th century, the U.S. State Department functioned like a bank that ensured financial support to docile governments in the Caribbean and Central America. The more independent governments in the region had to confront the Marines and the activities of the secret services that protected American mining enterprises and banana plantations. The political power of the United States was therefore at the service of private North American economic interests. The U.S. government carried out this function by developing a two-sided strategy: granting privileges to an array of local politicians to assure their collaboration, on the one hand, and intimidation by the Marines or the activities of the secret police and repressive forces on the other. Implementing this strategy between 1926 and 1933 led American troops to occupy several regions of Nicaragua for prolonged periods.

It was against this control and this military presence that General Augusto Sandino organized his long nationalist struggle that spread across the entire country (1927-1933). This armed challenge resulted in the retreat of American troops, but also led to the assassination of Sandino, who has remained the symbol of anti-imperialist struggle for the Nicaraguan people.

3. The Third Period 1932-1979

The third period is marked by the development in the political arena of a dictatorial system upheld by the ideology of national security (the Somocista period 1937-1979). This regime, put in place by the Americans, received their constant support, whether at the level of organizing and equipping the armed forces (the National Guard), or at the level of public finance (extension of the debt). This American presence "via interposed persons" fulfilled a double function.

First, it assured the U.S. government of the support necessary to pursue its foreign policy goals vis-a-vis the Axis powers (end of the 1930s and beginning of the 1940s), and then the communist bloc (1945 to the present).

In the second place, these dictatorships at the service of the United States also assured the multinational enterprises of a servile and cheap labor force for the production of consumer goods and even certain manufactured products.

It was American imperialism, and the Nicaraguan dictatorship that it sponsored, which gave rise to the movement catalyzed by the FSLN.

Since the revolution of 1979, the new regime has introduced Nicaraguan society to a process of rupture with the capitalist system. In terms of foreign policy, Nicaragua was integrated into the group of non-aligned countries. These events unfolded while in El Salvador, Guatemala and, to a lesser degree, Honduras, armed struggle took place. Rather than recognize the real causes of these movements, the American administration has argued for the need to set up a front against Soviet penetration of the hemisphere that it assumes the right to control (see confirmation of this in the Report of the Kissinger Commission, January 1984, Chapter 4). This is a new phase of U.S. geopolitics.

From that perspective, the Nicaraguan revolution constituted a breach in the line of defense in the Caribbean and Central America, not only by the transformations it creates in the relationship of forces within the region, but also because Nicaragua is evolving a new societal model that could appeal to the entire continent. The Sandinista experience is a symbol of hope, showing that change is possible.

Translated into diplomatic practice, the American ideology is expressed in indirect military intervention and direct action in the economic and political spheres.

IV. NICARAGUA IN SEARCH OF ITS IDENTITY

Despite innumerable obstacles created by the external aggression, Nicaragua has used the last five years beneficially, to reconstruct the state and the society in an original manner and to give men, women, and children new reasons to live. Even in these early stages, this process represents a promise and a hope to all the peoples of the world.

Even if the state has not yet attained its complete, formal legitimacy, the power structures have been profoundly transformed so as to give voice to the people and serve the real interests of the disinherited. Unlike most countries on the continent, Nicaragua is led not by individuals but by collectives (for example, the Government Junta, the Council of State). Power is therefore largely shared and is no longer the property of a few privileged groups or individuals.

The regime aims to be not only pluralist domestically but equally open to foreign countries; this is the reason for Nicaragua's solidarity with Third World countries, which it has demonstrated by participating in the "non-aligned" group and playing an active role there. It participates fully in the efforts of the Latin American countries to make the continent a nuclear-free zone, adhering to the Treaty of Tlatelolco.

At the same time, Nicaraguan society today is the locus of intense cultural and social activity (a literacy campaign reducing the illiteracy rate from 50% to 12%, a permanent program of adult education, health campaigns with massive vaccinations which most notably eliminated polio, the development of cooperatives in the agricultural sector, agrarian reform with distributions of land to the poorest farmers, the humanization of the criminal justice and prison system.

These reforms have been accompanied by a program for the construction of primary and secondary schools in the rural areas, with the participation of voluntary teachers. Many Nicaraguans have left their studies voluntarily to bring their energy and labor to the cotton and coffee harvests.

On the cultural level, the creation of libraries and the setting up of book vans, and the widespread development of workshops in poetry, dance, and theater began producing many positive results.

This all-encompassing cultural process profoundly changes the life of the people and people's relations with each another. The solidarity of the neighborhoods, and participation in the organization and the defense of daily life, are also manifested at the religious level. Popular religion, rather than being a source of alienation and the pretext for all sorts of excesses, is transformed into a growing awareness that real religious faith is a powerful force for the happiness and freedom of all.

With respect to the elections on November 4, 1984, 1,560,000 Nicaraguans over the age of 16, or 93.7% of the population eligible to vote, have registered. Thus it has been established that the people are mature enough to take political responsibility and freely conduct their own history. The dictatorship of the past is dead.

It is clear that the construction of a new society that was begun after the revolution of July 19, 1979 included some political errors and individual excesses. This was the case especially in the Atlantic Coast region, in relation to the indigenous minorities, who were victims of counterrevolutionary propaganda and of persons manipulated to oppose the Sandinistas. In this region, the situation of war, the security measures that war demands, and notably the resulting displacement of these populations along the Northern border considerably slowed down the correction of errors and the establishment of trusting, reciprocal relations. Nevertheless, and prominently since the amnesty measures of December 1, 1983, peaceful solutions and genuine reassurances have been pursued with sincerity and effectiveness.

V. PEACE EFFORTS

The government of Nicaragua, faced with the current war and facts that show the participation in it of Honduras and the United States, has from the beginning demonstrated a clear desire to negotiate a peaceful settlement. Nicaragua has acted in accord with the goals of the United Nations Charter, Article 1 (1), and has invoked the mechanisms of peaceful settlement contained in Article 33 of the Charter. It has even followed along the path of the courts of law, seeking validation in a judicial setting (request addressed by Nicaragua to the International Court of Justice on the April 9, 1984).

Specifically, the most significant expressions of Nicaragua's desire for peace include the following:

1. Contacts and Proposals for Direct Negotiations With the Government of the United States:

These began in Managua on August 12, 1981, with the meeting between Thomas O. Enders (Assistant Secretary of State) and Daniel Ortega Saavedra (Coordinator of the Government Junta of National Reconstruction). These were followed in April 1982 by discussions with Anthony C. Quainton, U.S. Ambassador to Nicaragua. They were taken up again in June 1983 with Special U.S. Ambassador to Central America Richard Stone and extended into 1984, at Manzanillo (Mexico), through discussions with Nicaraguan Deputy Foreign Minister Hugo Tinoco and Ambassador-at-Large Harry Shlaudeman.

2. Contacts and Proposals for Direct Negotiations With Honduras:

These have been conducted at the highest level, beginning with the 1981 visit of Daniel Ortega to Tegucigalpa, and in 1982, at the level of the Chiefs of Staff (May 2) and the Ministers of Foreign Affairs (October 8).

3. Favorable Responses to Initiatives of the Contadora Group:

Nicaragua's responsiveness has been shown in a very specific manner by its endorsement of the Document of Objectives relating to peace in the region, through its proposal for implementing those objectives entitled "Legal Bases to Guarantee the Peace and International Security of the States of Central America" (October 17, 1983). This proposal contains the following elements:

a. A draft treaty to guarantee mutual respect, peace, and security between the Republic of Nicaragua and the United States.

b. A draft treaty of peace, friendship, and cooperation between the Republics of Honduras and Nicaragua.

c. A draft accord concerning El Salvador, to contribute to a peaceful solution of the armed conflict within the Republic of El Salvador.

d. A draft treaty between the Central American republics, on the maintenance of peace and security and relations of friendship and cooperation between the republics of Central America. (This proposal was broadened on November 30, 1983 by a proposal concerning military questions, a policy declaration and an agreement aimed at promoting economic and social development in Central America.)

4. The Decision, in September 1984, to Sign the Contadora Act:

This meant that Nicaragua accepted the multilateral framework for peace (replacing the bilateral treaties indicated above) as proposed by the Contadora Group. It implies, for the five Central American countries, the beginning of implementation of the means to achieve a regional detente; commitments with a view to achieving national reconciliation in the areas of human rights, electoral process, etc.; measures to stop the flow of arms and to begin negotiations on arms control; the elimination of foreign bases and military schools on national territory; the progressive withdrawal of foreign military advisers; the elimination of extra- and intra-regional arms trade destined for opposition persons or groups that aim to overthrow governments, and the banning of support for these forces. In addition, important measures were outlined in the Contadora Act: the creation of a multilateral mechanism designed to channel and control economic and social aid and cooperation in the five Central American countries, and the creation of an impartial international commission for the verification and implementation of the agreements that are accepted.

In the face of the attitude of Nicaragua, which has shown itself to be favorable to negotiations, it should be pointed out that:

1. The demands of the United States for cessation of the arms traffic from Nicaragua to El Salvador — a traffic which has never been proven to exist — have created an impasse, making it impossible to reach any bilateral accord between Nicaragua and the United States.

2. Honduras has repeatedly refused to enter bilateral negotiations with Nicaragua. Meetings parallel to the Contadora gatherings have been organized among the Central American states, excluding Nicaragua. (Among these are the famous "Forum for Peace and Democracy" of October 1982, initiated by the United States, and the meeting in Tegucigalpa in 1984 of the Ministers of Foreign Affairs of the Contadora Group, El Salvador, Honduras, and Costa Rica; all such meetings are inconsistent with the actions proposed by the Contadora group itself.)

3. Although there were six meetings of the five Central American states under the aegis of the Contadora Group, for the purpose of guaranteeing respect for mutual interests, Nicaragua was the only one of the Central American countries that gave an affirmative response to the document setting forth the overall objectives.

4. The United States has not accepted the Contadora Act, and has exerted overwhelming influence on the other Central American countries, assuring their refusal to sign.

During the course of these developments, there has been no serious plan put forward on the part of the United States or its Central American allies to submit the conflict to a process of peaceful solution. Given the involvement of the United States and Honduras in the war against Nicaragua, it can be stated that these states failed to uphold the international obligation to seek peaceful settlement as it is formulated in Article 33 of the United Nations Charter.

Why this attitude? It must be pointed out that the Contadora peace efforts and the previous proposals by Nicaragua for negotiations have as their primary objectives peace in the region, the elimination of foreign military aid of any kind, and the conveyance of economic and social aid through multinational channels. These peace efforts represent a departure from United States policy toward Central America, a policy which, according to the documents submitted to the Tribunal, insists upon:

1. The fundamental principle of the hegemony of the United States in this zone, regarded as a strategic area for the security of the United States;

2. Interpreting and treating the Central American conflict as an expression of East-West tension;

3. The control of the United States over economic and social aid to the zone (bilateral aid subordinated to political conditions) in a manner that excludes Nicaragua.

The Contadora peace proposal overcomes and prohibits the isolation of Nicaragua — now considered by the United States as a country aligned with the East — and recognizes the reality that Nicaragua has undergone a national and non-aligned revolution.

VI. CONSIDERATIONS OF THE LAW

Nicaragua's Accusation

The government of Nicaragua accuses the United States of repeated violations of its sovereign rights. The most serious accusation concerns the international crime of aggression, of which the United States is guilty by virtue of multiple illegal interventions with the goal of depriving Nicaragua of its right to self-determination.

The crime of aggression has been perpetrated by various types of acts, all of which violate the rights of Nicaragua and which, moreover, even imply certain violations of the laws of war or incite war.

This illegal conduct is aggravated by the persistent refusal of the government of the United States to abide by the various procedures for the peaceful settlement of differences, as required by the rights of peoples (cf. Algiers Declaration), notwithstanding the constant efforts of the Nicaraguan government to negotiate a peaceful solution.

Specifically, Nicaragua contends that the United States has organized, trained, and armed counterrevolutionary forces established in Honduran territory, whose main objective is to overthrow the legitimate Sandinista government. Nicaragua contends that this entire policy violates rules forbidding the recourse to force and intervention in the internal affairs of other nations, set forth most notably in Article 2 (4) of the Charter of the United Nations, in Articles 18 and 20 of the Charter of the Organization of American States, and Article I of the Havana Convention of February 20, 1928 on the rights and duties of states in the event of civil war.

These various violations, orchestrated by the Central Intelligence Agency (CIA) on behalf of the U.S. government, have caused suffering and death for the Nicaraguan people and led to numerous illegal incursions into their territory, with the aim of terrorizing the civilian population, and in a time of great economic shortages have abusively deprived them of food resources.

In particular, Nicaragua accuses the government of the United States of having violated in the most serious manner its most basic rights as a sovereign nation by mining its ports, which caused considerable damage to its port installations as well as to several ships operating under foreign flags. These mining operations, which are acts of war, constitute an aggression on the part of a country which is officially at peace with Nicaragua and which still maintains diplomatic relations with it.

Nicaragua also accuses the United States of threatening a major invasion of its territory, a threat made credible by U.S. engagement in numerous air, sea, and land maneuvers on the basis of planned and disclosed strategic options. Such threats and plans constitute an aggression that makes a mockery of the sovereign rights of Nicaragua. The menace of this threatened invasion compels the Nicaraguan government to devote most of its already scarce resources to defense against these illegal activities, resources desperately required to meet the needs of its people.

Nicaragua contends that these illegal practices constitute criminal behavior, and entail personal accountability on the part of the Chief Executive of the United States and other policymakers in the sense of this term as defined by the Nuremberg Tribunal.

The Defense of the United States

In substance, the United States contends that it is acting in legitimate self-defense, according to the rights of peoples, and accuses Nicaragua of massive arms shipments to the Salvadoran rebels. This export of the Sandinista revolution constitutes, according to the United States, intervention in the internal affairs of El Salvador.

In this context, the United States claims that the mining of the ports of Nicaragua and the support given to the counterrevolutionary forces constitute an expression of the right of legitimate collective defense. Toward this end, the U.S. government relies on a broad and self-serving interpretation of Article 51 of the Charter of the United Nations, which confers the right of self-defense upon all states.

The United States accuses Nicaragua of supporting the rebel forces of El Salvador; and contends that such assistance constitutes an aggression according to the terms of Article 39 of the Charter and of the resolution on the definition of aggression adopted by the General Assembly of the United Nations in 1974.

The United States claims that its actions are a reasonable and appropriate effort to stop the flow of arms to El Salvador, with no intention of overthrowing the Sandinista government. It contends that it is no longer responsible for the conduct of the "contras" in their internal opposition to the Sandinista government.

The United States declares, finally, that Nicaragua has not fulfilled OAS norms regarding human rights and democracy, and that such deficiencies are sufficient to justify the external pressures exerted on Nicaragua to encourage respect for these norms.

The Facts

After having appraised the evidence presented, the Tribunal has arrived at the following conclusions:

— The government of the United States has not proven its principal accusation, that of the support given by Nicaragua to the rebel forces of El Salvador;

— The obvious objective of the rebel forces active along the border and in the interior of Nicaraguan territory is to destabilize, and if possible to overthrow, the government in Managua;

— By principal reliance on the CIA, an organ of the U.S. government, rebel forces are essentially equipped, directed, and controlled by the United States;

— The government of the United States has blocked efforts by Nicaragua to find a peaceful resolution of its disputes with foreign governments and has not shown good faith in trying to find a negotiated solution;

— The military and paramilitary operations have caused great suffering and great damage to the Nicaraguan people;

The United States has undertaken numerous military maneuvers which threaten Nicaraguan security, for purposes of provocation and intimidation, and has made plans for a large-scale invasion directed at Nicaragua.

Decision of the Tribunal

The facts herein reviewed demonstrate that the United States on many occasions has not respected the rules protecting the rights of peoples. The constancy and the gravity of these violations testify to a systematic policy that the Tribunal repudiates for its detrimental effects on the most fundamental rights of states and the most basic demands of the international community.

a) The foundation for this conclusion rests in the first place on the testimony presented and the documents produced which show that various American practices are contrary to the rules of general international law that govern relations between states. These practices also violate obligations contained in treaties that are normally a part of domestic as well as international law. Among the most pronounced of these violations is the discriminatory reduction of the sugar import quota (a violation of the General Agreement on Tariffs and Trade, GATT). Also notable are the violation, through support given to the rebel forces, of the Havana Convention of February 20, 1928 on the rights and duties of states in the event of civil war, and the abuses of rules protecting freedom of the high seas through naval maneuvers whose main objective is to threaten the security and stability of a small, menaced state.

There are accusations of imminent invasion by U.S.-backed forces that have been submitted to the Tribunal. These are backed by evidence, and are even more serious than violations of Nicaraguan sovereign rights by way of aggression and intervention.

This is one reason why the Tribunal cannot delay its decision until the World Court has acted. The Tribunal concludes that these invasion plans must be condemned. At the same time, the Tribunal rejects the U.S. policy of systematic nonrecognition of the sovereignty and independence of Nicaragua.

b) These conclusions are based on convincing evidence submitted to the Tribunal that the United States provides massive assistance to the forces attempting to overthrow the legitimate government of Nicaragua. This military aid takes the form of equipping and training armed personnel dedicated to counterrevolution. It is reinforced by U.S. tactics aimed at achieving the economic strangulation and diplomatic isolation of Nicaragua.

The United States policies constitute the most serious violation of the rules of international law that forbid intervention in the internal affairs of others and protect the basic rights of each people and each country to set up a regime of their choice through the dynamics of national self-determination. These legal conclusions reflect also the norms of the Charter of the United Nations, especially as specified in resolutions 2131 (XX), 2625 (XXV), 2734 (XXV), and 36/103 of the General Assembly of the United Nations. Those resolutions have been adopted with the approval of the United States and their validity cannot now be contested.

In this case, the evidence presented leaves no reason to doubt the democratic achievement of the Nicaraguan revolution. The Tribunal rejects the allegations made by the United States government concerning Nicaragua's failure to live up to its democratic promises, and denies the right of any government to judge the democratic character of other governments.

Under these conditions, there is no humanitarian justification for the intervention in Nicaragua. The problems existing in Nicaragua do not justify intervention, especially as the worst of these problems have been instigated by the United States itself.

c) Independently of the illegitimate intervention that has been established, the evidence presented supports a finding of aggression by the United States against Nicaragua, a basic repudiation in this setting of the rights of peoples.

Aggression is defined in Resolution 3314 (XXIX) of the United Nations General Assembly, whose provisions have been accepted unanimously by the member states who are empowered to interpret the Charter. Given this level of authoritative agreement, this U.N. resolution is properly treated as a declaration of law.

The evidence presented to the Tribunal establishes:

— that the mining of Nicaraguan ports by agents of the United States is a "use of armed force by a State against the. . .territorial integrity of another State" in the sense of Article 3 (b) of the resolution, even if it does not constitute an illegal blockade in the sense of Article 3 (c) of that resolution;

— that the support given by the United States to the rebel forces seeking to overthrow the legal government of Nicaragua, by the manner in which it has taken place, constitutes "a substantial involvement" on the side of the forces "which carry out acts of armed force against another State" as set forth in Article 3 (g) of the resolution.

These acts, which challenge the sovereignty and political independence of Nicaragua in a manner incompatible with the Charter of the United Nations, are of "such gravity" as to establish the Nicaraguan charges of aggression beyond any reasonable doubt.

There are no "other relevant circumstances," in the sense of Article 2 of the resolution, that might be invoked to qualify, much less to refute, this conclusion.

There is no serious ground to support the claim that the armed intervention by the United States can be justified as an instance of the right of legitimate defense. It is true, as argued by the United States, that legitimate collective defense is recognized by the Charter of the United Nations and by general international law. The Tribunal determines, however, that the conditions required for this legitimate defense, which the United States claims, are not present for the following reasons:

There has been no proof of the existence of armed aggression by Nicaragua against El Salvador. The United States government alleges that arms have been shipped from and by Nicaragua and are destined for rebel forces in El Salvador. No adequate proof of these charges has been offered. Even if it is assumed that these charges were established, such actions by Nicaragua would not constitute armed aggression in the sense of Resolution 3314 (XXIX). Therefore, recourse to force on the grounds of legitimate defense is not permissible.

Further, if the Tribunal were to assume that requisite aggression by Nicaragua had been established, it would remain true that the United States would be in violation of international law as a result of its failure to entrust the dispute to the competent organs of the United Nations and to honor the Charter obligation to find a peaceful solution. The threats made as part of the U.S. policy of intervention five years after it was undertaken are a continuous violation of the legal and sacred sovereign rights of the people of Nicaragua.

The doctrine of legitimate defense cannot, except under the terms and spirit of the Charter, be allowed to substitute for the collective mechanisms of security provided within the United Nations framework, which allows states to avoid resorting to military self-help. There is no credible legal basis for a U.S. claim of self-defense against Nicaragua; on the contrary.

The Tribunal fails to note any urgency of the sort that might allow the United States to act alone. Even in such instances, a state is obliged to inform the Security Council immediately if it acts in self-defense; similarly, the United States cannot claim a right to act alone because the U.N. organs are paralyzed, especially since the United States would itself be the state primarily responsible, through the exercise of its veto, for creating this paralysis. It should be remembered that the Sandinista leadership has consistently sought to turn the conflict over to a multilateral framework for resolution.

The same legal analysis pertains to the procedures and rules contained in the OAS system. The United States has avoided recourse to the OAS before undertaking its illegal program of multiple interventions. The Tribunal concludes then that the United States has violated the rights of peoples, both by the interventionary substance of its policies and by its consistent failure to work for a peaceful solution.

Finally, there exists the gross disproportion between the massive amount of power unleashed by the United States in its intervention to destroy the legal authority of Nicaragua, and the legitimate defense that it claims to be pursuing. The United States policy, moreover, has no foundation in terms of the force that would have been necessary to guard against alleged aggression by Nicaragua, assuming it had been established. That is, in any event, U.S. force is so excessive as by itself to condemn it as an abuse of the doctrine of legitimate defense.

On these various grounds, the Tribunal considers that the validity of the accusation of aggression made by Nicaragua against the United States is convincingly established beyond any reasonable doubt.

*   *   *

ON THESE GROUNDS, THE TRIBUNAL

CONDEMNS the policies followed by the United States in relation to Nicaragua as contrary to the rules of international law that forbid intervention in the internal affairs of a sovereign state and prohibit all associated acts of aggression;

RECALLS that these policies amount to violations of the most fundamental law of international society and constitute the commission of the most serious crimes against the rights of peoples;

DECLARES AND AFFIRMS the unconditional rights of the Nicaraguan people to enjoy self-determination, independence, and sovereignty;

CALLS UPON the international community to assure that these basic rights of the Nicaraguan people be preserved; to take steps to terminate the illegal policies of the United States government; to assure that crimes resulting from those policies are repudiated, and that those responsible are censured and if possible held accountable.

Message From the Tribunal

The jury of the Tribunal's session on U.S. intervention in Nicaragua presented this message when it issued its Judgment in Brussels on October 8, 1984.

Caught between dignity and contempt, Nicaragua is in the process of determining its fate.

A people who triumphed in 1979, after 25 years of strife and at the cost of 50,000 lives, now confront a country devastated by war and stripped by half a century of the Somoza family dictatorship.

Before 1979, of all the Latin American nations, Nicaragua spent the most on arms and the least on health and education. After the Sandinista revolution had dissolved the dictator's army and carried out profound social reforms, the nation found itself forced to live in a state of war.

This illegal, undeclared, and increasingly ferocious war of aggression is a means by which the United States refuses Nicaragua the right to the independence and self-determination for which the United States itself fought more than two centuries ago. Earlier, the United States refused Nicaragua the right to revolt against tyranny, a right recognized in its own Declaration of Independence.

This vast criminal project, financed in the name of human rights, invokes democracy to restore dictatorship and patriotism to re-establish colonization.

In carrying out its aggression, the United States uses an army comprised mainly of former officers and soldiers of the Somoza dictatorship, fugitives pardoned by a revolution which in its hour of triumph condemned no one. This army, whose goal is to annihilate Nicaragua, has its principal bases in Honduras and Miami; it is common knowledge that it is recruited, financed, armed, and directed by the government of the United States. North American military advisers participate directly in its actions. Although the principal target of aggression is Nicaragua, the war also affects the bordering countries, which are gradually being transformed into large military bases and thus function as part of an imperial, geopolitical strategy that sees Central America as an integral part of the United States.

There are already too many victims of the state terrorism that the present U.S. government is employing directly or indirectly against

Nicaragua. And this incessant harassment forces Nicaragua to sacrifice many of its development projects in order to meet its enormous expenditures for national defense — to redirect a great part of the country's meager human and material resources, resources which the revolution would rather put to creative ends.

Implicit in the aggression, and beyond the military attacks, commando raids, bombings, and sabotage, there is repression of the collectivity resulting from political, economic, and cultural pressures. The aggression points to an infinite violation of the laws of the United States as well as the norms of international law. An attempt is made to justify this aggression through a formidable international campaign to sway world opinion; it is a matter of designating the victim as the assassin and magically transforming the assassin into the victim.

In general the public knows little about the achievements of the Nicaraguan revolution which, in the midst of a war of aggression, has managed to teach a half million people to read and write and has succeeded, according to the most conservative estimates, in reducing the infant mortality rate by one third. Propaganda, on the other hand, portrays contemporary Latin American history only in terms of cold wars between opposing blocs, as though the Nicaraguan revolution and the revolutionary process developing in Guatemala and El Salvador were nothing more than echoes of foreign voices, the results of a conspiracy concocted in the caves of the Kremlin. Thus it distorts the reality of a region where to reach the age of 15 alive and in good health is an achievement and a privilege, and where North American democracy places and displaces dictatorships like pawns on a chessboard.

The United States, which owes its own independence and liberty to popular struggle, has denied the fighting people of Nicaragua the credit necessary to reconstruct a country ravaged by a dictatorship that the United States originally imposed. Rather, it has distributed and continues to distribute millions of dollars for the further destruction of Nicaragua.

For a system that relies on the exploitation of a number of countries by a few, the peril does not lie in the traffic of arms, which has never been proven, to the guerrillas of El Salvador. Rather, Nicaragua is dangerous in that it exports an example: the example of a small nation that does not allow itself to be humiliated, that manifests the strength of a national independence which is not reduced to a hymn and a flag, and that anchors in its very soil the fundamental principles of an authentic democracy.

Nicaragua is under attack not because it *is* democratic but rather to ensure that *it does not become so.* Nicaragua is under attack not because it *could become* a military dictatorship but to make sure that it *does.* Nicaragua is under attack not because it *could become* the satellite of a great power but rather to ensure that it *will.*

Here is a people in arms defending their right to life. For the first time in history, the Nicaraguan people are in control. They are the actors and the creators of their destiny. For the first time they are fully exercising their sovereignty. And for that, this impoverished, dignified country is not to be forgiven. Therein lies the defiance, the misfortune, and the wonder of Nicaragua.

List of Tribunal Members and Jurors for the Session on Nicaragua

Officers of the Permanent Peoples' Tribunal

President:	François Rigaux (Belgium)
Vice Presidents:	Ruth First (South Africa)
	Makodo Oda (Japan)
	Armando Uribe (Chile)
	George Wald (U.S.)
Secretary General:	Gianni Tognoni (Italy)

Members of the Jury of the Session on U.S. Intervention in Nicaragua, Brussels, October 5-7, 1984.

President:

| François Rigaux | Jurist |
| | *Belgium* |

Vice-President:

| George Wald | Nobel Prize laureate |
| | *United States* |

Members:

Victoria Abellán Honrubia	Professor of International Law
	Spain
Richard Baümlin	Member of Parliament and Professor of International Law
	Switzerland
Georges Casalis	Theologian
	France
Harald Edelstam	Diplomat
	Sweden
Richard Falk	Professor of International Law
	United States
Eduardo Galeano	Writer
	Uruguay

Giulio Girardi   Theologian and philosopher
                              Italy

François Houtart   Sociologist
                              Belgium

Edmond Jouve   Political scientist
                              France

Raimundo Panikkar   Philosopher
                              India

Adolfo Pérez Esquivel   Nobel Prize laureate
                              Argentina

Salvatore Senese   Magistrate
                              Italy

Ernst Utrecht   Sociologist
                              Indonesia

VI

SELECTED DOCUMENTS

This section contains some of the supplementary documents submitted for the jury's consideration; a full list may be found at the end of the section.

Report of the Commission of Inquiry of the Tribunal

The members of the Commission were Dr. Leo Matarasso, Dr. Gianni Tognoni, and Dra. Victoria Abellán.

The Commission, appointed by the Permanent Peoples' Tribunal to carry out an investigation into the present situation of aggression in Nicaragua, visited Nicaragua between August 1 and August 8, 1983. It had the opportunity to interview and obtain information from the following people and institutions:

— The President of the Supreme Court of Justice, Dr. Roberto Arguello Hurtado.

— The Foreign Affairs Committee of the Council of State.

— The Vice-Minister of Justice, Dr. Carlos Arguello.

— The Minister of Education, Dr. Carlos Tunnermann.

— The Minister of the Managua Reconstruction Junta, Dr. Samuel Santos.

— The Minister of the Interior, Commander Tomás Borge Martínez.

— The President of the Council of State, Commander Carlos Núñez, and the Directorate (Junta Directiva) of the Council of State.

— The Director of Public and Foreign Relations of the Sandinista Popular Army, Sub-Commander Roberto Sánchez.

— The General Director of Bilateral Affairs from the Ministry of Foreign Affairs, Aldo Díaz Lacayo.

— The Director of the newspaper *El Nuevo Diario*, Xavier Chamorro.

— The Director of the newspaper *Barricada*, Fernando Chamorro.

— Leaders of the member parties of the Patriotic Front of the Revolution: the Sandinista Liberation Front, the Nicaraguan Socialist Party, the Popular Social Christian Party, and the Liberal Independent Party.

— Representatives from the Antonio Valdivieso Ecumenical Center (an international center for documentation and information about the problems of religion in Nicaraguan society): Beatriz Arellano, a Franciscan; Claudio Vazuiz; Oscar Godoy, a pastor of the Assembly of God and coordinator of evangelical work.

— The Committee of Mothers of Heroes and Martyrs.

They also visited the wounded in the military hospital, and the border zone of Ocotal and Mozonte up to the Las Manos pass; and they had the opportunity to attend the Seventh Session of the Council of State on August 3, in which the Law of Political Parties was debated.

From the information and testimonies they received, the Commission was able to ascertain the following:

First: There is a state of undeclared war on the northern border, consisting of incursions by armed bands of Somocistas from camps based in Honduran territory.

According to information from the international press, these bands operate with the direct or indirect support of the governments of Honduras and the U.S., creating a situation of covert intervention in Nicaragua by those governments.

The border war caused approximately 400 deaths in 1983, and left an average of four to five soldiers wounded every day. There have also been assassinations of civilians (among them teachers) and massive kidnappings of the inhabitants of the border regions.

On the evenings of July 19 and 20, 1983, the Commission visited the city of Mozonte and interviewed the families of 150 kidnapping victims from that city. The testimonies all concur in affirming that the kidnappings were carried out against the victims' will by a Somocista band from Honduras, where the victims were taken; two deaths occurred in these incidents in Nicaraguan territory.

Second: One of the grave consequences of the war is the absorption of economic and human resources by military needs, which has extremely serious effects on the country's reconstruction and development (the reconstruction of the city of Managua, construction of housing, sanitary and social services) and education and production (as a result of the mobilization of workers and students).

In addition, restrictions on international trade and credit have been imposed by the United States, which in the past was the primary market for Nicaragua's export products (sugar, coffee, and cotton).

Third: In relation to human rights, basic rights and liberties are recognized and guaranteed in the Fundamental Statute (Decree No. 1 of July 20, 1979), and in the Statute of Rights and Guarantees of the Nicaraguan People (Decree No. 52 of August 21, 1979), Article 5 of which abolished the death penalty.

In addition, the following have been approved and ratified:

— the American Convention on Human Rights celebrated in San José, Costa Rica, in 1969 (Decree No. 174, published in the official Nicaraguan journal *La Gaceta*, November 26, 1979),

— the International Covenant on Civil and Political Rights adopted by the United Nations in 1966,

— the Optional Protocol to the Covenant on Civil and Political Rights,

— the International Covenant on Economic, Social and Cultural Rights adopted by the U.N. in 1966 (Resolution 2200 (XXI), attached to the three aforementioned documents, *La Gaceta*, January 30, 1980).

As a consequence of the war in Nicaragua, a State of Emergency exists at present, which limits the exercise of civil and political rights and, to a certain degree, establishes prior censorship of the press [official review of the contents prior to publication — Ed.]. A State of Emergency was declared in accordance with the provision in the Pact on Civil and Political Rights that permits the suspension of guarantees recognized by the pact "in exceptional situations that endanger the life of the nation."

With regard to *freedom of information*, the Commission was able to determine that press censorship is limited to the exigencies of the situation; it does not involve any discrimination whatsoever, thus complying with the requirements in Article 4 of the International Covenant on Civil and Political Rights. One proof of this is the regularity of publication of the newspaper *La Prensa*, which is clearly opposed to the government politically and ideologically.

With regard to *freedom of religion*, the Commission was able to ascertain that there is broad and total religious freedom, in terms of freedom to worship in the various churches, access to the media, and the existence of religious associations and meetings.

Fourth: The Commission paid special attention to the Miskito Question.

Based on testimonies and information received by the Commission, it was able to determine that the Somocistas sought to use the Miskitos and incorporate them into the war, given their location on both sides of the border of Honduras along the Río Coco. Methods used ranged from persuasion to threats, including the kidnapping of Miskitos and interning them in Honduran camps. In this regard, the Commission had the opportunity to hear testimony from Miskitos who escaped from the Honduran camps to which they were taken after being kidnapped.

The consequences of this situation in Nicaragua have been the following, among others:

a) the imprisonment of Miskitos for having joined or collaborated with the Somocista bands from Honduras. The Commission visited a semiopen prison farm where there are about 150 Miskito prisoners; on the other hand, on August 3, 1983, 46 Miskito prisoners were pardoned and freed.

b) the displacement of the Miskito population from the border, and their relocation in a zone to the interior, away from the scene of war.

The Commission confirmed the respect for the Miskito culture and language, as shown in the textbooks used by the literacy campaign.

The acts described above create a serious threat to peace in Nicaragua; a threat created not only by the continuous harassment of its borders, but also by the utilization of Honduran territory as a base of operations and training for the Somocista bands, as well as by the U.S. in its show of force in Nicaraguan territorial waters.

This situation demonstrates a clear intervention in the internal affairs of Nicaragua by Honduras and the U.S., which is in every sense contrary to the Declaration on the Inadmissibility of Intervention and Interference in the Internal Affairs of States adopted by Resolution 36/103 of the U.N. General Assembly.

The Commission understands that, based upon the facts and circumstances considered, the war in Nicaragua constitutes aggression according to the terms established by Resolution 3314 (XXIX) of the U.N. General Assembly, Article 3, Sections f and g.

Therefore, given that this intervention and the acts of aggression are clearly intended to change the existing political, economic, and ideological system in Nicaragua, which enjoys broad popular support, such acts of intervention and aggression constitute a violation of the principles of self-determination of the peoples recognized as a fundamental human right by Article 1 of Resolution 2200 (XXI), the Covenant on Human Rights, adopted by the U.N. General Assembly in 1966.

The Miskitos: Interview With Two Priests

This is an excerpt from an interview conducted by the Central American Historical Institute of Managua (Instituto Histórico Centroamericano, IHCA). As the introduction to the interview states, the two priests interviewed are familiar with the Atlantic Coast; both are also recognized throughout the Catholic Church in Nicaragua for their experience and moral authority. Father Francisco Solano, Vicar of South Zelaya, is viewed as the most important church official in the region after the bishop. A Capuchin, he was born in the U.S. and has worked for 15 years in Nicaragua. Father Augustín Sambola, also a Capuchin, was born on the Atlantic Coast and is a member of one of the Creole ethnic groups descended from slaves. Fr. Sambola has worked as a pastoral leader. Both have been threatened on various occasions by the contras; in one incident, Father Sambola was ambushed and attacked by gunfire.

THE ATLANTIC COAST: OPPRESSED RACES

IHCA: We have to begin by defining the Atlantic Coast — so often talked about and so little understood — and the nature of its inhabitants.

Solano: Some people believe that the Miskitos [also Miskitu — Ed.] live throughout all of Zelaya. This is one of many errors. It is important to distinguish the department of Zelaya from what is called the Atlantic Coast. The department was an English possession until 1894, when President Zelaya reincorporated it into Nicaragua. Strictly speaking, the coast itself is a strip of land on the edge of Zelaya, running along the Río Coco and down the Atlantic Coast to the town of Bluefields and a bit further south. The coast also includes a part of the mining zone, towards the Lagoon of Pearls. This is the coast, where there's a mix of ethnic groups and where the whole Miskito problematic has unfolded. In other words, the coast is only a fraction of the whole area of Zelaya, which itself represents 56% of Nicaraguan territory. The greater part of Zelaya is inhabited by mestizo *campesinos*, like those in the Pacific region, who have immigrated from Matagalpa, Boaco, and Chontales, in search of land. We do not have exact statistics, but there are around 250,000 mestizos, and around

The full interview was published in Envío, *the bulletin of the Instituto Histórico Centroamericano, in January 1984 (No. 31), under the title "The Miskitos and the Bishop Schlaefer Case."*

60,000 Miskitos. Creoles, either black or *garífono*, make up 27,000 inhabitants of the region; Sumos, about 8,000. There are also between 500 and 1,000 Ramas.

Sambola: Each of these groups has special characteristics. But they have one important thing in common: they all belong to oppressed races. British colonialism and American exploitation robbed them of their identity. My ancestors were not allowed to speak *garífono*, and they slowly lost their history and their roots along with their language. The Atlantic Coast peoples are races without identity. Their cultural framework was broken by the large companies that came to exploit the region and that led the indigenous peoples to end up identifying themselves with their employers rather than with their own peoples. This is the drama: on the Atlantic Coast there has been no Nicaraguan national identity. And this is the challenge: to develop such an identity. It is a very slow process. Of all these races, the Miskitos are best known outside Nicaragua. Since 1980 the Miskitos have been an important concern for many people. Nothing is said about the mestizos or about the poor *campesinos*. But the reality of the Atlantic Coast goes beyond the situation of the Miskitos and the reality of the Miskitos is more complex than people think.

IDEOLOGICALLY, THE COAST BELONGED TO THE CHURCHES

IHCA: How has the Catholic Church developed in Zelaya and above all in the coastal strip?

Solano: In the immense underpopulated parts of Zelaya, occupied by mestizo *campesinos*, the Catholic Church traditionally worked through occasional missions in the relatively populated areas. Missionaries might visit once or twice a year. The Capuchin missionaries are the Church's most important representatives in Zelaya and the Atlantic Coast.

The 1968 Latin American Bishops' meeting at Medellín, Colombia, totally changed Zelaya's pastoral structure. From that time on, base communities began to develop. Above all, lay Church leadership was encouraged, through the Delegates of the Word program. In 1969 Zelaya had only 35 priests. It was the Nicaraguan Church's most ignored region. Today we are even fewer: there are between 20 and 25 priests and 18 women religious. But the lay structures that were created after Medellín are working well. There are now 1,700 Delegates of the Word in the department, the majority of them men. The role of *campesino* women has been most developed in Siuna, where some have become Delegates of the Word for their communities. There are 36 permanent deacons in Zelaya, both mestizos and Miskitos. We can say that today 95% of Zelaya's pastoral work (catechism, religious celebrations, administering the sacraments, etc.) is done by lay leaders who have emerged from the *campesino* communities.

IHCA: Does the Catholic Church in Zelaya have special characteristics that differentiate it from the Church in the Pacific region?

Solano: I think so. The massive participation of lay people is one factor. For example, in the Pacific region there are no permanent deacons. These deacons are chosen by their communities. Their wives, parish priests, and communities vouch for their work over a period of five years, and the bishop then ordains them. Another feature here is that, despite differences of opinion, greater unity has been maintained within the Church. This unity has been strengthened by the practice, established several years ago, of holding large meetings for dialogue and sharing among pastoral workers, priests, and religious in the region. There is a clear desire for dialogue, a desire to deal with differences in a fraternal manner. This has been encouraged by the complex reality of the zone and by the personality of Bishop Schlaefer, who has been Bishop of Bluefields since 1970.

Another special factor in Zelaya is ecumenism. Unlike the other parts of Nicaragua, in Zelaya the Catholic Church has worked alongside other Churches: the Moravians, the Anglicans, and the Baptists. Though early on there was an attitude of competition between the Churches, since Vatican II there have been great efforts to change this attitude and to develop more unity. There are now close relations, with dialogue, mutual respect, communication, and no proselytism. The Ecumenical Council of Christian Churches of Bluefields is a recent expression of this ecumenism. Thus, despite all the racial and historical differences, there is no religious rivalry on the coast, neither between Church leaders nor among the people.

Sambola: Before the revolution there were already two clear tendencies among the priests and religious, tendencies that were passed on to those with whom they worked, the Delegates of the Word. There was a more open tendency, and one that was more conservative. When I arrived at Waspam after having worked in Siuna — where there has been much renewal in the Church — I was surprised by the conservatism of the Church in Waspam. I came from a place where we had worked in communities, in popular organizations, and with new lay ministries. But I found myself in Waspam in a church reminiscent of the 16th-century Council of Trent.

These two tendencies led to two different responses on the part of the people to the resistance to the Somoza dictatorship and then to the changes brought on by the revolution. People's current reactions to agricultural cooperatives, to the Miskito resettlements, and to so many other new things to a large degree depend upon which Church tendency has been present in their community.

IHCA: And what about the Moravian Church, the Atlantic Coast's first Christian Church?

Sambola: The Catholic Church helped in the organization of mestizo *campesinos* in the 1960s, and even of Miskitos, through the Río Coco

Association of Farmers' Clubs, probably the first Miskito organization and
the root of what was later to become MISURASATA. But the Moravian
Church has been the only real basis of Miskito nationhood. The Moravians arrived on the coast in 1849, and have always worked among Miskitos, with deacons and other forms of lay participation. The Moravian
Church is an evangelical one, the "Unitas Fratrum" that came from Germany to Nicaragua at the request of the British government, which then
controlled the Miskito area. Because of the Moravian evangelization, by
the end of the 19th century all the Miskitos identified themselves as Christians. At the beginning of this century, the Sumos began to convert to
the Moravian Church.

Thus, when the Catholic Church arrived on the coast, the Moravians
already had a well-established pastoral structure. As the Miskito people
did not have their own national identity, the Moravian Church gave them
such an identity through religion. Accordingly, it is an ethnic religion,
an almost national religion. This has given the Miskito people a special
ideological make-up. The Moravian Church is at the root of their identity as a people. Their history is in the Church. Even now, if one enters
a Moravian church, one hears religious hymns brought over by the first
European missionaries in the 19th century. The people's mental structure finds security in repeating received tradition again and again. There
is a fear of the new, and naturally also of the revolution. Medellín opened
doors in the Catholic Church, but there has not been a parallel renewal
among the Moravians. So I would say that in Zelaya the Catholics are
on average more open to the revolution. The Moravians, in general, are
more hesitant. The Anglican Church is a minority. It is centered in
Bluefields and in the towns of the Lagoon of Pearls and around the mouth
of the Río Grande in Matagalpa. The Baptist Church is also in Bluefields.

IHCA: Do religion and church institutions, whether Catholic or Moravian, have more influence on the coast than in the rest of Nicaragua?

Sambola: Economically, the coast belonged to the big companies. Ideologically, it belonged to the Churches. This is the historical reality. And
such a reality doesn't change in a few years. Moreover, for years the majority
of Church representatives, whether hierarchy, missionaries, priests, pastors, or religious, have been foreigners, mostly Americans. This is true
even today. The revolution's anti-imperialist message is not as well received
on the Atlantic Coast as on the Pacific. Many of the groups on the coast,
and especially the Miskitos, were 100% with the American companies.
Why? Because from the companies they received not only work and wages,
but also everything they wanted: salt, tools, and many other exotic products
that they had never had before. Thus it was hard for them to understand
the exploitative structures that lay behind the paternal image of these
companies. They saw only the immediately visible aspects of the compa-

nies; they didn't see how the wood and gold that left the coast made other people rich. They also had the experience that the missionaries and other foreigners, mostly Americans, had helped them, providing health care, education. . . .

So the American domination of Nicaragua was experienced quite differently on the Atlantic Coast than in the Pacific region. Nor was Sandino understood, with his anti-imperialist struggle. This is a serious problem! The only real historical roots are in religion, and the picture is further complicated by the fact that the churches never questioned the companies or organized any opposition against them. Rather, over the years they inculcated passivity.

IHCA: But did the Catholic Church not develop certain social programs?

Sambola: The Somoza dictatorship abandoned the coast to its own backwardness and to the greed of the American companies. The Church picked up whatever the Somoza government failed to do. Health care, education, and agrarian organization should be the responsibilities of the state. In Zelaya, these functions were basically undertaken by the Moravian and Catholic Churches, out of necessity and with a certain paternalistic attitude.

IHCA: What has the new government done with such Church projects?

Solano: In Central Zelaya, for example, in 1976 the Church launched an ambitious educational project. Since there were no schools in the mountains, pastoral workers trained rural teachers who would in turn teach in their own communities. Now education is one of the basic goals of the revolution; the Sandinista government recognized the project's value and took it on, developing it further, providing more human and material resources than we ourselves could have provided. We continue to participate in the project. Some religious are fully involved, and their congregations receive funds for the work from the United States. No religious, no Christian, has been pushed aside.

In the health field, a welfare-type approach seemed to predominate. The Moravians ran a hospital in Bilwaskarma and the Catholics had one in Waspam. Health has been a point of conflict with the Miskitos. Several years ago, a health program was organized along the Río Coco, also with the support of Catholic community leaders. It was efficient, well-structured, and appreciated by the people. After the insurrection, this project was dismantled and another one established. The new one may have been better, but it was an error nevertheless.

The Miskito communities were used to the old project and did not understand the change. Maybe those responsible thought that the new project would be so much better and they did not consider the consequences of dismantling the old system. Maybe the religious who ran the

former project were very protective of their "turf." In any case, the Miskitos were upset. It is clear that there have been cases of enthusiastic government officials arriving on the coast and thinking they were starting from
zero, without taking enough time to understand the previous history of
things. In wanting to help the people, they may have destroyed traditions
that are important to the indigenous people. But at times problems are
also caused because the Church does not know how to let go of its projects.
Health care and education should be public (not just denominational)
concerns. Though the Somoza dictatorship did not assume these responsibilities, the new government does, and sometimes the Church does not
know how to adapt to its new role of participant or helper in government-
run projects.

   IHCA: Since you say the churches were the ideological rulers of Zelaya
and the Atlantic Coast, the revolutionary government must cooperate with
them. Does this lead to manipulation? Many have accused the Nicaraguan
government of using religious people for now but later, when it's no longer
necessary, they'll be tossed aside. What has been your experience in this
regard?

   Solano: I personally see relations based upon sincerity, fraternity, and
a desire to cooperate so as to serve the people. This has been the pattern
from the beginning. As many Christian values are also revolutionary values
there is much that can be shared. We also have goals in common. But
I think we have to ask what manipulation is. If there have been occasions
in which the revolution has tried to manipulate the Church, there have
also been occasions when the Church has tried to manipulate the revolution.

   Sambola: I've had the same experience and found great sincerity in
the majority of cases. I've often heard government officials say that if the
Gospel were lived as Jesus taught, the revolution would be fulfilled. Their
occasionally critical attitudes have encouraged us to purify our faith. This
is not a hypocritical relationship, but one of collaboration, that can help
purify the Church. So I would answer the question in terms of purifica-
tion rather than manipulation. There are also good relations with the
Moravians. For example, the ongoing meetings between William Ramírez, the Minister in charge of the zone, and the Moravian pastors who
work with the Miskitos, have been important. William has been a brother
to them. He is a leader of much patience, the long-standing patience of
the poor. He doesn't try to change everything from one day to the next.
For on the coast patience is needed, not just revolutionary enthusiasm.

   Solano: In South Zelaya, the minister in charge, Lumberto Campbell,
has also been patient. He is a black Creole. He shares the culture, the
mentality, and the life-style of the Creoles and understands how to work
with his people. Thus errors and conflicts have been kept to a minimum.

What remains then is not an ethnic or regional problem (vis-a-vis the Sandinista government on the Pacific Coast), but rather a local racial one. The blacks have a very visible participation in the new structures of revolutionary power. The aspirations of the black Creoles are being fulfilled. This is not true of the Miskitos.

THE ASPIRATIONS OF THE MISKITOS ARE VERY MODEST

IHCA: How exactly would you define the "Miskito problem"?

Sambola: It's a historic problem. A social, cultural, and economic problem. The counterrevolution has also turned it into a political and military problem.

At first the revolutionary government basically neither knew nor understood the Miskito people. This is not so much an error; it's a limitation. The government thought: now we are all Nicaraguans, we are all equal. And they wanted to establish the same organizational structures on the Atlantic Coast as on the Pacific. The Miskitos reacted. They did not understand the changes. Miskito leaders such as Steadman Fagoth *did* understand the changes, but they took advantage of their positions of leadership to encourage suspicion. This is where the Miskito problem begins. In the last two years, many aspects of the problem have been overcome with the decentralization of government administration in the various regions of the country. Now, while goals are established at the national level, the specific means of applying those goals are worked out in the First Special Zone (North Zelaya) itself. Regionalization has meant a qualitative leap forward in the resolution of the Miskito problem. One must remember that the Miskitos do not understand what the *Guardia* was, what *Somocismo* was, nor what the revolution and the counterrevolution are. The Miskitos have never been part of Nicaraguan national life. They have lived apart for years upon years, used by the English, by the Americans, by Somoza. So the revolution comes to the Miskitos saying: we're all Nicaraguans and we're equal and we'll all participate together. The revolution *could* have said: "We'll leave this group alone, we don't understand it." But to neglect a group in this way goes against the principles of the revolution. So the burden of the Miskitos had to be taken up. But it's no easy matter to address the reality of such a special group, so different in its worldview. . . . And so this revolutionary commitment has had very serious consequences.

IHCA: What were the main mistakes made by the new government in its approach to the Miskitos?

Solano: Given the idiosyncracies of the Miskito worldview, certain concrete actions have taken on a highly symbolic and very negative meaning for the Miskitos. The military situation, the war in the border area of the Atlantic Coast, can explain these errors, but...for example: some Miskitos have come to understand that it was necessary to move the villages along the Río Coco, and they can understand that the decision to evacuate the area saved many Miskito lives. But they still ask why the evacuation came so suddenly and with such force. They understand the evacuation, but not its urgent and obligatory nature. For the Miskitos, movement itself is neither new nor bad. They are accustomed to moving. Throughout their history they have been a wandering people. But with the sudden evacuation, houses were burned and cattle were killed. There were reasons for doing this, to prevent the contras based in Honduras, the *guardia*, to use the houses or to find food in the evacuated area. This is understandable, but the negative symbol remains: the people saw their houses burned, they saw years of work destroyed in minutes. And they ask why there wasn't time to save the zinc roofs. Some were allowed to, but most could not return. For the people, the roofs symbolize much work, and the same with the livestock. They still haven't got cows in the new settlements. So the children don't have milk and can't have their *cuajada* [a milk product]. The fire that burned their homes, the destruction they themselves witnessed, the lack of milk for their children...these are powerful symbols that touch life itself. The Miskitos cannot understand all of this.

IHCA: Wasn't there enough time to explain the reasons for the evacuation?

Sambola: I was in the zone at the time. No, there really wasn't time. The choice was between evacuating them or letting them die there. At that time the attacks were already very strong and the Miskito people in those areas were sandwiched between the Somocistas and the Nicaraguan army. I figure that, given the way Miskitos are, it would have taken a year or two to convince them of the need for the move. And there really wasn't that kind of time at all.

Solano: Military considerations also explain other problems with a high symbolic content. The Miskitos were not allowed to travel by river in their *pipantes*, their home-made canoes. For the Miskitos, travelling by river in their canoes is a vital part of life. It's as if we were forbidden to walk on our two legs. The river is part of their life, as is fishing and travelling by river. The ban was meant to keep contras from using some Miskitos to transport arms or food by river. I wonder if it might not have been better to accept the fact that some of them would do this, because I think that the widespread opposition to the ban is worse. Another measure with symbolic importance has been the occupation of chapels and churches. Occasionally, the military situation led the Nicaraguan army to base itself in Catholic and Moravian chapels. These are the largest and safest buildings in the communities, built out of cement. Their usefulness is easy to understand. But the Miskitos are super-religious in the sense of natural religion, and for them sacred places are untouchable. To find uniformed and armed people inside these sacred places is a tremendous shock. They see the occupation and don't reflect on the reasons why. This has caused discontent and destroyed trust.

IHCA: What has the revolution given the Miskitos?

Sambola: The most important thing has been a feeling of identity as a people. Ten thousand Miskitos were born, along with the revolution. By this I mean, for example, they began to speak their own language. Many people used to avoid speaking Miskito because they felt ashamed. Those who spoke Spanish enjoyed a higher social status, while those who spoke Miskito were automatically at the bottom. Thousands of Miskitos were afraid to speak in their own tongue outside their community lest they be taken for thieves or sorcerers. And now they speak Miskito with pride in their race. Miskito is openly spoken on the buses now, and in Managua one can hear Miskitos speaking their own language when they meet, even if strangers are present. This is the most important thing, this is number one: dignity. On the basis of this dignity, a Miskito identity is being born. The revolution removed the obstacles to this and so it developed. First came dignity, through the use of language, and then organization. This is where the counterrevolution entered the picture, taking advantage of the political space that the revolution was opening up.

With the triumph in 1979 a space was created so that certain community organizations that already existed could flourish. Steadman Fagoth and others took advantage of this situation and took the structures in another direction. For example MISURASATA, under Fagoth's direction, was responsible for the literacy campaign in the area. Many people learned to read, but we believe that even during the campaign, seeds of distrust toward the revolution were already being planted among the Miskitos. The fact that Fagoth was able to direct everything is a sign of how the revolution works. The fact that he had been a security agent under Somoza was known, but he was nevertheless given this great responsibility. I don't think this was owing to either naivete or revolutionary euphoria, but because it is a principle of this revolution that everyone can participate. The revolution has faith in people and, because of this, people are given opportunities. The Miskitos too have been given opportunities through health care, education, new roads, and cooperatives. But remember that for the Miskitos to own something is not important. Miskito aspirations are very modest, unlike those of the mestizo *campesinos*, who do want to own land. The Miskitos don't want to own anything, they only want to live as they please, to have freedom of movement. In the mountains of Siuna, I have seen *campesinos* cut up to 17 acres of hillside a year for wood. The Miskitos cut only what is absolutely necessary. Their goal is simply to live, while the goal of the *campesinos* is to have. The challenge of this revolution is to join living and having, in order to learn how to share.

A PEOPLE USED TO WAR

IHCA: There are many Miskitos among the Somocistas and counterrevolutionary mercenaries of the FDN. How do you explain this phenomenon?

Sambola: Various factors have allowed sympathy for the counterrevolution to become almost a part of the Miskito identity. There are the great limitations on the part of the revolution in dealing with the Miskito question, certain errors on the part of the government and, above all, manipulation by the American government, working through leaders such as Fagoth. After the evacuation from the Río Coco to Tasba Pri, 10,000 Miskitos left for Honduras. One cannot interpret this simplistically as their fleeing from "repressive Nicaragua" to "free Honduras." There is a historical reality behind the flight of the Miskitos. The Miskitos have never recognized the border. They have always crossed the border in both directions looking for an easier situation. Why did they go? There are problems here? — let's go where there aren't any. When they heard there was going to be an evacuation they crossed the river, and they are still over there. A Miskito who goes from Nicaragua to Honduras is not strictly speaking a refugee. The Miskito region covers parts of both countries. But once there, many were recruited in the contra camps prepared beforehand by the Somocistas.

IHCA: How many?

Solano: It's very hard to know. Nicaraguan authorities estimate that there are 5,000 Miskitos who have taken up arms and are now operating in either Honduras or Nicaragua. No doubt there are camps where they are well trained militarily and well armed. And we know that the U.S. government, via the government of Honduras, is supporting this war which is mainly counterrevolutionary, but also Miskito in nature.

IHCA: What leads the Miskitos to get involved in the counterrevolutionary war? What do they hope to gain?

Solano: The only aspiration of the Miskitos is to return to their lands. Throughout their individual and communal history, they have gone up and down the rivers, fishing, doing as they wished. This is what they long for, and this is what they're fighting for. Radio Miskut incites them to fight, with its propaganda telling them that in this way they will soon be able to return to their rivers. This is the heart of their lives. They don't want money. They don't want to be rich. They only want to do what they did before. The radio station also makes use of religious motivations and biblical themes: the history of the exodus, of the exile. This affects them greatly because they are a religious people. . .

One should add that the Miskito culture is accustomed to war. English pirates used the Miskitos as mercenaries in their attacks on the Spanish cities of the Pacific Coast. A historical tradition makes them "men of war." The counterrevolution plays upon this tradition, for example by using the names of Miskito warriors of the past. This historical reality is used to express their nationhood, their race. Such arguments also work to mobilize the Miskitos.

THE OPEN VEINS OF THE ATLANTIC COAST

IHCA: While the Miskitos struggle to return to the rivers of their ancestors, Miskito leaders outside Nicaragua are talking of "independence" for the Atlantic Coast and an autonomous Miskito nation. What do you think of this proposal?

Solano: It is an idea which lies totally outside the historical context of the coast and of Zelaya. This zone lacks the resources to maintain itself as an independent nation. It lacks the basic products, the means of production, and the human resources. With what's here no nation can be created. To put it simply, to exist as a nominally independent nation, the Miskitos would have to become totally dependent on the American empire. Dependence upon the government in Managua would be exchanged for dependence on the government in Washington. The coast would return to what it was before, to what it has always been. . . .

IHCA: And what was the coast and Zelaya in the hands first of the British empire and then the American?

Solano: Zelaya became a totally dependent region and then was abandoned as a disaster area. Its wood, bananas, and gold were exploited. It appeared to be a prosperous region with happy people. But this was an illusion. The people were taught to consume only foreign products, and nothing remained in the region. When the possibilities of further exploitation were exhausted, the companies took off and left an even greater dependence behind. Guadalupe along the Rama River, Muelle Real along the Sikia River, La Cruz del Río Grande, La Barra del Río Grande: these are all ghost towns now. Whatever concern the U.S. government now claims to have about the welfare of the coast is not sincere. They just see the coast as a way of dividing Nicaragua. And they continue to think as they have always done, about an alternative canal through Central America, should problems arise in Panama because of the new treaties. In addition, from the Atlantic Coast they can control the Caribbean. So the American government is not concerned about the rights of the Miskitos, it is looking after its own interests.

Sambola: What did the U.S. companies leave on the coast? Hundreds of Miskitos exploited in the mines, victimized with diseased lungs. Thou-

sands of acres of land without trees. Old machinery, not even a good airport for access to the mines. They left behind a chronically ill population. And the saddest thing is that thousands of Miskitos do not know
that their lungs were wasted in making other people rich and that their
gold was used to develop another country. So this is what the U.S. presence
bequeathed to the revolution on the Atlantic Coast. How can the counterrevolution be concerned for the well-being of Miskitos, when those who
really control the counterrevolution have never cared about the Miskitos?. . .

IHCA: To conclude, what do you think is the greatest challenge that
the Miskito people present to the revolution?

Sambola: One of the main challenges is to seek greater participation
of the Miskitos and other coastal peoples in the overall development of
the area and the country. This involves moving slowly, at the grass-roots
level. That's where we are. I think a great help has been the fact that
some Miskitos can go to study in the Pacific region and in other countries. This helps to expand their viewpoint, so that they see reality differently when they return, and can go beyond a merely local perspective.
This is not a matter of isolated cases, but of an entire project. This will
help to encourage participation.

Solano: An important goal is to train officials in all areas so that
administrative dependence upon the Pacific can be overcome. In local
governments the participation of inhabitants of the coast is almost 100%;
the same in education. But not in health. The only health care workers
from the region are auxiliary nurses and a few doctors. The judges are
also "imported," and this is a sensitive area, because as a judge one should
be immersed in the mentality of the people. Most military officials are
also "imported."

Church leaders are also from outside the region. Not lay leaders; they
are almost all locals. I would like to point out that the dynamic of participation is very important and that the behavior of the government is not
paternalistic. Rather, it seeks to respond to the people's own participation, further it, and strengthen it. This aspect of initiative, participation, and ongoing, deepening awareness is key. I know that all of this is
easier in times of peace. Clearly the war has slowed down the development on the coast. . . .

Sambola: Everything was already difficult there. With the war, even
more so. On the coast, everything remains to be done. Even to have a
key made in Bluefields one has to go to Managua. And Bluefields is the
most developed place on the coast. There are many great challenges. If
the revolution in the Pacific region is a "four-year-old child," on the Atlantic
Coast it is a child that has not yet been born. But together we will help
it be born.

The International Court of Justice:
Interim Order of Protection From U.S. Activities

On May 10, 1984, the International Court of Justice at The Hague issued a historic order favorable to Nicaragua's complaint against the United States for laying mines in its ports and other actions. The Court also rejected on a temporary basis the U.S. position that the World Court had no authority in the case (on the technical grounds that Nicaragua had never officially recorded its 1929 decision recognizing the Court).

A few hours before the original filing of Nicaragua's complaint, President Reagan had said the U.S. would not submit to World Court jurisdiction on Central American disputes for two years.

On November 26, 1984, the Court ruled permanently that it did have authority in the case and it rejected Reagan's declaration. A full hearing on the case was expected to take place in May 1985.

Here are excerpts from the Interim Order of Protection of May 10, 1984, which reflects worldwide opinion that Nicaragua's charges are justified. The Court's decision also embodies the concept of a community of nations in which relationships must be subject to forms of global order. In the first excerpt, the Court reviews the charges brought by Nicaragua; the second contains the main part of the ruling itself.

ORDER

Present: *President* Elias; *Vice President* Sette-Camara; *Judges* Lachs, Morozov, Nagendra Singh, Ruda, Mosler, Oda, Ago, El-Khani, Schwebel, Sir Robert Jennings, de Lacharrière, Mbaye, Bedjaoui; *Registrar* Torres Bernárdez.

The International Court of Justice,

Composed as above,

After deliberation,

Having regard to Articles 41 and 48 of the Statute of the Court,

Having regard to Articles 73 and 74 of the Rules of Court,

Having regard to the Application by the Republic of Nicaragua filed in the Registry of the Court on 9 April 1984, instituting proceedings against the United States of America in respect of a dispute concerning responsibility for military and paramilitary activities in and against Nicaragua;

Makes the following Order:

1. Whereas in the above-mentioned Application the Republic of Nicaragua, invoking the declarations of acceptance of the jurisdiction of the Court deposited by both States under Article 36 of the Statute of the Court, recounts a series of events over the period from March 1981 up to the present day, as a result of which Nicaragua claims to have suffered grievous consequences, and claims that

> "the United States of America is using military force against Nicaragua and intervening in Nicaragua's internal affairs, in violation of Nicaragua's sovereignty, territorial integrity and political independence and of the most fundamental and universally-accepted principles of international law";

and whereas, on the basis of the facts alleged in the Application, it requests the court to adjudge and declare:

> "(a) That the United States, in recruiting, training, arming, equipping, financing, supplying and otherwise encouraging, supporting, aiding, and directing military and paramilitary actions in and against Nicaragua, has violated and is violating its express charter and treaty obligations to Nicaragua and, in particular, its charter and treaty obligations under:
>
> — Article 2 (4) of the United Nations Charter;
> — Articles 18 and 20 of the Charter of the Organization of American States;
> — Article 8 of the Convention on Rights and Duties of States;
> — Article I, Third, of the Convention concerning the Duties and Rights of States in the Event of Civil Strife.
>
> (b) That the United States, in breach of its obligation under general and customary international law, has violated and is violating the sovereignty of Nicaragua by:
>
> — armed attacks against Nicaragua by air, land and sea;
> — incursions into Nicaraguan territorial waters;
> — aerial trespass into Nicaraguan airspace;
> — efforts by direct and indirect means to coerce and intimidate the Government of Nicaragua.
>
> (c) That the United States, in breach of its obligation under general and customary international law, has used and is using force and the threat of force against Nicaragua.
>
> (d) That the United States, in breach of its obligation under general and customary international law, has intervened and is intervening

in the internal affairs of Nicaragua.

(e) That the United States, in breach of its obligation under general and customary international law, has infringed and is infringing the freedom of the high seas and interrupting peaceful maritime commerce.

(f) That the United States, in breach of its obligation under general and customary international law, has killed, wounded, and kidnapped and is killing, wounding, and kidnapping citizens of Nicaragua.

(g) That, in view of its breaches of the foregoing legal obligations, the United States is under a particular duty to cease and desist immediately:

From all use of force — whether direct or indirect, overt or covert — against Nicaragua, and from all threats of force against Nicaragua;

from all violations of the sovereignty, territorial integrity, or political independence of Nicaragua, including all intervention, direct or indirect, in the internal affairs of Nicaragua;

from all support of any kind — including the provision of training, arms, ammunition, finances, supplies, assistance, direction or any other form of support — to any nation, group, organization, movement, or individual engaged or planning to engage in military or paramilitary actions in or against Nicaragua;

from all efforts to restrict, block, or endanger access to or from Nicaraguan ports;

and from all killings, woundings and kidnappings of Nicaraguan citizens.

(h) That the United States has an obligation to pay Nicaragua, in its own right and as *parens patriae* for the citizens of Nicaragua, reparations for damages to person, property, and the Nicaraguan economy caused by the foregoing violations of international law in a sum to be determined by the Court. Nicaragua reserves the right to introduce to the Court a precise evaluation of the damages caused by the United States";

2. Having regard to the request dated 9 April 1984 and filed in the Registry the same day, whereby the Republic of Nicaragua, relying on Article 41 of the Statute of the Court and Articles 73, 74, 75, and 78 of the Rules of Court, urgently requests the Court to indicate the following provisional measures to be in effect while the Court is seised of the case introduced by the above-mentioned Application:

" — That the United States should immediately cease and desist from providing, directly or indirectly, any support — including training, arms, ammunition, supplies, assistance, finances, direction, or any other form of support — to any nation, group, organization, movement, or individual engaged or planning to engage in military or paramilitary activities in or against Nicaragua;

— That the United States should immediately cease and desist from any military or paramilitary activity by its own officials, agents or forces in or against Nicaragua and from any other use or threat of force in its relations with Nicaragua";

THE COURT,

A. Unanimously,

Rejects the request made by the United States of America that the proceedings on the Application filed by the Republic of Nicaragua on 9 April 1984, and on the request filed the same day by the Republic of Nicaragua for the indication of provisional measures, be terminated by the removal of the case from the list;

B. *Indicates,* pending its final decision in the proceedings instituted on 9 April 1984 by the Republic of Nicaragua against the United States of America, the following provisional measures:

1. Unanimously,

   The United States of America should immediately cease and refrain from any action restricting, blocking, or endangering access to or from Nicaraguan ports, and, in particular, the laying of mines;

2. By fourteen votes to one,

   The right to sovereignty and to political independence possessed by the Republic of Nicaragua, like any other State of the region or of the world, should be fully respected and should not in any way be jeopardized by any military and paramilitary activities which are prohibited by the principles of international law, in particular the principle that States should refrain in their international relations from the threat or use of force against the territorial integrity or the political independence of any State, and the principle concerning the duty not to intervene in matters within the domestic jurisdiction of a State, principles embodied in the United Nations Charter and the Charter of the Organization of American States.

IN FAVOR: *President* Elias; *Vice-President* Sette-Camara; *Judges* Lachs, Morozov, Nagendra Singh, Ruda, Mosler, Oda, Ago, El-Khani, Sir Robert Jennings, de Lacharrière, Mbaye, Bedjaoui.

AGAINST: *Judge* Schwebel.

The U.S. Presence in Honduras: Tables

Table 1: U.S. MILITARY AND ECONOMIC ASSISTANCE TO HONDURAS 1946-1984
(for U.S. Fiscal Year, figures in millions of dollars)

	1946-1979	1980	1981	1982	1983	1984
Military Aid						
1) Military Assistance Program	5.6	0	0	11.0	27.5	77.5
2) Credit Financing	12.5	3.5	8.4	19.0	9.0	0
3) International Military Education and Training	8.5	0.4	0.5	1.3	0.8	1.0
Economic Support Fund (ESF)	2.4	0	0	36.8	53.0	112.5
Economic Aid (Agency for International Development)	213.8	45.8	25.7	31.2	35.1	32.0
TOTAL	271.8	49.7	34.6	99.3	125.4	223.0

Source: *United States-Honduras Relations*, Central American Historical Institute, Georgetown University, Washington, D.C., May 1984. [Updated in April 1985 — Ed.]

Table 2: U.S. MILITARY PERSONNEL STATIONED IN HONDURAS 1980-MAY 1984

Date	Total Personnel Stationed in Honduras	Troops Participating in Maneuvers (approximate figures)
1980		
Feb.-Dec.	26	0
1981		
Jan.-June	7	0
July-Dec.	21	130
1982		
Jan.-March	104	0
April-June	45	0
July-Dec.	50	180
1983		
Jan.-March	62	1,600
April-July	346	3,500
Aug.-Dec.	346	5,500
1984		
Jan.-Feb.	227	2,700
March-April	2,000	800
May	(Information not available.)	1,800

Source: *United States-Honduras Relations*, Central American Historical Institute, Georgetown University, Washington, D.C., May 1984.

List of Documents Submitted to the Jury

This list does not include documents which are written versions of verbal presentations; it is a list of supplementary documents or substantially expanded versions of verbal presentations.

I. Tribunal Documents

Report of the Commission of Inquiry (August 1983).

Text of the Nicaraguan Complaint.

II. General Aggression

"Ciento treinta años de intervención y de agresión de los Estados Unidos en Nicaragua." Document prepared by the Instituto de Estudios Sandinistas, Managua.

Nicaragua Fact Sheets. Chronological account of U.S. "Covert Activities" in and against Nicaragua. Filed at the International Court of Justice, The Hague, April 9, 1984.

Discurso del Comandante Daniel Ortega Saavedra, 4 de mayo, 1984.

"The Mining of Nicaragua's Ports." Central American Historical Institute, *Update*, Vol. 3 No. 13, April 5, 1984.

International Court of Justice, Orders of May 10 and May 14, 1984 in the Case Concerning Military and Paramilitary Activities in and Against Nicaragua (English and French).

The Impact of Aggression (author unlisted).

III. Military Aggression

"Into the Fray: Facts on the U.S. Military in Central America." *Defense Monitor*, Vol. XIII, No. 3, 1984.

"La présence Nord Américaine au Honduras." September, 1984.

"International Arms Transfers to Central America since 1969." Central American Historical Institute, *Update*, Vol. 3, No. 21, July 6, 1984.

IV. The Contras

"Who's Who in Nicaragua's Military Opposition." Central American Historical Institute, *Update*, Vol. 3, No. 24, July 23, 1984.

V. Economic Aggression

"El boycott económico y los efectos económicos de la agresión a Nicaragua."

Alejandro Dubois and Véronique Staes. A study prepared by the Instituto Nicaragüense de Investigaciones Económicas y Sociales (INIES), Managua.

VI. Nicaraguan Peace Efforts

"Fundamental Commitments to Establish Peace in Central America." Ministry of Foreign Relations, Managua.

"Chronology of Attempts at Bilateral Negotiations Between Nicaragua and the U.S."

"New Nicaraguan Peace Efforts." Central American Historical Institute, *Update*, Vol. 3, No. 16, June 1, 1984.

"Le Groupe de Contadora." Karin Jurion.

VII. The U.S. Position

"Reagan's Central American Policy: A New Somoza for Nicaragua." Marlene Dixon, Institute for the Study of Militarism and Economic Crisis, San Francisco. (Written presentation, English and Spanish.)

"International Lawlessness in the Caribbean Basin." Dr. Francis Boyle.

"Background Paper: Nicaragua's Military Build-up and Support for Central American Subversion." U.S. Department of State and Department of Defense, July, 1984.

VIII. Domestic Issues

"El derecho de los humildes: la defensa de una revolución original — Balance de 5 años del proceso Sandinista Nicaragüense." Instituto Histórico Centroamericano, Managua, *Envío*, Año 4, No. 37, July, 1984.

"Les Neuf Points de la Coordination" (coordinadora).

"Population et Histoire Economico-Politique de la Côte Atlantique: La minorité Miskitu et les autre groupes ethniques." Centre Tricontinental, Belgium, September 1984.

Position of the Government Junta of National Reconstruction on its policies toward minorities.

"The Miskitos and the Bishop Schlaefer Case." Instituto Histórico Centroamericano, Managua, *Envío*, No. 31, January, 1984.

"The Reason for the Settlements." *Tasba Pri,* Managua, 1982.

"Los refugiados misquitos en Honduras." The Marianella García-Villa International Committee for Human Rights in Central America and the Caribbean, July, 1984.

"Problemática religiosa en la revolución sandinista y intervención norteamericana." Luis Serra.

"Nicaragua 1983." Centro de Comunicación Internacional, Managua.

Informe del EPS-Ejército Popular Sandinista.

"Nicaragua's Elections: Voter Registration." Central American Historical Institute, *Update*, Vol. 3, No. 27, August 13, 1984.

"Nicaragua Prepares for November 4 Elections." Central American Historical Institute, *Update*, Vol. 3, No. 19, June 25, 1984.

IX. Juridical Documents

"The Role of the International Court of Justice." Richard Falk, *Journal of International Affairs*, Vol. 37, No. 2, Winter 1984.

Charter of the United Nations; Charter of the Organization of American States; U.N. General Assembly Resolution on the Definition of Aggression (3314); U.N. General Assembly Resolutions 36/103, 2225, 2160, 2625 and 2131; and Convention on Duties and Rights of States in the Event of Civil Strife (No. 70 of the Havana Convention on Civil Strife, 1929).

"El Principio de la No Intervención en los Asuntos Internos de los Estados y su Aplicación a las Relaciones USA-Nicaragua tras 1981." Dr. Joan Piñol, Barcelona.

X. The European Perspective

"Europa Occidental frente a Nicaragua en el marco de la crisis centroamericana." Cristián Parker G. and Pablo Salvat B. from the Centre Tricontinental, Belgium.

Afterword

by Gregory L. Colvin

In the months since October 1984, when the session of the Permanent Peoples' Tribunal on U.S. intervention in Nicaragua was held, a number of critical events have occurred which show the continuing breaches of international law practiced by the Reagan administration in its relations with Nicaragua. They provide additional evidence in support of that session's conclusion, that U.S. policy toward Nicaragua is "contrary to the rules of international law that forbid intervention in the internal affairs of a sovereign state and prohibit all associated acts of aggression."

These intervening developments include steps taken by the U.S. government to disregard the proceedings of the International Court of Justice (the "World Court"), Reagan's explicit embrace of the contras and their goal of overthrowing the government of Nicaragua, efforts made by Nicaragua to pursue negotiations, and efforts made by the United States to prevent successful negotiations. There have been further revelations concerning atrocities committed by the contras and the nature of the instruction, direction, and financial support provided by U.S. agencies. There have been further examples of the United States threatening the use of force against the territory of Nicaragua, as well as U.S. acts of interference in the Nicaraguan elections held in November 1984.

THE WORLD COURT

In the case brought by Nicaragua against the United States before the International Court of Justice, there were several rulings in late November rejecting the positions taken by the U.S. government. The Court found unanimously that the Nicaraguan complaint was admissible, that it had jurisdiction in the matter, and that the U.S. improperly attempted to exempt itself in advance from court authority.

On January 18, 1985, the U.S. refused to appear any longer in the World Court proceedings. The last government that refused to appear in a case brought against it was the government of the Ayatollah Khomeini.

Gregory L. Colvin, who received his J.D. from Yale University (1971), is the Executive Secretary of the North American Chapter of the Antimperialist Tribunal of Our America (TANA) and a practicing attorney in San Francisco, California.

In this case, as with Iran, the World Court can proceed to a final judgment without the participation of the accused nation, and sanctions could be imposed against the U.S. If the U.S. attempts to block enforcement measures in the U.N. Security Council by veto, the World Court decision could be turned over to the General Assembly under the Uniting for Peace Resolution of 1950. This resolution, proposed and used by the United States against the Soviet Union's exercise of veto power during the Korean War, would authorize the General Assembly to recommend that all U.N. members adopt sanctions against the U.S. government for its willful refusal to obey the World Court decision. These measures could include the complete or partial interruption of economic relations and of rail, sea, air, postal, telegraphic, radio, and other means of communication, and the severance of diplomatic relations. Any nation could take these steps without being held legally responsible for violating international law.

Meanwhile, since May 10, 1984, the Interim Order of Protection issued by the World Court has been in effect, not only prohibiting the laying of mines in Nicaragua's ports, but also generally stating that the right to sovereignty possessed by the Republic of Nicaragua should not in any way be jeopardized by any military or paramilitary activities. The U.S. government has ignored this order, and pursued a policy of encouragement and material support for the contras. Whether or not the U.S. appears in the remaining proceedings of the World Court, it is obligated by the U.N. Charter and the Court's enabling statute to abide by this order. Its failure to do so could make the Reagan administration liable to suit in a U.S. domestic court for breach of a treaty obligation.

REAGAN ADMINISTRATION GOALS

On February 21, 1985, President Reagan admitted under questioning at a press conference that the U.S. wanted to "remove" the elected government of Nicaragua "in its present structure." The original justification given to Congress and the American people for aid to the contras — that they would interdict arms shipments bound for El Salvador — has been virtually abandoned. (Reagan has gone beyond previous rhetoric in support of the contras, to the point where he has now referred to them as "our brothers," "freedom fighters," and the "moral equivalent of our Founding Fathers.") Nicaragua's legal case against the United States is strengthened by Reagan's more explicit admission of intent — to overthrow the Nicaraguan government in direct violation of its U.N. Charter Article 2 (4) obligation to refrain from "the threat or use of force against the territorial integrity or political independence of any state."

NEGOTIATIONS

Under Article 33 of the United Nations Charter and Article 23 of the

OAS Charter, it is the obligation of nations to seek peaceful resolution of disputes. Contrast the records of the United States and Nicaragua following the Tribunal's session in October 1984:

Since Nicaragua boldly announced in September 1984 that it would accept the draft Contadora treaty without any changes, the United States has backed away from the negotiation process and demanded more conditions to be met.

At the same time that the U.S. walked out of the World Court case, the Reagan administration announced that it was suspending participation in the bilateral talks it had been holding with Nicaraguan representatives at Manzanillo, Mexico.

In March 1985, Nicaragua announced it would voluntarily reduce the number of Cuban advisers, abide by a moratorium on purchase of new weapon systems, and allow full inspection of its military facilities by a U.S. congressional delegation. The United States rejected this initiative out of hand. In addition, Nicaraguan President Daniel Ortega has recently undertaken extensive travel and contacts with other nations in Europe and Latin America in the search for a peace agreement in Central America, but without serious response from the Reagan administration.

MILITARY AND PARAMILITARY ACTIVITIES

In the last six months, evidence has continued to mount indicating that the contras in Nicaragua engage in systematic terrorism against the civilian population. In March, extensive studies were released by several organizations, including Americas Watch, an investigative group headed by attorney Reed Brody, and the International Human Rights Law Group, with verification by *New York Times* reporters. Under Article 29 of the Fourth Geneva Convention of 1949, support of the contras creates liability on the part of the U.S. government for the grave breaches of international law committed by its "agents," whose acts also constitute war crimes under the customary international law of war.

A specific example of the extent and nature of U.S. Central Intelligence Agency direction of contra activity, coming to light in October 1984, was the publication of a manual dispensing CIA advice to the contras on "psychological" warfare, including the selection of targets for assassination and the creation of "martyrs" by inducement of violent incidents. In addition to the clear breach of international law, violations of American domestic law appear to have been committed in the preparation and oversight of this manual.

The response of the American people as manifested in congressional legislation reached a decisive point in the fall of 1984, when Congress halted any further covert funding to the contras until after February 28, 1985, when Reagan would be required to return to Congress with a justification for any continued aid to the contras. Despite this prohibition, the administration has acted to encourage private groups to funnel aid to the contras. To determine public reaction to other means of supporting the contras, administration officials have floated ideas such as overt aid, aid to contra families living in Honduras, and funding channeled through other nations, particularly Asian countries. Regardless of whether the support comes from private or public sources, the U.S. Neutrality Act makes it a crime to prepare, organize, finance, take part in, or launch a paramilitary expedition against a country with which the U.S. is at peace, like Nicaragua.

U.S. THREATS TO USE DIRECT FORCE AGAINST NICARAGUA

In November, on the night that the U.S. election returns came in, administration officials took advantage of the media coverage to generate a rumor that Soviet MiGs were arriving in Nicaragua. As this story persisted over several weeks, the Reagan administration appeared to be moving toward development of an international incident which would justify some level of overt U.S. military attack against Nicaragua. American warships violated the territorial waters of Nicaragua as they sought to harass the Soviet freighter *Bakuriani* while it was docking and unloading at Corinto. Nicaraguan airspace was violated by U.S. SR-71 reconnaissance aircraft deliberately causing sonic booms over Managua. Finally, the administration admitted that the MiG-21 story was "almost certainly" untrue. From a 1983 classified Defense Department document, we now know that the Defense Department, with help from the CIA and the State Department, was implementing a program of "perception management" designed to make the threat of invasion as real as possible to the people and government of Nicaragua.

It is hard to imagine a more intentional violation of the OAS Charter language in Article 18, prohibiting any "attempted threat against the personality of the State," and the U.N. Charter language in Article 2 (4), prohibiting "the threat or use of force."

INTERFERENCE IN THE NICARAGUAN ELECTIONS

Finally, the United States took a number of measures to try to disrupt, impair, or least undermine the legitimacy of the Nicaraguan elections held in November 1984. It successfully pressured opposition candidate Arturo Cruz to stay out of the Presidential race altogether, and U.S. diplomats persuaded the candidate of the Liberal Independent Party to withdraw just two weeks prior to the vote. Financial offers were made to the Democratic Conservative Party to try to get them to stay out as well. On the military side, the contras murdered people at voter registration tables and kidnapped a candidate for the National Assembly. The U.S. attempt to delegitimize the election generally failed, as the FSLN Presidential candidate Daniel Ortega received 67% of the vote with seven parties on the ballot. Those measures were taken in violation of the OAS Charter, Article 18, statement that no state has the right to intervene, directly or indirectly, in the internal affairs of any other state.

CONCLUSION

As the Permanent Peoples' Tribunal concluded in October 1984, upon hearing the evidence presented in this book, "These policies amount to violations of the most fundamental law of international society and constitute the commission of the most serious crimes against the rights of peoples." The additional evidence against the U.S. government that has developed in the past six months is massive, and shows that the United States efforts to destabilize Nicaragua and overthrow its government are more intense and diverse than ever before.

As this book goes to press, the Reagan administration is making a major move in Congress for approval of $14 million in aid to the contras. As an explicit tactic to attract congressional support for renewal of covert aid, Reagan has proposed a "cease-fire" in Nicaragua, coupled with resumption of military support if the Sandinistas do not negotiate with the contras within 60 days. Under the U.N. Charter, all use of armed groups, irregulars, or mercenaries by one nation against another is characterized as aggression. The United States is the appropriate party to be negotiating with Nicaragua. The contras have never qualified as legal combatants under international law, and are entitled to be treated by the Nicaraguan government as common criminals.

The fate of international law is the fate of humanity. We are faced with a crisis of survival, not only for progressive movements in Central America, but also for the fragile peace and security of a world that lives a few seconds from nuclear holocaust. There is not much to hold together the system of global, mutual understanding on the key issues which are addressed by the U.N. Charter and the OAS Charter: non-aggression, peaceful settlement of disputes, non-intervention, sovereign equality of states, and self-determination of peoples.

As Daniel Ortega wrote in the *New York Times* in March 1985, "Why care about international law? Because disrespect breeds chaos. When a powerful nation repudiates international law — and its highest symbol, the World Court — it threatens the entire legal order and sets a dangerous precedent."

April 17, 1985

About the Editor

Marlene Dixon is Director of the Institute for the Study of Militarism and Economic Crisis in San Francisco, and editor of its journal, *Contemporary Marxism*. She has edited three books on Central America; the two previous volumes were *Revolution and Intervention in Central America* and *Nicaragua Under Siege*, also published by Synthesis Publications. She has traveled several times to Nicaragua.

A leading activist and community organizer in the civil rights, anti-war, and women's movements for many years, Dr. Dixon was also a professor of sociology at the University of Chicago and at McGill University in Canada. She has published numerous books and articles on issues of international affairs, domestic politics, and the workers' movements. In addition to those listed above, her books include *The Future of Women, World Capitalist Crisis and the Rise of the Right, Grassroots Politics in the 1980s, The New Nomads, Things Which Are Done in Secret, Contradictions of Socialist Construction, In Defense of the Working Class,* and *Health Care in Crisis.*